THE
STRATEGIC
CUSTOMER
SUCCESS
MANAGER

A Blueprint for Elevating Your Impact and Advancing Your Career

CHAD HORENFELDT

Foreword By: Kristi Faltorusso
Chief Client Officer at ClientSuccess

PRAISE FOR CHAD HORENFELDT AND *THE STRATEGIC CUSTOMER SUCCESS MANAGER*

I've known Chad Horenfeldt since the early days of Gainsight, and I've seen first-hand how he's helped shape the customer success profession into what it is today. His insights come from lived experience, and his ability to communicate them clearly and powerfully is unmatched. In The Strategic Customer Success Manager, Chad distills years of battle-tested lessons into a playbook that every CSM—from rookie to veteran—needs right now.

— **Nick Mehta**, CEO at Gainsight and author of *Customer Success* and *The Customer Success Economy*

What sets this book apart is its clarity of purpose. It is unapologetically designed for strategic CSMs. These individuals set the tone for a company's most valuable customers but are underserved when it comes to guidance on navigating complexity, building trust, and proving impact. Few people bring the credibility, candor, and lived experience that Chad offers in this actionable blueprint.

— **Gemma Cipriani-Espineira**, Head of Digital Success at Atlassian, Founder of CS Angel

The Strategic Customer Success Manager is a must-read for CS professionals who want to drive measurable impact for their organization while developing critical skills to accelerate their career growth. Chad offers a first-of-its-kind playbook that is relatable, practical, and easy to read.

— **Rod Cherkas**, CEO of HelloCCO and author of *The Chief Customer Officer Playbook*

Customer Success is at an inflection point. The days of reactive, support-focused CSMs are behind us. Today's Customer Success Managers (CSMs) must be consultative, commercially savvy, and capable of delivering meaningful value to their customers. "The Strategic Customer Success Manager" meets this moment. Chad Horenfeldt has written an engaging, practical, and powerful guide that helps CSMs become true business partners ready to thrive in an AI-driven world. Every Customer Success team should have this on their desk, and in their enablement programs.

— **Donna Weber**, Customer Value Realization Expert and author of *Onboarding Matters*

The Strategic Customer Success Manager is a thoughtfully written guide that offers a transformative path for anyone striving to become an intentional and impactful customer success manager. With actionable frameworks and deeply personal insights, Chad provides the kind of strategic playbook many in the profession have long needed but rarely received. Thank you, Chad, for writing this invaluable resource. Your work will undoubtedly elevate the practice of customer success and help countless professionals show up as their best selves.

— **Emilia D'Anzica**, entrepreneur & author of *Pressing ON as a Tech Mom*

With customer expectations evolving at record speed, this book is the essential guide for forward-thinking CSMs. It builds on existing resources and elevates customer success to a strategic discipline.

— **Wayne McCulloch**, Chief Customer Officer at Alkami Technology, author of *The Seven Pillars of Customer Success*

Chad is one of my longest-standing friends in Customer Success—and one of the most thoughtful students of the craft. He's spent years not just doing the work, but teaching it, evolving with it, and now documenting what the best CSMs do to drive real business outcomes. This book is a field guide for that journey.

The CSM of the future isn't buried in tickets—they're in the boardroom, speaking the language of value, building trust, and guiding accounts toward outcomes. That's the vision this book delivers.

If you're building a CS org or developing your own practice, The Strategic Customer Success Manager is required reading. It's not just timely—it's timeless.

— **John Gleeson**, General Partner at Success Venture Partners, Former VP of Customer Success at Motive

With customer expectations evolving faster than ever, The Strategic Customer Success Manager is the definitive guide to staying ahead. This book redefines what it means to be a CSM and elevates the entire profession.

— **Diane Gordon**, Founder at Customer Growth Consulting

In working with Chad, I've come to see him as perhaps the most giving leader and thinker in customer success today. True to form, with this book he generously provides a comprehensive and simple to understand roadmap for any customer success professional or account manager who wants to enhance their career.

— **Bob London**, Founder & Chief Listening Officer at Chief Listening Officers

This is an entirely practical and thoroughly field-tested book for strategic CSMs, from those just starting out to those who want to professionalize their approach to our field. If you are looking for a complete guide to thriving on the front lines of Customer Success, you found it!

— **Kristen Hayer**, Founder & CEO at TheSuccessLeague.io

Chad's leadership in the CS space has always impressed me, and this book captures his thoughtful, no-nonsense approach perfectly. It's full of real-world stories, practical frameworks, and curated recommendations that equip CS pros to thrive in this evolving profession.

— **Cinthia Silva**, Enterprise Customer Success Manager, Board Member at Latinos in Success

This is not just a book; it's a masterclass in transforming from a reactive CSM to a proactive, strategic business partner. Chad has given the CS community a field guide that delivers proven frameworks, battle-tested strategies, and practical exercises that create real change. Every CSM and CS leader needs this on their shelf—and in their onboarding programs.

— **Nils Vinje**, CS Expert & Founder of Glide Consulting

As a former management consultant turned CS leader, I know what it means to be strategic—and this book gets it. Chad turns abstract advice into practical tools CSMs can use every day. If you're ready to move from reactive to respected, this is the blueprint.

— **Ejieme Eromosele**, VP of Customer Growth at Quiq, Founder of Success in Black

I've had the privilege of knowing and learning from Chad for a decade, and have always respected his authenticity and thoughtful approach to leadership. He brings a mix of empathy, curiosity, and strategic thinking to every conversation. He's someone people naturally trust and learn from, especially in the CS community.

— **Shari Srebnick**, CS influencer and thought leader

Chad brings a unique blend of empathy, strategic thinking, passion and practical wisdom to his approach as a CSM. His insights come from lived experience, and his ability to communicate them clearly and powerfully is refreshing. Chad's customers loved him and he made the organizations that he worked with better. I know everyone that cares deeply about customer success will truly enjoy this book.

— **Joe Payne**, Former Eloqua CEO

Chad's depth of experience and practical frameworks make this book a must-read for any CSM looking to elevate their impact. He brings clarity to what it means to be truly strategic in customer success, and his actionable insights will help CSMs at every stage of their career

— **Irit Eizips**, Chief Customer Officer & CEO at CSM Practice

Few people have the credibility and depth of experience Chad brings to this book. His journey, insights, and frameworks combine storytelling and strategy in a way that resonates and empowers. This is the CS book we've been waiting for.

— **Maranda Dziekonski**, CS Executive, Customer Success and Insights MBA Program Advisor at the University of San Francisco School of Management

The Strategic Customer Success Manager nails the human frameworks—trust, executive storytelling, value mapping—that transform a helpful rep into a strategic advisor. As AI reshapes our companies into smaller teams, those foundations become the guardrails that let CSMs guide co-pilots and audit agentic workflows. Chad keeps AI tactics evolving on his website; the book stays timeless by cementing the critical thinking your team can apply today and tomorrow.

— **Jan Young**, Founder, StepUpXchange

For more information, email chad@strategiccustomersuccess.com.

strategiccustomersuccess.com

ISBN: 979-8-218-69426-5 (paperback)

THANK YOU FOR BUYING THIS BOOK!

Visit strategiccustomersuccess.com to sign up for my newsletter, access additional free resources, and download templates mentioned in this book.

Scan the QR code below to access the bonus chapter "What May Be Holding You Back from Being a Strategic CSM".

To Allie, Matthew, Judah, Amelia, and Timbit. Without your love, support, and encouragement, I wouldn't have been able to complete this.

CONTENTS

FOREWORD

When I started in customer success in 2012, I walked in thinking, *I got this.*

I wasn't a fresh college grad trying to break into software as a service (SaaS)—I was a former customer for the product I was now responsible for supporting. I knew the technology inside and out, I understood the use cases, and I figured that would be enough to set me up for success.

Spoiler alert: It wasn't.

It took me about two weeks to realize that knowing the product didn't mean I knew how to be a customer success manager—and it certainly didn't mean I understood what it meant to be a strategic CSM. I had no framework, no structured onboarding, and no real guidance on what "customer success" was supposed to look like, beyond "Make sure the customers are happy."

So, like a lot of early CSMs, I did what I thought I was supposed to do. I focused on product adoption, answered customer questions quickly, and made myself as helpful as possible. And while that sounds like a good approach, I quickly learned being helpful doesn't always translate to being valuable.

That lesson hit me hard when I lost my first renewal.

I had worked with this customer for months. I'd answered every email, jumped on every call, and helped troubleshoot every issue. When renewal time came, I naively thought, *Of course they'll renew. Why wouldn't they?*

Then, they didn't.

When I asked why, their answer floored me:

"We love working with you. But we're just not seeing enough impact to justify the cost."

That was the moment I realized that customer success is not about how much your customers like you—it's about how much business value they see.

And here's the thing: I had zero playbook for how to actually drive business value. I had no structured way to tie customer goals to outcomes, no framework for how to handle strategic conversations and no clue how to own renewals and expansions instead of just hoping for them.

If I'd had this book, I could have avoided so much wasted time and guesswork.

The playbook I wish I'd had

The biggest challenge I faced early on—and the one I see so many CSMs struggle with today—is the transition from *reactive customer support* to *proactive strategic partnership*. It's the difference between being a nice-to-have and being an undeniable, indispensable driver of revenue and retention.

And that's exactly what this book will teach you how to do.

Chad Horenfeldt has built a framework that every CSM needs—whether you're brand new to customer success (CS), or have been at it for years but still feel like you're spinning your wheels. This book isn't generic advice about "delighting customers" or sending thoughtful follow-ups. It's a real, practical, step-by-step guide to becoming the kind of CSM that moves the needle for your customers *and* your business.

What makes this book so valuable is that it gives you tactical, proven strategies for:

- Building trust quickly—so customers see you as a true partner, not just another vendor.
- Running strategic conversations that actually drive impact (instead of endless "check-in" calls).
- Managing renewals and expansions like a proactive owner, not an order taker.
- Learning how to align customer success with business objectives—both for your customers and your own company.
- Understanding how to work cross-functionally with sales, product, and marketing to deliver real results.

I cannot stress this enough: If I'd had this book in 2012, I would have been ten times more effective in half the time.

The problem no one talks about

Here's what makes all of this even harder:

Most CSMs are told to "be more strategic," but they are not given any real direction on what that means or how to do it.

I've worked with hundreds of CSMs over the years, and I can't tell you how many times I've heard the same frustration:

- "My manager keeps telling me to level up and be more strategic, but I have no idea what that actually looks like."
- "I keep hearing that I need to drive impact and tie value to business outcomes, but no one has ever shown me how."
- "I want to be proactive, but I'm drowning in reactive work and don't know where to start."

Sound familiar?

The truth is that CS leaders are great at asking for more—but they're not always great at providing the frameworks, training, and support to make it happen. So CSMs keep struggling, trying to figure it out as they go, hoping they're on the right path.

This book fixes that problem.

It doesn't just tell you to be strategic—it shows you how. It gives you the exact tools, frameworks, and examples you need to stop guessing and start leading.

Why this matters more than ever

Customer success isn't just evolving—it's being *redefined* in real time.

When I started, CS was still seen as a cost center—something companies *needed* but didn't always know how to measure or scale. Today? It's a revenue driver.

That means CSMs are no longer just problem solvers—we are growth enablers, strategic consultants, and trusted business advisors. The best CSMs don't just ensure customers are using the product; they ensure customers are getting so much value that renewal is a no-brainer and expansion is the next natural step.

And yet, despite all of this, most CSMs are still figuring it out as they go.

They're handed a book of accounts, told to "own the relationship," and left to piece together what *strategic* actually means. Some make it work. Others burn out. But no one should have to guess their way to success.

That's why this book is so important.

It gives you the playbook that most CSMs never get. It demystifies what it really takes to become a high-impact, high-value CSM—one who isn't just managing accounts but driving real business outcomes.

This isn't just a job—it's a career accelerator

I say this all the time, but I'll say it again:

The best CSMs don't wait for a seat at the table—they pull up a chair and make it impossible to ignore them.

And if that's the kind of CSM you want to be—the kind that executives trust, sales teams rely on, and customers actually see as a partner—then you're holding the right book.

Because customer success isn't about how *helpful* you are. It's about how much impact you drive.

And after reading this book, you won't be just another CSM. You'll be the one they call when they need a strategic partner who actually moves the needle.

So, read every page. Take notes. Apply the frameworks. Do the exercises provided.

Because once you start *owning* your role and leading with strategy instead of just reacting, everything changes. And trust me—you won't want to go back.

—Kristi Faltorusso

INTRODUCTION

"**Y**ou need to be more strategic." Have you ever received this feedback from your manager? Most likely, the person who said this to you didn't define what they meant or provide you with any practical guidance on improving. I struggled with this same challenge for many years.

So how do you become more strategic as a customer success professional? You must shift your mindset and be very deliberate in your actions. I've written this book to pass on the knowledge that I've accumulated over my twenty-plus years in customer success. It won't be an overnight transformation, but with focused and deliberate practice guided by this book, I can guarantee that you will see improvements in your performance.

But who am I, and why should you listen to me? Let me tell you about how I started in customer success.

My customer success story

"You have experience with B2B, right?" It was early August 2005. I was sitting across from Paul Teshima, who was the head of the CS team at Eloqua. At the time, Eloqua was a young tech start-up in Toronto, Ontario. I was interviewing for a customer success manager (CSM) role, which was originally called a *solutions manager*. I recognized this as a pivotal moment that could elevate my career—if only I understood what Paul meant when he mentioned "B2B."

As I considered Paul's question, beads of sweat gathered on my forehead, and I did everything I could to keep my hands from shaking. I didn't know exactly what to say, so I mumbled, "I have experience with B2B." I had no idea that B2B stood for *business-to-business*. I'm sorry, Paul, if you're reading this, but I'm not sorry for my response.

I want to make it clear that I don't condone lying in interviews. Trust is a cornerstone of my definition of customer success and one of my core personal values. That said, I felt justified in bending the truth a smidge at the time. I had the right background for the role, and I was confident that I would kick ass on Paul's team. I was ready for a career in customer success even though CS didn't exist yet. But was this the right role for me?

Let's go back a few years before that interview, when my career was in the toilet. I was wrapping up a Master of Arts degree in history and deciding what I wanted to do with my life. I loved history but didn't see a future where I could make a living at it. I'm sure many of you with liberal arts degrees can relate. As I was finishing one of my last academic papers, I was presented with an opportunity to run a charity that taught children about water conservation and protecting the environment. It was by far the most rewarding role I've had in my career and was my first exposure to the power of the internet, which I used to expand the reach of our cause.

With ongoing school debts, I decided I needed to make more money. I reluctantly quit the charity and embarked on a European adventure with my best friend to put myself in further debt and have some much-needed fun. At the tail end of our tour through Scotland, we started an impromptu "friendly" game of soccer in the beautiful town of Loch Lomond near Glasgow. We were down 2–0 (or 2–nil for you football fans), and I was fed up. I huddled my team together and declared, "We're not letting them score another goal. No matter what!" These words come from someone who might rank among the worst soccer players ever to play but is fiercely competitive and hates losing.

We broke from the huddle, and within thirty seconds, this huge Aussie on the other team had a breakaway on our goal. I put my head down and sprinted after him. When I looked up, I somehow found myself within five feet of him and had a chance to stop this guy from scoring. I made the quick decision to use a slide tackle, where you extend one leg with the intent of knocking the ball away from the opposing player. The problem was that I had no idea what I was doing. I slid my right leg between his tree-trunk limbs, which were in full stride. Big mistake.

In an instant, a massive *crack* that sounded like lightning splitting a tree permeated the air. My right tibia and fibula bones snapped, and I was lying there in excruciating pain. I prevented the other team from scoring, but my European trip was done. What I didn't realize, while I was clutching my leg, was that things would get much worse.

I was rushed first to one hospital and then to a larger one in the town of Paisley, as my leg was in rough shape. I was given heavy doses of morphine to control the pain and told that I needed to be operated on immediately. I dozed off after being administered anesthesia, with the hope that I would wake up with a few screws in my leg and a one-way ticket home.

I slowly opened my eyes and fought to regain control of my senses. I could see doctors and nurses scurrying about with concerned looks on their faces. My surgeon bent down by my side and said in a thick Scottish accent: "We couldn't operate on your leg, lad. You're lucky to be alive." I wasn't fully awake, so I didn't process what the doctor had just told me. He continued "The bone marrow from your broken leg caused a blood clot in your lungs. You developed a pulmonary embolism and your oxygen levels had become drastically low. We weren't sure if you'd wake up." The doctor's words started to sink in. Right up to that moment, I had felt young, dumb, and indestructible. My innocence was now gone.

This was one of the lowest periods of my life. After three weeks in the hospital, I was finally discharged and flown home in an air ambulance. It took almost a full year before I was walking without a cast. My mobility was severely limited, I had mounting college debt, I was living at home, and I had no idea what I was going to do with my life. After a few days, I stopped feeling sorry for myself and resolved not to play it safe anymore when it came to pursuing my dreams. I wasn't going to squander my second chance in life.

I decided to explore my interest in web technology, which was sparked during my time in the nonprofit sector. I took a fifteen-month crash course in programming, database management, and project management and put myself further in debt. When I graduated, I felt that things were finally looking up for me, until I realized how poor my job prospects were. We were still feeling the remnants of the dot-bomb era, and it was going to be tough for an inexperienced history grad, now in technology, to get my first real break.

It was early 2002 when I came across a small technology firm in Toronto that had an opening for a consultant. I leveraged my technology and nonprofit background to somehow convince the president, Jeff Chapleau, to hire a debt-laden history major, who was a failed developer and going nowhere in life. I spent three years there, honing my skills and cutting my teeth in the tech industry. During that time, I realized my true passion: helping customers solve their business problems by leveraging technology.

From there, I ended up at the SaaS company Eloqua, where I lied in my interview and officially began my career in customer success. I didn't realize then that I was embarking on a career path that would transform my life. After five years as a CSM, I moved into leadership roles, where I've helped build high-performing customer success teams for several SaaS companies, including Eloqua (Oracle), Influitive, Bluecore, Updater, and Kustomer (Meta), among others.

The route to a career in customer success can be unconventional and unpredictable. I'm sure the ups and downs of my story resonate with many of you, as you've had similar career challenges. Customer success is still like the Wild West—much of it has yet to be defined or standardized. This book is my attempt to inspire others to continue to aim higher and improve our profession.

The customer success game has changed

As my CSM career progressed, I learned that remaining relevant required me to shift my methods in response to evolving practices and heightened customer expectations. It was during this period that my vision of a strategic customer success manager first took shape. But it took a long time to materialize and perfect.

When I first started as a CSM, I viewed myself as a *customer success helper*, which earned me a strong following among my customers. An early highlight of my career was attending an Eloqua user group meeting in Austin, Texas, and receiving a standing ovation from my customers. Being overly helpful to my clients proved effective to a certain extent, but ultimately, it held me back.

After losing a handful of customers, I began to question my skills. I asked myself, "My customers love me. Why are some of them still churning?" It dawned on me that my efforts to win over my primary customer contacts and create advocates often left me invisible to the key decision-makers responsible for renewal decisions. More alarmingly, I lost customers that I never imagined were at risk. I realized that I was slowly failing at customer success.

This book is the culmination of years of hands-on experience, thought leadership through blog posts and other content, and the collective wisdom of the amazing customer success community and beyond. The outcome is a fresh perspective on the role of a CSM, which I refer to as a strategic customer success manager.

So, what's changed in the world and why do CSMs need to transform how they operate? As it has become more affordable and straightforward for software companies to introduce new products, customers have gained access to an unprecedented range of options and greater ease in switching to competitors. I saw that firsthand at Eloqua, as our main competitors, such as Marketo and HubSpot, started picking off our customers after we had dominated the market for years. It's even easier to build out powerful applications today with the advent of AI.

In addition, customers now expect and deserve a better experience, and the COVID pandemic has further accelerated this transition.[1] According to the recent *Global Consumer Trends Report* by Qualtrics, 53 percent of consumers will seek out alternatives if they have a poor experience.[2] Our customers want to feel truly understood and expect a personalized approach that caters to their needs. According to the same report, nearly two-thirds (64 percent) of consumers favor purchasing from companies that personalize their experiences based on their preferences and needs.[3]

The good news is that many B2B companies have recognized these trends and increased their focus and spending on retaining customers.[4] More organizations are realizing that a greater investment in customer retention can increase customer lifetime value (CLV) and increase profits.[5] As a result, customer success has exploded in the last ten years despite the economic slowdown in the technology sector. This has led to many people flocking to the CSM profession.

---

1 Niraj Ranjan, *How the Pandemic Has Impacted Customer Expectations*, Forbes, February 4, 2021, https://www.forbes.com/sites/forbesbusinesscouncil/2021/02/04/how-the-pandemic-has-impacted-customer-expectations/?sh=44be38913185.

2 *2025 Global Consumer Trends Report*, Qualtrics, accessed October 15, 2024, https://www.qualtrics.com/ebooks-guides/customer-experience-trends/.

3 *2025 Global Consumer Trends Report.*

4 "2022 Customer Success Leadership Study," ChurnZero, accessed November 14, 2022, https://churnzero.com/wp-content/uploads/2022/11/2022-Customer-Success-Leadership-Study-ChurnZero-ESG.pdf.

5 Fred Reichheld, "Prescription for Cutting Costs," Bain & Company, September 2001. https://media.bain.com/Images/BB_Prescription_cutting_costs.pdf. This research demonstrated that a 5 percent increase in customer retention produces more than a 25 percent increase in profit.

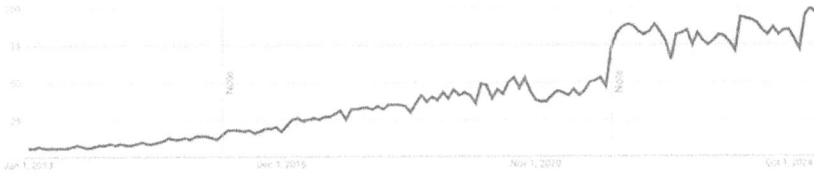

Figure 1.⁶ The rise over time of people worldwide searching for "Customer Success" on Google.

Many customer success professionals follow the traditional CSM 1.0 playbook of the "customer success helper." But this positions the CSM role as more like customer support than being a strategic advisor and leads to a disproportionate amount of unnecessary customer churn and CSMs not receiving the recognition they deserve.

It's time for customer success professionals to command greater respect from their customers and from within their organizations. Being a CSM isn't just about being responsive to customers' needs or providing assistance when they beckon for help. Being a strategic CSM isn't just about being empathetic; it's about being deliberate and tenacious. It's not just about being supportive; it's about being consultative and analytical.

Many CSMs have not been trained in the critical abilities required to develop trust with key stakeholders and identify their clients' underlying aspirations. This can limit their effectiveness with clients and within their organizations, ultimately impacting their career growth.

Who this book is for

If you've ever been ignored by your customers, been passed over for a promotion, or become frustrated at not receiving the recognition you felt was warranted, you're not alone. You've also picked up the right book. I will provide

---

6 Google Trends, "customer success, worldwide, 1/1/13–3/31/25," https://trends.google.com/trends/explore?date=2013-01-01%202025-03-31&q=customer%20success#-TIMESERIES. From the Google Trends data starting in 2013, we can see a meteoric rise in interest in the search term "customer success" across the world.

you with the tools and strategies to transform you into a strategic CSM and help you achieve greater heights within customer success and beyond.

Is being a strategic customer success manager easy? Hell no. It will take time and practice to master these skills. There are no shortcuts here. Strategic CSMs need to perform at a higher level and constantly uplevel their skills. The good news is that I've laid out various strategies and frameworks to become a complete strategic CSM. My recommended approaches come from someone who has been there, done that, and lived to tell the story. There is no fluff here—just real and proven approaches that you can start leveraging right away.

Although I've authored this book for CS professionals and those who want to break into customer success, anyone who regularly works with customers—in account management or sales, for example—will find it insightful. It was also designed for customer success leaders and other executives who are looking to build high-performing customer success teams.

What you will learn

This book is not meant to be a primer on customer success. I didn't write this to waste your time learning about the history of customer success or to debate whether customer success or sales should handle renewals (it's customer success, by the way). It was written to improve your stature and make you invaluable to any company.

You will find everything you need to transform yourself into a strategic CSM, whether you are just starting in customer success or are a ten-year veteran.

There are five main parts in this book:

Defining What a Strategic Customer Success Manager Is provides definitions of customer success, what it means to be a strategic customer success manager, and practical approaches for quickly building trust with your clients. I also cover the skills and behaviors you need to exhibit as a strategic CSM.

Your First Ninety Days as a Strategic CSM and Beyond covers everything you need to know when starting a CSM role to give you the best chance of being successful. We start with the basics to ground you on the core aspects of your role, raise your sights, and direct you on where to focus for your first ninety days. This also includes best practices for tracking and managing your at-risk customers.

Taking Your Customer Success Career to the Next Level builds on these basics by introducing some of the more advanced concepts for being a strategic CSM.

How to Conduct Strategic Conversations with Your Customers includes the most critical sections of the book and will transform how you conduct your customer meetings by using strategic conversation strategies.

Key Moments in the Customer Journey provides practical advice on leveraging your newly learned strategic CSM skills to transform your client kickoffs and quarterly business reviews (QBRs), and manage renewals and expansion opportunities.

Though these parts work individually, the material flows most effectively when read chronologically, with each concept laying the groundwork for the next.

To supercharge your learning, complete the exercises in the *Putting this into practice* sections at the end of each chapter. You'll have an opportunity to reflect on what was covered as well as incorporate and practice the new skills that you'll develop. The only way to truly transform yourself is to follow a concept called *deep practice*, defined by Daniel Coyle in his book *The Talent Code*. It's a structured approach to skill mastery requiring focus, deliberate effort, and learning from mistakes.

While I will provide you with the blueprint for this transformation, it's up to you to apply these concepts. They may make you feel uncomfortable at times, but you need to stay the course. As Coyle states, "Deep practice isn't a piece of cake: it requires energy, passion, and commitment."[7] Don't skip over these exercises—they're carefully crafted to deepen your grasp of these concepts.

In addition, I've included several templates and additional resources at strategiccustomersuccess.com. I aim to keep this site updated as a source of customer success information, so please check it out and sign up for updates.

Note to the reader: Throughout this text, I will use "client" and "customer" interchangeably.

I hope my experiences and insights motivate you to begin your journey in customer success or reach new milestones in your career. Thank you for joining me on this path and sharing in my mission to elevate customer success to new heights.

---

7 Daniel Coyle, *The Talent Code: Greatness Isn't Born. It's Grown. Here's How.* (Bantam, 2009), 314.

PART I

Defining What a Strategic CSM Is

CHAPTER 1

What Exactly Is a Strategic CSM?

If you've ever been a customer success manager, you remember when you lost your first significant customer. You felt horrible. My first major client loss is etched in my mind like a late-night infomercial on repeat. I had just started my CSM career at Eloqua and worked with small- to medium-sized businesses. This particular client was using Eloqua's marketing automation platform to launch email campaigns to their prospects. My main point of contact was a friendly Texan who always responded with a "Well, thank you kindly" in her strong Southern accent when I offered assistance. Unfortunately, this seemingly gentle person was about to rip my heart out—she would become my first churned customer.

Writing about this years later, I realize I should have seen it coming. Underneath my client's polite exterior, there was a hint of anxiety that made me uneasy. It was clear that she was overwhelmed by the complexity of our product and didn't seem to enjoy what she was doing. Was I up for the challenge? Of course! I believed that I could make anyone successful. I was very naive in my younger CSM days.

I did everything in my power to encourage her to use our product. I painstakingly built her email templates so she didn't have to, uploaded her list of email recipients to ensure that we maximized her reach, and even executed the email campaign on her behalf to ensure there were no snafus. As you can probably guess, none of this mattered. Even after all this effort and my willingness to donate my left kidney to this client, she told us that our platform was too complex for what they needed and that they weren't renewing. I was crushed and felt betrayed. It was like my best friend had just stabbed me in the back.

I then compounded the problem by blaming everyone else. I blamed our product for its excessive complexity. I blamed the client's unwillingness to learn how to use our product. I blamed the sales team for overselling. What I didn't realize at the time was that I was part of the problem. I needed to take a different approach to decrease the chances of this happening again.

I used to think my job as a CSM was to be helpful—like those concierge people at those fancy schmancy hotels that always offer timely and spot-on advice. But helping your clients and making them happy will only take you so far. You must elevate your CSM game and establish a more profound connection with your clients. Being a strategic customer success manager is all about focusing on your client's business, not just your product. It's about building relationships with the right stakeholders in your client's organization and aligning with their business goals rather than solely prioritizing product adoption. It's more than being customer-centric—it's about building trust and delivering value for your clients and your company.

To begin this journey, let's look at some definitions used throughout this book. We'll start by defining the most nebulous term in our industry: customer success.

The foundation of customer success

Over the past twenty-plus years, working with hundreds of clients, building several high-performing customer success teams, and collaborating with numerous leaders in the CS field, I've concluded that customer success has two foundational elements: trust and value.

Yes, customer success is about customer retention, revenue growth, and achieving business outcomes, but those are just outputs of customer success, not the foundational elements. Therefore, I define customer success as a balance between the inherent trust your customers have in you and the value they realize.

Customer Success = Trust + Value

When customers trust you, they are more open to listening to you and working with you to achieve value from your product. When customers have found value in your product and your company, they will develop a higher degree of trust in you. On the flip side, when you erode that trust, your customers will be less inclined to see the value you offer and may churn.

The idea of customer success goes well beyond a group of people in your company; it's a philosophy that your organization must embody. That said, I firmly believe in the need for a customer success department, as CS should play a central role in fostering a customer-centric culture. It should also be the voice of reason within an organization to prevent actions that can compromise your customer's trust.

The good news is that you can contribute to the change necessary to create an environment where customers come first. You can influence your company's culture and set the standard. This is customer-led growth, a core component of being a strategic CSM.

What is a strategic customer success manager?

The most important objectives of a CSM, according to Gainsight, are the following, listed in order of priority:

- Higher retention rates
- Driving revenue growth

- Improved product adoption[8]

Customer success managers tackle these objectives differently from company to company, depending on their role, their company's product offerings, and the structure and processes of the CS team. For example, some CSMs are directly involved in renewal negotiations, while in other organizations, this task may be reserved for renewal specialists or the sales team. Some CSMs handle onboarding new clients, while at other organizations, they're solely focused on product adoption and achieving value once the initial onboarding phase has concluded.

While customer retention, revenue growth, and product adoption are critical to the CSM role, CSMs don't own the relationship with the customer. I'm in agreement with the Disney philosophy that "No one owns the customer, but someone always owns the moment."[9] You need to leverage your entire company to drive value for customers. You can't do it alone. I'll expand on this later, as it's a central tenet of being a strategic CSM. Given that the responsibilities of CSMs differ by organization and their success hinges on support from other teams, how can you drive meaningful results? At the heart of this lies building trust and delivering value.

As a CSM, you have a general guideline for your day-to-day responsibilities, but much of your role comes down to thinking on your feet and adapting to the circumstances that present themselves. That's why in chapter 3 I'll discuss certain skills and behaviors that CSMs need to hone.

The issue is that even when you're building trust and delivering value with a high level of precision, you may still experience surprise customer churn. Companies are seeing a higher amount of churn in general in the

---

8 Vaidyanathan and Rabago, Customer Success Professional's Handbook, 22–23.
9 "At Disney, Someone Always Owns the Moment," Customer Experience Matters, November 16, 2011, https://experiencematters.wordpress.com/2011/11/16/at-disney-someone-always-owns-the-moment/.

post-COVID economic downturn.[10] The old CSM playbook isn't good enough anymore. CSMs and CS leaders need to take a different approach if they want to maintain or improve their renewal rates and potentially uncover revenue opportunities. Enter the strategic customer success manager.

Breaking down what it means to be a strategic customer success manager

A strategic customer success manager (SCSM) builds on the core aspects of a CSM but takes the role to another level. Let's start by defining what we mean by *strategic*. Richard Rumelt is an expert in this space and defines strategy as follows: "A good strategy is a set of actions that is credible, coherent and focused on overcoming the biggest hurdle(s) in achieving a particular objective."[11] Let's break this definition down to understand how it perfectly applies to the role of the SCSM:

- Focused on overcoming the biggest hurdle(s): An SCSM must first uncover the customer's biggest challenges. Once you understand these, you can work with your customers to formalize a solution. It's one of the reasons I recommend using the 3C framework (company, customers, and challenges) discussed in chapter 2, so you come to meetings prepared with foundational knowledge of your customer.
- Achieving a particular objective: SCSMs go beyond helping their customers with product adoption. They focus on defining and achieving their customers' business outcomes. Business outcomes

---

10   Alex Wilhelm, "As Net Retention Plummets, AI Could Be the Savior Software Companies Need," TechCrunch, August 18, 2023, https://techcrunch.com/2023/08/18/ai-could-save-the-day-for-software-companies; Matt Eldridge, Greg Fiore, Simon Heap, and Kenzie Haygood, "Why Software Companies' Customer Success Is Failing," Bain, accessed September 25, 2024, https://www.bain.com/insights/why-software-companies-customer-success-is-failing-tech-report-2024.
11   Julie Zhou, "How to be Strategic," The Year of the Looking Glass, October 2, 2018, https://medium.com/the-year-of-the-looking-glass/how-to-be-strategic-f6630a44f86b.

are high-level objectives that indicate whether your customers have achieved value from your product.

- A set of credible and coherent actions: SCSMs don't take a scattered approach to helping their customers achieve their outcomes. They work with their clients to create detailed joint customer success plans (see chapter 17) to organize a set of actions into a concrete path forward.

Putting that together we have: Strategic CSMs focus on their clients' business rather than just their organization's products. They go beyond product adoption to uncover and help deliver their customers' business outcomes, and they then turn these outcomes into concrete actions and use a joint success plan to measure their client's progress. By following this approach, strategic CSMs provide more value for their customers and deepen the level of trust with them. But wait—there's more.

Being a strategic CSM is not just about customers

Customers come first for a strategic CSM, but aligning with other functions within your company is key to driving greater overall impact as a strategic CSM. SCSMs understand that they can't go it alone and that their success depends on their relationships with their colleagues in sales, product, engineering, and marketing, as well as their colleagues in customer success and support.

So they also need to build trust with their teammates. SCSMs can be catalysts for change within their respective companies to ensure the customer is represented. Therefore, as a strategic CSM, you must strike a balance between being customer-centric and company-centric.

To achieve this, SCSMs:

- Immerse themselves across their organization to spread the wealth of their customer knowledge. For instance, they share customer stories with their sales and marketing teams and assist their product and engineering teams by bringing forward common customer feature requests and issues.

- Don't see these other departments as obstacles but as allies in achieving their customers' business outcomes. They cultivate collaboration, replacing the us-versus-them mindset with teamwork. They assume the best of others and demonstrate extreme empathy for their peers. When internal problems surface, they strive to pinpoint and resolve the root issue.

- Recognize that they have the power to transform their company's culture into one that is more customer-centric. They believe that they can also break down barriers between departments. We'll delve into this area further in chapter 11.

Being an SCSM also means getting rid of bad habits

Successful strategic CSMs recognize that it isn't just about doing more; it's about doing what matters and cutting out the rest. It means reducing or eliminating certain activities and behaviors, including the following:

Providing direct troubleshooting and other forms of product support—SCSMs shouldn't be triaging or addressing product issues. While the customer may appreciate the CSM's direct assistance, it lowers the perception of the CSM in the eyes of the client. They see you only as a product expert, not someone who can help them drive their business forward. Performing product support also distracts the CSM from uncovering customer challenges and delivering business outcomes. I've seen very few CSMs who can straddle the worlds of product support and maintaining relationships with senior customer stakeholders. Leave support to the support team. You should only have to assist the support team with client escalations, and when context is needed to resolve issues.

Doing the work for the client—It's tempting to complete tasks directly for your customers, but this should be the exception, not the rule. CSMs should only be completing product configurations or other services for their clients if they are early-stage start-ups. You only have a limited number of hours in your day, and you should be focused on strategic conversations and executing success plans—not turning knobs and other tasks that professional services, a partner, or the customer can perform. SCSMs recognize when they are performing too many tasks and either delegate them or recommend product changes to reduce the tasks that fall on CS.

Accepting the status quo—SCSMs don't just accept things as they are. They question why their clients have been implemented or configured in a certain way. They challenge their customers when they decide to go down a path the product wasn't designed for. They proactively look for issues rather than sidestepping or ignoring them.

Becoming a strategic CSM leads to a complete transformation of your mindset. You need to distance yourself from these four roles: the firefighter, waiter, fixer, and entertainer.

- **The firefighter:** You shouldn't constantly need a firehose to put out fires raised by your customers as part of your role. You should have other resources such as a support team you can leverage to douse these flames. You'll need to strap on your helmet and run into a fire or two from time to time, but it should be more about managing the client relationship than directly troubleshooting product issues.
- **The waiter:** Your job isn't always to please the customer and give them whatever they've asked for. Providing them with an exceptional experience is important, but your main purpose as an SCSM is to ensure that your clients achieve value. This may require that

you push back on their requests. For instance, you may need to decrease the meeting cadence with some customers so you can spend your time where it will have the greatest impact.

- **The fixer:** As mentioned, it's very tempting to do the work for your clients because you know what's required to drive value. It's okay to do this occasionally, but your focus should be on teaching your customers how to fish rather than fishing on their behalf. Then your customers will take greater ownership of your product and will be better off in the long run.

- **The entertainer:** You aren't there to make your customers happy or feel warm and fuzzy. You can have the most wonderful and intimate relationship with your clients and then have them give you a churn notice a week later—I've seen it too many times. You're there to ask difficult and uncomfortable questions to ensure your customers are on the right path to achieving their business outcomes. If you're too cordial, you may not have the chutzpah to probe deeper into your clients' usage drop-off or recent meeting absences. Customer success isn't about making your customers happy—it's about helping them achieve the success they envisioned when they purchased your product.

You can put this on a sticky note on your computer to remind yourself: "You are not a firefighter, a waiter, a fixer, or an entertainer. You are a strategic CSM." Do whatever it takes so you don't embody these roles.

Strategic CSM defined

So, let's put this all together. Strategic CSMs aim higher by going beyond the standard tactical CSM duties. Your role as an SCSM is to address your clients' overarching needs and objectives. You focus on their long-term success rather than short-term gains. You see the CSM–customer relationship as a game of chess rather than checkers, as you're focused on the bigger picture and thinking three moves ahead.

Being a strategic CSM is not just about securing the upcoming renewal but creating customers for life. You're not just a product expert but someone who can improve your customers' overall business and even assist them in advancing their careers. Furthermore, as a strategic CSM, you represent the customer's perspective within your company and actively advocate for improvements to the overall customer experience.

Therefore, a strategic CSM is someone who builds trust and creates value for their customers and their own organization.

Typical CSM versus Strategic CSM: Summary

Typical CSM	Strategic CSM
Expert in their product	Expert on their customer's business
Drives adoption	Drives business outcomes
Customer-centric	Customer and company-centric

Figure 2. The differences between a typical CSM versus a strategic CSM.

Putting this into practice

Take a moment to go through these questions and write down your answers:

- Name a company that you trust and find value from. What value do they provide you? Why do you trust them?
- Write down an example of a trusted relationship you built with a customer. Why did they trust you?
- Write down an example where the trust between you and your customer was broken. Outline what happened and what the result was.

- Write down an example of how you provided value to a customer. How did the customer react?
- Provide details on how you've provided value to other departments as a CSM.

Summary and key takeaways

The core responsibilities of CSMs include retaining customers, uncovering growth opportunities, increasing product adoption, monitoring customer health, handling escalations, and identifying advocates. An SCSM goes beyond that to:

- Focus on their clients' businesses rather than just their products.
- Be company-centric and not just customer-centric, acting as a catalyst for cultural transformation within organizations.
- Limit or avoid distracting habits such as direct troubleshooting or performing product tasks for their clients. They don't accept the status quo.
- Forgo the roles of firefighter, waiter, fixer, and entertainer, as these lower their impact.
- Build trust and create value for their customers and their organization.

Remember, customer success is all about trust and value.

CHAPTER 2

How to Quickly Build (and Lose) Trust

Early in my career, I learned the importance of building trust with my customers and the impact of a strong first impression. In early 2007, I was invited to meet with Cognos (IBM), the largest customer I had been assigned up to that point in my CS journey. I have two distinct memories from visiting Cambridge, Massachusetts, in winter: I was freezing—even as a Canadian—and I was scared out of my mind.

Cognos brought me into their global marketing kickoff meeting to get me up to speed on their key priorities and challenges. It was a fantastic opportunity to be immersed in their business, as I had just been assigned to them. It was also a big responsibility, as they were one of Eloqua's most important customers at the time. To top it off, Drew Clarke, Cognos's vice president of marketing, was a Harvard alumnus, so the meeting was held there, adding to the excitement.

I was still getting my feet wet as a CSM and felt intimidated by all these superintelligent marketers—especially Drew. In addition to being a Harvard grad, he was a captain in a US Army armored cavalry regiment. His booming voice told you who was in charge, and it was clear how well respected he was by his team. The senior employees in the room paid Drew their full attention, and the junior people kept trying to one-up each other to impress him.

When I entered the meeting room, I felt like I was in a scene from *Good Will Hunting*. The room was spacious, and everything was wood—the walls, the floors, the desks—everything. The tables had been arranged into a large square so everyone could sit facing each other, with Drew holding court in the center of the square.

I was in complete awe of one of the most advanced B2B marketing organizations at the time. As I was brand new to the Cognos account, I decided to mostly be a silent observer during this time and absorb as much as possible.

Although I felt like a fish out of water, I kept my composure and thought I had admirably represented my company. I flew home with optimism and excitement for what was to come. The problem was that the experience hadn't gone as well as I thought.

It turned out that Cognos was displeased with my lack of participation and questioned whether I was the right CSM for their organization. They felt that I just sat there all day—preoccupied with my laptop. They saw me as aloof and disengaged. When this got back to me, I worried I was going to be kicked off this account after just a few weeks.

Their impression of what I was doing couldn't have been further from the truth. While I did have my laptop open the whole time, I was busy taking detailed notes and trying to follow along. It didn't matter though. The damage was done, and things didn't get off to a great start for me with Cognos. I hadn't determined what they expected from me at that meeting. I learned a valuable lesson that day about building trust and providing value in every interaction, and I vowed never to repeat that mistake.

If only I'd received some of the advice in this book back on that freezing day at Harvard, I could have set a more positive tone with my Cognos stakeholders and helped them achieve better results more quickly.

Twelve tips to quickly build trust with your customers

Follow these tips to take on new customers like a boss and to strengthen your relationships with your existing customers. While these suggestions may demand extra time upfront, they'll save you trouble down the line. If you forge trusted relationships with your clients early on, your job will become immensely easier.

1. Learn about your customer's business: The 3C method

You need to immerse yourself in your customer's business if you want to serve them better and quickly build rapport. The more you speak in their language, using terms and phrases that they use, and the more intimate you become with their core challenges, the more they'll be willing to open up to you. This will require you to be part historian and part private investigator.

When learning about your customer's business, focus on these three things that make up what I call the 3C method:

- Learn more about how their *company* operates.
- Learn about who their *customers* are.
- Understand their current *challenges*.

Demonstrating to your customers that you understand the three Cs—their company, customers, and challenges—will help you cross the invisible trust barrier and put you on a better path.

I. Company: What do they offer and how do they make money?

To fully grasp your customer's business, you must understand what they do. You should be able to answer most of these questions:

- What are the products they sell or the services they offer?

- How do they make money? What are their different revenue streams, and which lines of business are the most profitable? Which area seems to be growing? Which is stagnating? Where are the biggest opportunities for growth, if any?

- Who do they compete against, and how do their offerings differ? You may be able to determine this from Crunchbase, G2, or other review sites. Industry reports such as Gartner's *Magic Quadrant* provide competitive comparison data.

- What is most unique about their offerings? From your research, what makes them different from anything else on the market?

- Have they had any recent layoffs? Are they hiring?

- If they are a public company, how is the company currently performing, and what is its future outlook? Read the latest financial reports and SEC filings as well as investor briefs that summarize the current state of the company.

- If they are a private company, when was the last time they raised funding, and how much did they raise? Look for reports on the company's valuation to understand its worth. Also, look for any trouble on the horizon, as it could impact their need for your products or their budget availability.

You should now have a clearer view of your customer's business, their competitors, and how they make money. Take note of their preferred terminology and adopt it in your discussions.

Much of the information you'll need can be accessed from public materials. You can review recent Google News posts, the company's website, social media such as LinkedIn, quarterly earnings reports, and other industry information. As a starting point, leverage AI tools, such as ChatGPT, which can summarize the most relevant information in seconds. You can also have your client fill in the blanks and provide their perspective when you meet with them.

II. Customers: Which type of customers do they value the most and why?

Next, focus on learning more about who your client sells to, their customers. These end customers ultimately pay your invoices and are whom your client cares the most about.

Aim to identify the various types of customers who buy their products and determine which customer segments they prioritize and why. For instance, does your client offer special treatment to repeat customers, or are they targeting a new market? As you learn more about their customers, you will uncover your client's priorities and what is most important to their business.

III. Challenges: What challenges are they facing?

You must be in tune with your customers' goals, challenges, and priorities to ensure your products deliver what they're trying to achieve. Your customer's challenges are often deeper and more intricate than they seem at first. Imagine them as an iceberg. What you see above the surface is just a small part; roughly 90 percent of an iceberg is underwater.[12] Your client's challenges are similar.

For example, your client may have financial troubles, so they need to cut expenses, including paying less for your product. Your client champion may have been saddled with too many responsibilities or with technologies that they don't have the skills to handle. Unfortunately, instead of taking responsibility, they may blame your company for their failings.

It falls on you to dive deeper so you can understand the extent of their problems. You don't want to just solve the issue at hand—you need to get to the root challenge. It's easy to label a client that is having budget challenges

---

12 "Icebergs," AntarcticGlaciers.org, last modified August 18, 2022, https://www. antarcticglaciers.org/glacier-processes/glacier-types/icebergs/.

as "difficult." It's harder to seek out the truth and find out what's behind their behaviors, so you can ensure they are on the right path. You'll likely need to explore their challenges further when meeting them (see part IV on how to conduct strategic conversations).

> **Expert tip: Review podcasts and videos about your customers.**
> Review podcasts and YouTube videos about your clients, especially if the CEO or senior leaders are featured. They can provide tremendous insights into your customers' businesses and personal lives, which you can leverage to build stronger connections when you meet. These resources are also easy to consume, especially when you're on the go. When speaking to your customers, you can mention the podcast or video you listened to, increasing your credibility. It signals that you're committed to learning about what makes their business successful. AI tools should soon be able to stitch this data together for you, saving you valuable time.

2. Review past notes and correspondence

You should strive to understand your customers at a deeper level, including knowing their hobbies, families, and what makes them tick. A human-centered approach shows genuine care for your customers, so when a client is handed off to you, take the initiative to gather all the key details about their history, background information, and overall satisfaction. At Eloqua, we had a saying: "If the customer tells us something, they shouldn't have to tell it to us again." Do your best to emulate this mindset. The idea is that anything the customer shares with sales, professional services, CS, or support should be captured in a central location. If this doesn't exist in your organization, look for ways you can make improvements.

Examine any client notes you have, past correspondence, and other interactions as well as chatting with your colleagues. For example:

- Look at any recent support interactions with your team to see your client's recent issues, questions, and priorities. Look for any concerns they have and note the tone of the communication. Is it cordial, hostile, or similar to the norm you see? Are there any escalations? Not seeing any support interactions may also be a red flag—it all depends on your products.

- Find out if they have submitted any feature requests or have challenges caused by outstanding bugs.

- Review pertinent meeting notes and previous correspondence. Determine the last time someone from your organization met with key stakeholders and the context of the meeting. AI tools can quickly summarize all of this for you so you can narrow your focus.

- Avoid asking customers questions they've already answered or scheduling a QBR too soon after the previous CSM held one. This is unprofessional and erodes trust. Try to uncover as much as you can about the client from the information you already have.

- Review past recorded calls to understand the different customer personalities and gather additional context before your first meeting. Like a historian, you can review the past to uncover what sales may have promised or what the client thought was promised. Review all past contracts, renewal agreements, upsells, and other major milestones. Preparing will require some effort, but it will be worth it.

3. Review product usage and adoption

A common mistake CSMs make is prioritizing their customers' product usage data instead of first understanding their customer's business. This is why I placed reviewing your client's product usage at number three to stress the need to focus on their business first.

Your organization may use specific criteria to determine which clients are high and low performers. This may be part of a customer health score. Are they leveraging the key features that have proven to provide value? Do you have data-driven indicators that highlight the outcomes or benefits your client is experiencing?

You may also have key product usage areas, such as license utilization, which tells you if a client isn't fully utilizing what they're paying for or is ripe for an upsell. Last, reviewing the top and bottom product users may make sense so you can understand who the "power users" are and who may need additional attention. Many power users are also your top supporters or advocates. By identifying them, you can reach out and see if they would like to provide referrals or reviews, or be part of a case study.

After reviewing your product's usage and adoption, you should have several questions to ask your customers and some ideas on how to help them. You may find that certain new features were never used, or other components were never fully configured, or need to be reconfigured based on their company's growth. When taking on a new customer, you have a golden opportunity to establish yourself as a trusted advisor by bringing your client insights they were never aware of. Use this to your advantage.

I prefer to compare my customers' current product usage to our most successful customers that have similar characteristics, such as the same industry. Your company may have a customer maturity model or benchmark metrics that make this type of comparison easier. Even if you don't have these tools, always be prepared with relevant customer stories to drive home certain points. You can make a great impression by bringing insights, examples, and ideas to the table.

4. Draft an account plan

The best way to determine what you know and don't know about your newly assigned client is to gather all the relevant information in one place: an account plan. With account plans, you gain a comprehensive understanding of your customers, ensuring successful renewals and identifying areas for growth. Leverage the intelligence you gathered about your client in steps 1 to 3 to complete this task.

Will you have all the details needed to complete your account plan? No, and that's OK. I look at customers like jigsaw puzzles. It takes time to put the pieces together to get the full picture, but you need to start somewhere. The first draft of your client account plan is like starting with the corners and outside pieces of the puzzle. It gives you a jumping-off point to determine where the rest of the pieces go.

I'm using the term *account plan* rather than *success plan* because, though they are often used interchangeably, they convey different meanings. I describe an account plan as an internal document that provides a snapshot of a client's current situation, outlines key objectives, and details the actions of various internal teams to support the client in reaching those goals and exploring future opportunities. Success plans are similar but are shared with your customers, so they can't contain sensitive client information such as their future growth potential. We'll come back to success plans in chapter 17. Include these recommended elements in your account plan:

Contractual elements: the basic elements of the customer's contract that you need to know.

- ARR/MRR: ARR is annual recurring revenue, and MRR is monthly recurring revenue. Most SaaS businesses leverage one or the other to determine how much your client is paying you on a recurring basis. It indicates their current value to your organization.
- Contract start date: This is the start date of the current contract.
- Contract end date: This is the renewal date, which you should be intimately aware of. If you have opt-out dates, include those as well.
- Customer start date: The customer start date indicates when the client started doing business with you and tells you how long they have been a client.
- Launch date: The launch date is when the client starts achieving value with your product.
- Product(s) purchased: List of all the products purchased.

You may want to include other critical contractual elements.

Company summary: Include a summary of the details from your 3C assessment in this section. Add any pertinent details that could influence the overall account plan. For example, if the company has recently gone through a large layoff, this could indicate their business is struggling, which could impact how they leverage your products. Last, include any relevant historical details such as a recent CSM change or possible challenges during onboarding—anything that can provide more context on the relationship and its current state.

Client health: The *health score* tracks your client's health. It indicates the likelihood of your client renewing. This can be an automated score from your customer success platform (CSP) or a grade you manually assign to clients based on your health assessment such as green, yellow, or red. It usually includes several factors, including product usage and customer engagement data, as well as CSM sentiment.

If you don't have a formal health score, you can approach it manually using this structure:

- Green: There is a greater than 90 percent chance that your client will renew.
- Yellow: There is a 50–90 percent chance that your client will renew.
- Red: Under a 50 percent chance that your client will renew.

If your client is considered at risk—marked as red or yellow—you should clearly identify the primary reason for this status. Common causes include stakeholder changes, feature gaps, product or support issues, lack of perceived value, financial concerns, and more. While a client may be at risk for several reasons, focus on the core issue driving their low health score. Client health is covered in greater depth in chapter 8.

Key stakeholders: Create a condensed list of the key client stakeholders, their exact titles, and the strength of the relationship. Use the following contact roles (or similar ones that your organization uses):

- Decision-maker: This is your most important client stakeholder, as they will decide whether to renew their subscription with you. They are typically in senior roles—director level and up. Although several senior stakeholders may be involved in the renewal, depending on the cost of your products, there is usually one primary decision-maker.
- Primary contact(s). These are your day-to-day contacts, the primary people you converse with. They are often the administrators and can sometimes be the decision-makers.
- Influencer(s): Influencers are usually individuals in senior positions who can sway the decision about renewing your product, though they aren't the final decision-makers. For example, the CEO or

CTO can be an influencer. Sometimes, influencers can overrule the decision-maker. You need to identify all influencers and ensure that you address their concerns directly or through your primary contacts or decision-makers. In addition, if your decision-maker leaves, influencers can gain more power, so you need to know who they are and keep them in the communication loop.

Other roles to consider identifying include billing and technical contacts, depending on the nature of your product and the individuals involved on the customer's side. It's also a good idea to pinpoint your client *champions*. These are your loyal supporters who will endorse your company when called upon.

Once you've completed this first step, indicate the strength of the relationship with each client contact—either weak, moderate, or strong. This indicates how connected you are with the client and where you must invest your time further to prevent surprises.

- Weak: Someone who is unresponsive or difficult to connect with, or someone that no one in your organization has engaged with in over a year.
- Moderate: Someone who either is slow to respond or hasn't engaged with your organization for at least three months but has within the last year.
- Strong: Someone who responds within a few days, or someone who regularly engages with your organization.

A new customer stakeholder should be labeled *weak* until you can establish a trusted relationship. If you aren't sure what the relationship strength should be, mark them as weak until you determine the right level. I also recommend mapping out your stakeholders' reporting relationships to better understand your customer's organizational structure and identify the key players.

As you get to know your customer stakeholders, it's also important to capture their personal goals. Are they trying to learn additional skills? Are they trying to get a promotion? Including these details in your account plan will help you tailor your future communication to help your customers along their career journeys.

Once you have completed this exercise, you should know how strong the relationships are for each key role and if you have any gaps in the stakeholder relationships that need to be prioritized. In addition, this exercise will tell you if any of them are *detractors*—people who have a negative view of your company and may be opposed to renewing.

Expert tip: The 1–2 punch and 3 × 3

As a rule of thumb, identify one decision-maker and two primary contacts to ensure you're well-connected with your customers. This is what I call the 1–2 punch. It protects you if one of your main contacts leaves. For enterprise clients with multiple stakeholders, Wayne McCulloch, author of *The Seven Pillars of Customer Success*, recommends following a 3 × 3 model.[13]

The 3 × 3 model involves building relationships across three organizational levels, such as VP, director, and manager, with at least three individuals at each level. This approach helps establish broad and deep connections within the customer organization. While it may be difficult to achieve, it's an easy framework to remember.

A classic mistake is relying too much on relationships with primary contacts while neglecting to cultivate strong connections with decision-makers and influencers. This is a common precursor to churn,

---

13 Wayne McCulloch, *The Seven Pillars of Customer Success: A Proven Framework to Drive Impactful Client Outcomes for Your Company* (Lioncrest Publishing, 2021), 303–304.

because though the client appears to be green, the decision-maker may have decided to switch to a competitor without your knowledge. Don't be caught flat-footed. It's part of your role to ensure you develop a close relationship with the right customer stakeholders at the right level. While you own this relationship, that doesn't mean you can't leverage others in your organization, such as the CS leader or other executives, to assist with engaging these senior customer stakeholders (see chapter 9 for how to engage decision-makers).

Reason for purchasing: Why did your client originally do business with you? This is usually documented by the sales team. Don't forget to capture this detail and any particular use cases they envisioned for your product. Then determine whether the original reasons for purchasing your product are still relevant. Businesses evolve over time—they expand, downsize, and transform. Customers who were once a perfect match for your product may no longer align with your *ideal customer profile* (ICP). Your organization may innovate to match their new requirements or you may decide that they're no longer a good fit and that it's OK to let them churn. Your job is to identify the risk and bring it forward to your company to determine what can be done to save them.

Product adoption: This section will offer an overview of how effectively your clients leverage your products. You can break this section out by product, feature, or use case—it depends on your organization and your products. For example, I've seen account plans that list specific use cases and indicate the level of maturity the client has reached in each area. This section illustrates the breadth and depth of your client's product usage.

Business outcomes: Business outcomes are the high-level objectives that indicate whether your customers have achieved value from your product. Examples of business outcomes include improving efficiency, increasing sales, or improving employee satisfaction. These should be written from your customer's perspective and in their language—not yours. Each business out-come should have at least one success metric that demonstrates the impact of your product. An example would be something like "increasing revenue by 10 percent by the end of Q2." Last, list out the goals with associated tactics that, if completed, should lead to achieving the stated measurable result (see chapter 17).

Risks: In this section, you should detail all possible risks or threats associated with your clients. These should emanate from the client health section mentioned previously. Include the risk type (similar to the at-risk reason described above), the possible impact (low, medium, or high), and the risk mitigation strategy to get things back on track.

A common risk mentioned in an account plan is a client stakeholder change. For example, if there is a new decision-maker, that should be noted in this section as a possible risk, and there should be a plan to ensure you meet with that person to determine their priorities and business outcomes. The overall impact should be marked as *high* because it's unclear what this person's priorities are, and you need to establish trust. Another common risk is a known product gap, which usually includes a specific feature request your customer has made.

If you observe anything unusual during the transition of the account to you, record it in the risk section and assess the severity. As the slogan of the NYC transportation authority goes, "If you see something, say something."

Opportunities: The next component of an account plan documents any potential growth opportunities. The opportunities section outlines new features your clients may be interested in and potential expansion opportunities that they need to pay for. There may also be additional divisions that you want to sell into. This section is very helpful when you have multiple customer-facing teams involved, such as account managers or sales reps. This also indicates future potential and provides more visibility into how valuable a client is to your organization based on their current and potential spend. For more on ways to seek expansion revenue, see chapter 20.

Next steps: The last component of an account plan outlines the prioritized actions that you and your client are responsible for. This section focuses on *how* to address your client's needs. Don't go into too much detail here; this isn't a project plan—it's a high-level summary. Include an estimated due date for each action, assign a task owner, and track the progress. As an example, given the client's desired outcomes and recorded risks, you might consider pairing an executive from your team with your client counterpart.

Should you create account plans for all your clients? It depends. If you manage more than fifty clients, creating account plans for each one would be extremely challenging. Begin with your most important ones, based on their value to your organization. Ultimately, you or your manager decide which clients to create account plans for. See Figure 3 for an example of an account plan and go to strategiccustomersuccess.com to download an account plan template.

Account Plan

Maple Software

General Information

ARR	$76,000	Product Package	Enterprise	CS Owner	Sasha
Contract Start Date	11/1/2026	# of Seats	23	AE	George
Contract End Date	10/31/2027	Additional Products	Insights, Chat	Exec Sponsor	Patti
Original Start Date	11/1/2026	GTM Segment	Strategic	Onboarding Manager	Jen
Live Date	12/15/2026	Implementation Type	Full Serve		
HQ State	Ontario	Client Health	Green		
HQ Country	Canada				
Website	maplesoftware.com				
Industry	Technology				

Customer Stakeholders

Full Name	Title	Contact Type	Relationship Strength	Champion?	Notes
Sarah	Head of CX	Decision Maker	Strong	TRUE	Very difficult to negotiate with
John	Manager of CX	Primary Contact	Medium	FALSE	Just joined. Still training
				FALSE	

Business Outcomes

Outcomes	Success Criteria (Target)	Priority	Status	Notes on progress
	10% of volume handled by chatbot by end of Q2	Medium	On Track	Chatbot volume is at 7%
Improve efficiency	Improve first response time by 10% by end of Q2	High	Derailed	First response time has only improved 2%

Product Adoption

Channels Used	Email, WhatsApp
Integrations	Shopify

Figure 3. An example of an account plan.

5. Establish your credentials

When being introduced to a customer for the first time, share your relevant experience and expertise to speed up the trust-building process. For instance, you could say, "I've been a CSM for over three years, have spent the past two years in this industry, and have worked with organizations such as X, Y, and Z to deliver outstanding results." Take a moment to write out your intro and even practice saying it a few times so you can say it with confidence.

It's a simple step that will put your clients at ease, as they'll know they're in capable hands, which is one of Robert Cialdini's principles of psychological influence, "authority," as depicted in his book *Influence: The Psychology of Persuasion*. The more you position yourself as an expert in your field, the greater the chances that your clients will take you seriously and follow your instructions.[14] Just as a doctor conveys authority with a stethoscope and diplomas displayed in their office, you should position yourself as a trusted advisor capable of driving your client's business success. You may not have a stethoscope, but you can ensure your LinkedIn profile is up to date with your experience, education, certifications, and any other relevant information. Consider listing the clients you've worked with in your experience section and highlighting how you contributed to their business success. The more recognizable and relatable those clients are, the better. Familiarity breeds trust.

Whenever possible, ask someone the client is familiar with, like the account executive or onboarding manager, to introduce you. This is known as a *warm handoff* and helps carry the trust already built up between the client and the other person over to you.

---

14   Robert B. Cialdini, *Influence: The Psychology of Persuasion* (HarperCollins, 2009), 164.

Expert tip: Talk about your experience—not how long you've been at your company

If you're new to your company and just taking on new clients, you don't need to tell the client that you're a rookie and still learning the ropes. Focus on your overall experience as a client-facing profession-al. Many new CSMs say, "I'm new here," thinking it will earn the client's sympathy and forgiveness for potential missteps, but it may have the reverse effect.

Revealing to clients that you're new may prompt them to be cautious about accepting your guidance. They may wonder, "What can this person do to help me?" Clients may perceive that they aren't important enough to merit a more seasoned CSM, leaving you in a *trust gap* that's hard to bridge. If they inquire about your tenure, it's crucial to be transparent. That said, there is no reason to divulge this information unless asked, as it can work against you.

6. Share something about yourself

Customer intimacy "is the pinnacle relationship where the CSM knows the customer better than anyone else," says Mary Poppen, an author and renowned customer success and customer experience leader.[15] How do you cultivate that level of intimacy? A simple way to achieve this is by revealing something personal about yourself. I often share a brief story about my kids or our dog. It usually goes something like, "Apologies if you hear some noise in the background; my kids have friends over." This small gesture often encourages your customers to share something personal in return. You can also ask about their weekend or holiday plans. Always remember to see your clients as people, not just a checkbox to check off.

---

15 Ashvin Vaidyanathan and Ruben Rabago, *The Customer Success Professional's Handbook: How to Thrive in One of the World's Fastest Growing Careers—While Driving Growth for Your Company* (John Wiley & Sons, 2020) 75.

Besides mentioning personal details in conversations, use visual cues to spark a more personable conversation. For example, in my home office, I created a collage of my kids' art on the wall behind me, including colorful pictures of rainbows and hearts. It's become the perfect Zoom background and deepens the level of intimacy with other meeting attendees. Roaming pets can also bring levity to your meetings.

Other suggestions include displaying concert posters, sports memorabilia, or whatever else interests you—as long as it's professional. Since displaying your actual home environment may not be possible, a virtual background that tells a personal story can suffice. By sharing something personal, you show your customers that it's okay for them to do the same.

Expert tip: Keep track of your customer's personal details

When your clients reveal where they live, their children's names and ages, their upcoming honeymoon location, their favorite muffin recipe, or even their dog's favorite food, write it down! Mentioning these personal details later in your conversation or at a subsequent meeting can build a stronger bond with your customer that goes beyond work. Little things matter, and the more you treat your customers as people, the greater the trust you'll form with them. My bonus tip is to send your customers personalized gifts based on what you learn about them.

7. Call out the large issues right away

One of the worst things you can do when taking on a customer is to ignore existing issues or try to sidestep them. This will only lead to frustration and damage trust. The best approach is to acknowledge any major challenges in the relationship upfront and tackle them head-on. You can't overlook past problems just because you weren't part of them. They are now your problems too. Acknowledging known issues will release customer tension and build a trust-based foundation. They'll see you as a problem solver and a strong advocate on their behalf.

8. Focus on what you know rather than what you don't

It can be daunting taking on new clients. You may tell yourself, "What if I don't know enough? They'll think I don't know what I'm talking about." Use the knowledge and resources you already have and focus on your strengths. Be confident in your skills and rely on your prior experiences, even if you're new to the role. You know more than you think you do. Trust me. With that said, the more product and industry knowledge you have, the more value you can provide your customers. It's not just about being a product expert but knowing how to apply your product knowledge to meet your client's needs.

9. Stop telling lies so you feel better

It seems obvious that you shouldn't lie to your clients, but we do this more than we realize. You may feel that customers will think less of you if you can't answer their questions, but the reality is that it's a lot worse when you provide false information. If your client discovers the truth (which they almost always do), you've just put yourself in a tough spot for no reason.

If you don't know the correct response to your client's inquiry, just tell them you aren't sure and provide a timeframe when they can expect to hear from you. Providing incorrect or incomplete information just so you feel better can erode your customer's confidence in you when they realize you lied to them. While it's tempting to just spit out an answer—don't do it.

10. Clarify your role and reset communication expectations

A change in CSMs is a good opportunity to reset your client's expectations of the CSM role and the other resources they may have access to, including support. Their requests might include regular technical consultations or frequent meetings, but this approach may not maximize the value you can deliver. Call a time-out and reestablish both the rules of engagement with your client and the meeting cadence.

A reset allows you to clarify your duties and review the various resources and services they have access to. For example, instruct your customers to contact your support team for all product-related issues instead of sending them to you. If your clients resist, simply explain that your support team can more adequately track their items and leverage their collective product expertise to provide a more accurate response. If your customers continue to reach out to you, try and understand if your client has any underlying issues with your support team.

To assist in this process, remind your clients of the different resources available to them, including who they should go to for what and the expected response times. This could consist of your customer community, training portal, or other similar resources if those exist. There shouldn't be any ambiguity about where your customers should go when they need assistance or the expected turnaround time.

In addition, define how often you will meet with your customers, what the meetings will consist of, and who should be present at these meetings. For example, set a cadence for QBRs and outline what they'll include. Ask them for their communication preferences. Some clients prefer to meet quarterly but want to receive regular tips/best practices or know about upcoming product features. Others prefer to receive text reminders when they are behind on a jointly agreed-on task. Clearing this up in the transition call will set you up for future success.

11. Send a detailed follow-up

Don't waste a great first impression by falling down on the follow-up. Send a detailed meeting recap, including the decisions made and action items, within twenty-four hours of your first meeting. Knock out any easy tasks quickly and set expectations for when you will respond to the other items. This avoids any confusion regarding what was covered and what needs to happen next.

> **Expert tip: Ask who else should receive regular updates**
> Meeting new customers can be overwhelming, as you may meet with several new stakeholders. Don't assume that all the stakeholders can make the initial meeting. If they aren't there, simply say: "I want to share these positive results with others in your organization. Who should we include in the follow-up that isn't present at this meeting?" This way you get to know all the stakeholders. I've uncovered some important client stakeholders that I didn't know existed with this easy tip. Record those contacts in your account plan and indicate their contact role.

12. Respond as if the renewal depends on it

Your new client may send you a simple question or make a small request during your first meeting. For instance, they may ask for an update on a feature request. How you address these initial requests can set the tone for the rest of the relationship. Respond to them as if the renewal depends on it, but you don't need to rush back with an answer just for the sake of answering. Get the details you need from your team and respond appropriately—just don't forget about it. If it will take you a few days to get back to them, let them know when they should expect to hear back from you. Even if it's not you that will follow up, let them know who they should expect to hear from. This creates a perception that you are someone they can trust.

Expert tip: Push off the intro

When a client is transferred to you, defer the introduction until you've had the necessary time to get acquainted with the client's background and setup. One of the worst things you can do is meet with a new client without adequate preparation. If you're unaware of the client's current onboarding status, key frustrations, or pressing priorities, you may start the relationship on the wrong foot. All it takes to destroy your credibility is asking a question you should know the answer to or answering it in a way that demonstrates that you know nothing about their business. Don't be that person.

By rushing the client transition, you risk making a poor first impression and putting the entire relationship at risk. One of the most common pet peeves customers complain about is repeatedly explaining their history to a new CSM. If they feel they're wasting their time, you may not get a second meeting. At Kustomer, I encouraged CSMs to refuse to do client transition meetings until an internal information-sharing session had been held and the previous CSM had completed the transition process. Push for something similar if your organization doesn't have such a process.

Putting this into practice

Go to strategiccustomersuccess.com to access "The Strategic CSM Client Transition" checklist that includes many of the items mentioned in this chapter. Complete this the next time you take on a new customer and keep track of how many elements you used.

Create an account plan: Leverage what was covered in this chapter to create an account plan for one of your clients (past or present). Remember, you don't need to know all the elements of your account plan right away. Use it to capture what you need to start on the right path with your new client.

Optional: Go to strategiccustomersuccess.com to download the "Account Plan" template.

Summary and key takeaways

Taking on new customers shouldn't be something you fear. It's important to build trust with your clients early on.

To build trust when taking on a new client:

- Don't dig yourself holes that will be impossible to get out of.
- Establish your expertise, be prepared, be vulnerable, be honest, set expectations, follow up, be responsive, and do the necessary work to make your clients successful.
- Don't forget that trust is a foundational element of customer success. While there are ways to speed up the process of building trust, trust can be easily broken.
- Use the 3C framework to focus on your client's business rather than their use of your product. This includes understanding their company, their customers, and their challenges.
- Review past notes and correspondence and their use of your product before you meet with a client.
- Create an account plan that contains everything you know about the customer: contact details, company information, client health, key stakeholders, reasons for purchasing, product adoption, business outcomes, identified risks, and possible opportunities.
- Properly introduce yourself by focusing on your prior experiences and successes. Don't play the *new employee* card. Your customers don't care, and it can work against you.
- Speed up intimacy by sharing something about yourself with customers and asking for the same in return. Be vulnerable.
- Call out their larger issues immediately and determine how you will deal with them.

- Remember you know more than you think, even if you're new to your company. Focus on your skills and expertise rather than what you feel you lack.
- Send a detailed follow-up with clear action items, owners, and due dates.
- Respond to your customer's first request as if the renewal depends on it.

Follow these tips to set the right tone for your relationship and to create an atmosphere of trust. Go show your new clients what you're made of!

CHAPTER 3

Skills and Behaviors that Strategic CSMs Need to Master

Several years ago, while at Eloqua, I had one of my strangest experiences as a CSM. I received a call from one of my clients, who started going off on me. He had just received an email from one of our sales reps that wasn't meant for him. You heard that right: For some reason, the rep accidentally cc'd the client on an internal email. The email contained some unprofessional details I won't go into here.

My client ended the call by saying, "That was really unprofessional. What's going on over there?" As I hung up the phone, I remember having a hollow feeling of shame inside me and a few veins on my head pulsing from my anger. Regrettably, my initial instinct was to call the sales rep and vent my frustration. It was impossible at the time for me to wrap my head around how that mistake could have happened.

Freaking out and allowing my emotions to dictate my decisions led to some very negative consequences. While no lasting harm resulted from the sales rep's actions, I made my sales colleague into an enemy that day and gained a reputation as a hothead who couldn't control his emotions. I didn't demonstrate enough empathy or self-regulation, and I regret it.

Admittedly, I still wrestle with controlling my emotions, but I've come a long way. SCSMs need to be self-aware and show empathy to build trust and deliver value internally and with customers.

Along with being self-aware, strategic CSMs need to develop other soft skills. While you may already have mastered some of these, others may require more time and practice. So your objective is to gain awareness of what is required to be an SCSM.

In the past, I've struggled to define the skills and behaviors I expected my customer success teams to emulate, so I took the time to document these. This led to the creation of these four main skill and behavior categories:

- Emotional intelligence
- Ownership and growth
- Teamwork and influence
- Entrepreneurship and leadership

These four categories are interrelated. Don't be discouraged if you currently lack some of these skills and behaviors. The rest of the book will assist you in developing and mastering them so you can transform yourself into an SCSM.

Emotional intelligence

Emotional intelligence is about recognizing, understanding, and managing one's own emotions and recognizing, understanding, and influencing the feelings of others. You inherently acknowledge that what you do and say can impact others positively or negatively. Your emotional intelligence can help you resolve conflicts, handle stressful situations, and prevent disagreements from happening in the first place.[16]

---

16 "What Is Emotional Intelligence?," Last Eight Percent, accessed December 10, 2024, https://www.ihhp.com/meaning-of-emotional-intelligence/.

To achieve emotional intelligence, focus on:

- Self-awareness
- Empathy
- Adaptability
- Openness in communication

Self-awareness is being in tune with and monitoring one's own emotions. Cultivating this skill will enhance one's ability to connect with others effectively. As mentioned, I've struggled with this area over the years. In the heat of the moment, stress can take over, and I can either blow up or become too defensive. I've also let my passion for the customer get the better of me, which I exhibited when I lashed out at my sales colleague.

Bringing emotion into a conversation can be beneficial, but only to a certain extent. If you dismiss your colleagues' opinions or snap at your manager in front of others, you'll alienate yourself. It's also important to stay calm and avoid raising your voice with your customers, even when you feel attacked. My advice is to always take the high road—no matter what. To work on this skill, see chapter 18 on handling upset clients.

Self-aware people recognize their weaknesses and shortfalls. They realize when they need help and seek it out. They are skilled at keeping cool under pressure and can assess what is happening around them to determine the best course of action.

In addition, someone with high self-awareness has excellent interpersonal relationships across their organization. They can read the room and exhibit a strong sense of maturity. They consider the consequences of their actions and the impact of their words.

Empathy is about imagining yourself in others' shoes, internalizing their needs, and connecting with their emotions. It extends to customers and your teammates.

Someone with a high degree of empathy practices active listening techniques, which are critical to developing strong bonds with others and having strategic conversations (see part IV). They assume the best of others and don't pass judgment or blame.

In the past, I would immediately jump to blame mode. This, of course, would usually backfire because there are always two sides to the story. To help me keep my emotions in check, I start with the facts. I ask myself and others, "What actually happened here?" and then replay the facts. In most cases, a miscommunication or a simple mistake has occurred.

Adaptability lies in skillfully navigating the rapid shifts within your organizational landscape and that of your clients. You must be good at rolling with the punches and not get too hung up when things go haywire, such as a major product bug. This behavior is especially needed within fast-growing start-ups.

Someone with a high degree of adaptability can easily handle multiple demands flying at them, shifting priorities, and a high degree of ambiguity. They demonstrate resilience in the face of adversity. They are OK with working through broken or incomplete processes and stepping in to improve them. They are comfortable with being uncomfortable. They also exhibit a tremendous amount of grit, which Angela Duckworth, the authority on this subject, defines as having "passion and perseverance for long-term goals."[17]

The previously mentioned former VP of CS at Eloqua, Paul Teshima, once placed what seemed to me an impossible retention goal in front of the entire customer success organization at a quarterly kickoff. Paul seemed completely disconnected from reality, and my frustration must have been written all over my face. At the time, Eloqua was doing a complete overhaul of its user interface, causing tremendous pain for our customers and the CS team as we wobbled through this transformation. My team was at the

---

17 Angela Duckworth, *Grit: The Power of Passion and Perseverance Young Readers Edition* (Simon & Schuster/Paula Wiseman Books, 2020), 956.

epicenter of our client's disgruntlement, making Paul's target a hard pill to swallow. I eventually accepted this goal, but it took some time to get behind it. I understood that we had to look beyond our current situation and keep moving forward. I kept reminding myself: Adapt, adapt, adapt.

Openness in communication involves being clear and transparent, which creates strong connections grounded in trust with customers and peers alike. You foster an environment where information flows freely and openly, and you are receptive to ideas and opinions. You ensure that critical information is regularly shared internally and externally and that messages are conveyed clearly and concisely.

SCSMs who have mastered communication openness regularly share their expertise with their customers and within their organizations. They broadcast positive news, such as hitting a new milestone, but they don't shy away from telling a customer that a certain feature isn't on the immediate roadmap. They appreciate and respect customer feedback despite how crazy it sounds, and they maintain a high degree of professionalism in all their communication.

Ownership and growth

This category is arguably the most critical. Embodying ownership, believing in one's ability to grow, and fostering growth in others are essential for success as a strategic CSM. Being an owner means committing to one's responsibilities, goals, and targets. Even more importantly, it means being committed to the success of one's customers.

Someone who embodies the idea of constant growth is committed to enhancing their skills, how their company operates, and their customers' results. They actively pursue learning and self-development opportunities and are open to feedback. Both concepts require a high degree of drive that will push you to improve your customers, yourself, and everyone around you.

Work on cultivating the four main elements of ownership and growth:

- Drive
- Growth mindset
- Customer centricity
- Accountability and bias for action

Drive is an inner motivation to excel and make progress. It also involves a steadfast commitment to your team's mission. This could include finding creative ways to address your customers' needs or leading a project to improve your team's productivity. High-performing SCSMs are a fountain of energy and set the pace for the rest of their CS organization.

Someone with a high degree of drive has an intrinsic desire to push the envelope and improve their environment. They are relentlessly committed to achieving their own goals and are dedicated to securing their customers' goals, and even assisting their teammates in attaining their goals. They embody the concept of proactiveness and typically operate well beyond their core responsibilities.

Drive is a core competency of mine, but it can also be a double-edged sword. It pushes me to do everything I can to achieve specific targets, but it can also cause me to work well beyond regular business hours, impacting my personal life. If you're a highly driven person like me, you must set limits to protect yourself from burnout and from negatively impacting your friends and loved ones.

A **growth mindset** is rooted in a belief in self-improvement achieved through consistent effort in learning and refining behaviors. The term originates from Stanford professor Carol Dweck's book *Mindset: The New Psychology of Success*. Someone with a growth mindset runs toward difficult challenges rather than away from them. They remain curious even in challenging situations, stretch themselves outside their comfort zone, and perceive setbacks as stepping stones on their path to attaining higher levels of achievement.[18]

People who embody the idea of a growth mindset also foster an environment of continuous improvement. They recognize that growth requires mastering new skills and sharing their insights and abilities with others. Someone with a growth mindset doesn't get bogged down in perceived issues and constraints. They know that "shit happens," and they deal with it. In addition, those with a growth mindset can see past short-term problems without getting mired in a sea of negativity. Top-performing SCSMs leverage their growth mindset to champion change within their customers' organizations and their own.[19]

Being **customer-centric** involves being obsessed with your customers and representing their voice within your organization. Customer-centric individuals feed off the success and satisfaction of their customers and take it personally when mishaps occur or customers churn. The ultimate achievement of someone who is customer-centric is generating long-term relationships beyond their current role and even their current company. For instance, customers I met more than ten years ago at Eloqua still engage with me on LinkedIn. This reflects my dedication to putting the client first, and it stands out as one of my proudest achievements as a customer success professional.

Customer-centric people aim to build personal connections with their customers and strive to understand their needs rather than feigning interest. They are curious about their customers as people outside of work and take the time to explore their customers' needs by delving into their challenges. Strategic CSMs go a step further by anticipating their customers' requests.

---

18 Carol S. Dweck, *Mindset: The New Psychology of Success* (Ballantine Books, 2007), 81.

19 Swati Somineni, "The Power of Growth Mindset in Customer Success," SmartKarrot, April 12, 2021, https://www.smartkarrot.com/resources/blog/customer-success-growth-mindset/.

In addition, customer-centric SCSMs look for new ways to add value to customers. The end result is an engaged customer base with many customers who will advocate on your company's behalf through testimonials, case studies, and other means (see chapter 9 for examples of building unbreakable customer relationships).

Someone with high **accountability** is committed to their role and responsibilities and takes the lead in resolving complex customer problems. They bring forward viable solutions rather than just raising issues. They have a *bias for executing ideas* rather than just suggesting them.

Accountable and execution-focused individuals prioritize the most important items over urgent ones. In this way, they focus on tasks that will have the most impact, such as QBRs, rather than client busywork that can suck up their time and attending to clients who scream the loudest. Successful strategic CSMs take ownership of challenging projects and understand when to seek assistance from others. For more on this topic, see chapter 12 on productivity.

Teamwork and influence

Customer success teams rely on highly collaborative environments where individuals put their egos aside and help each other. While strategic CSMs care about their individual performance metrics, they embody the feeling that they are "in this together" and assist their teammates as needed.

My proudest achievement as a customer success leader at Kustomer was the camaraderie we forged when we were in hypergrowth mode and then acquired by Meta. Our team culture reminded me of the atmosphere of HBO's *Band of Brothers* miniseries. Between the acquisition announcement, the deal's formal closing, and the divestiture from Meta, there was complete chaos at times.

My team could barely hang on, but they didn't let the pressure overcome them. They didn't want to let their teammates down, as their success was tied to the team's success. That is what teamwork is all about.

Influencing customers requires a blend of empathy, critical thinking, and effective coaching abilities. For instance, guiding customers away from their legacy processes requires uncovering obstacles to change and creating a strategy to address them. You can't force them to drastically alter their workflows when they've become accustomed to their familiar routines (see part IV on how to have strategic conversations).

To be a team player:

- Collaborate
- Coach and mentor others

Collaboration involves fostering an environment of team cohesion in which everyone supports each other, actively shares their knowledge, and relies on each other's expertise. It involves being present when your teammates need you the most, without being prompted. Those with a collaborative mindset recognize their teammates' contributions, big or small. Their spirit of collaboration also extends to their customers and their desire to partner with them.

Someone who is highly collaborative demonstrates a high degree of humility and places team success above any individual rewards. They embrace diversity among their colleagues and celebrate people's uniqueness. They have established strong connections across their team and their organization and can help uncover and resolve team conflicts. While they may not agree with every company policy or decision, they commit when it's clear that their company has made a firm decision.

Coaching and mentorship involve educating, influencing, and developing those around you—whether your customers or colleagues. By doing so, you uplevel their abilities and deepen their trust in you.

Those adept at coaching and mentoring excel in facilitating insightful customer discovery conversations. More experienced SCSMs can mentor their teammates and may move into leadership roles.

Entrepreneurship and leadership

As a strategic CSM, you're the CEO of your book of business, and you should act as if you're running your own small company. It might feel unusual to think of yourself as an entrepreneur within your own company, but successful CSMs need the same skills required to create a thriving business.

Leadership might traditionally be associated with guiding people, but it also entails making sound decisions, setting the right strategy for your customers, and managing them effectively. Last, to effectively lead your customers and influence your company as an SCSM, you need to be a product expert and adept at analyzing data.

To be an effective entrepreneur, you need:

- Business acumen
- Client management
- Decisiveness
- Product expertise and an analytical mindset

Business acumen can refer to several different competencies. For an SCSM, it means having a thorough understanding of the financial dynamics within your customer portfolio and your company. It also includes recognizing your customers' business objectives, mastering the art of negotiation to align outcomes, and identifying opportunities to enhance customer value and drive revenue growth.

Strong business acumen means having a clear understanding of the amount of revenue you manage, the business value your clients have achieved, and the customers within your patch who have the best chance of increasing their spend with you.

In addition, you also demonstrate a keen interest in understanding your customers' business, including their products, target audience, and the challenges they encounter (the three C's mentioned in chapter 2). You also leverage customer engagements to uncover your customers' priorities and business outcomes. Last, experienced strategic CSMs have negotiation experience in high-stakes environments—especially those who work with enterprise customers. This can include finalizing a renewal agreement, presenting various expansion options, or influencing which features your product team should focus on.

Client management involves the key behaviors and strategies CSMs use to nurture, retain, and expand customer relationships. This includes aligning with customers' business outcomes and employing QBRs, success plans, and other tools to provide value and achieve results. It can also involve revenue management duties, such as renewals and expansions.

SCSMs with strong client management skills create comprehensive plans aligned with their customers' business outcomes and set clear expectations to avoid misunderstandings. They also need to be effective project managers to keep the customers on track and are willing to challenge them constructively. Moreover, they are comfortable engaging customer stakeholders at all levels and don't fear having tough conversations.

Decisiveness requires gathering key details, making rational and timely decisions, and guiding your customers to do the same. With this, you exude confidence and aren't afraid to make mistakes. This could mean making a concession to the customer in a very tense negotiation or holding firm when a customer makes an unreasonable request.

Someone who is decisive collects as much information as possible and can discern what additional information is required before determining the best next step. They can break down multiple issues and focus on what is most pressing. Strategic CSMs need to break out of analysis paralysis and make difficult choices despite missing key details. Even if they don't make the right decision every time, they keep moving forward and learn from their mistakes. They also guide their customers to make the best decisions possible and push them to act.

Having a **deep understanding of your product** is an essential aspect of being a successful SCSM. Not only do you know the ins and outs of your products, but you can also mesh your product knowledge with your customers' needs to generate the best solutions possible. A strong component of being a solutions-focused CSM is the ability to interpret and analyze data. The degree of skill required will depend on how technical and complex your products are and the breadth and depth of the data produced.

Someone who possesses extensive product expertise will have mastered the fundamentals of their products and be up to date on the latest feature releases. They show a high degree of curiosity and may experiment with new ways of using their products. They may also put forward several high-value feature enhancements based on the challenges they've witnessed on the front lines. Those who excel in this area are often called upon by other members of their organization for their insights.

A person with a powerful **analytical mindset** employs data from diverse sources, including product usage, benchmarks, and industry data, to assist customers in making optimal decisions. They are comfortable either working with existing reporting tools or busting out Excel, ChatGPT or business intelligence platforms to dive further into the data and discover meaningful insights. Top-performing SCSMs will leverage data to not only influence their customers but also drive change within their company.

Do you seriously want me to do all of that?

If you're a bit overwhelmed by what is required to be a strategic CSM, that's OK. Acquiring these skills takes years and requires exposure to situations that will test your abilities. The skills are challenging to develop, and they require deep practice. You can't get there by reading a few books or taking some courses on customer success and calling it a day.

On a positive note, you've probably noticed the overlap across the four different skill and behavior categories, which means that learning one skill can help you become proficient in others. So focus on one or two areas as a starting point and go from there. To assist in this process, complete the exercise in the *Putting this into practice* section to better understand your current level of proficiency.

The last thing to keep in mind is that you'll most likely never master all these skills and behaviors. That's why I've stressed the significance of collaborating with other team members. Utilize your colleagues' talents whenever feasible. Accept that others will have expertise that you don't, and be OK with that.

Putting this into practice

What are the skills and behaviors you should focus on? Go to strategiccustomersuccess.com and download the SCSM Skills & Behaviors Matrix. Evaluate where you feel you currently stand in each section to gain insight into your strengths and areas for improvement. I also recommend completing the CliftonStrengths assessment to understand your top five strengths, so you have a sense of where you should double down and where you should lean on others.[20]

Summary and key takeaways

To become an SCSM, you need soft skills in emotional intelligence, ownership and growth, teamwork and influence, and entrepreneurship and leadership.

---

20 Go to https://www.gallup.com/cliftonstrengths/ to complete a CliftonStrengths Assessment.

These skills include:

- self-awareness
- empathy
- adaptability
- communication openness
- drive
- decisiveness
- a growth mindset
- accountability and a bias for action
- collaborativeness
- ability to coach and mentor others
- business acumen
- client management
- customer centricity
- product expertise
- an analytical mindset

Learning these skills and behaviors won't happen overnight. They take time and deep practice to develop. There are no shortcuts. So focus on one or two skills to start, and remember you don't need to master all of these skills and behaviors, although you should be proficient in as many as possible.

PART II

Your First Ninety Days as a CSM and Beyond

CHAPTER 4

Starting Your CSM Role with the Basics

Awkwardness is the best way to describe how I felt when I started a CS role earlier in my career. I was trying to soak up as much as I could as quickly as possible to stop feeling useless and helpless. Everyone else seemed to have their stuff together, yet I didn't even know how to schedule a meeting, let alone find the meeting room I was invited to.

On my second day, I was asked to shadow a client call. I felt uncomfortable being introduced as the person "just listening in," which is often code for "Ignore them; they're not important." All I could do was sit there like a five-year-old child in advanced algebra class. Everything went over my head.

I had to remind myself that this is a normal feeling and to slow down and take things one step at a time. No one expected I would become an expert in my first week, and I shouldn't have put so much pressure on myself. I began crafting my own onboarding plan to navigate the challenges of these initial months. This personalized approach complemented my company's onboarding process, setting me up for success in my role. The next few chapters will outline this in greater detail.

As a new CSM, you need to start with the basics, including learning about your company, the customers you serve, and how to use your products. These building blocks will lay the foundation for making sense of the other parts of your onboarding and will help you to eventually become a strategic CSM.

Get to know your company

You did it. You made it through the grueling interview process and landed that coveted role you dreamed about. Now comes the hard part—you'll need to prove to your new employer that you're up for the challenge. But are you conscious of the full reality that you find yourself in? Most likely not. Regardless of what you learned during the interview process, the veil will now be pulled back, and you'll see how things truly operate at your new company. As a starting point, focus your energy on what your company does, the products it offers, the industries it plays in, and its culture. That will give you the foundation to be more comfortable in your role.

Learn about your company's messaging and product offerings

During your onboarding, it's tempting to only focus on learning how to use your products inside and out, but that will only get you so far. You must grasp how the different components of your products align to fulfill your customers' needs and how your products' advantages outweigh those of your competitors.

Many organizations offer an employee orientation program that includes a company overview, the value proposition of their products, and their market positioning. Unfortunately, these are typically generic and not geared to your specific role. Strategic CSMs push for a much more in-depth understanding of their company and its products.

Use the following questions to enhance your understanding of how to position your company in the competitive landscape:

What is your company's elevator pitch? How would you describe it to someone you met on the street? You should be able to explain what your company does succinctly. If you're unable to, ask someone on the sales team what their elevator pitch is and how they describe what your company does.

I prepare three types of elevator pitches that I use for different occasions:

- *A simple one-liner that I use at networking events*: I always had a one-liner description of my company ready for when I met people at various networking events. For example, I described Kustomer as a customer relationship management (CRM) support platform that competes with Zendesk and Salesforce. This summary offers enough context for most people to understand what our products do, allowing them to ask follow-up questions if they want to dive deeper.

- *A more in-depth explanation of what my company does*: This version goes beyond the one-liner by providing more details on what my company does and the products we sell. It's perfect for situations when a new stakeholder joins your meeting and knows very little about what your company does. In this extended company narrative, you might highlight the size of the companies you serve—be it small to midsize, midsize, or enterprise—along with some of your notable customers and any distinctive details that could captivate your audience. For instance, you could mention recent achievements like securing funding, reaching a significant revenue milestone, or receiving a prestigious award.

- *A version my parents would understand*: When I had to explain what Kustomer did to my parents, or I was at a party that included people who had no concept of what a CRM is, I made sure I had a simplified version at the ready that focused on how our products helped the end customer rather than describe my company. For instance, I explained to my mom that Kustomer is a customer service application designed to resolve customer support issues, such as helping her return a purse she mistakenly ordered.

What products do you offer? Become familiar with the various products your company sells. Beyond learning your lineup of products, you'll also want to get a sense of what the typical purchase process looks like. For example, do customers purchase certain products upfront and then add on others over time? Is there a certain combination of products that tend to be purchased together? Having a broad understanding of this can reveal the typical product bundles your customers choose, their buying patterns, and the types of products in your portfolio.

Why do your customers buy from you? There's usually certain pain points your product was brought in to address. This ties directly to your value proposition—the set of promises your product is expected to deliver. Your sales team has the best take on why customers buy, so I would ask the top sales reps this question.

How much do you charge for your products? Once you understand your product offering and value proposition, it's time to examine your pricing strategy. To effectively support your clients and ensure they see a return on their investment, you must understand the details of their contract fees and the factors that influence the price. Some products are priced based on the number of licenses, while others are charged based on actual product usage, such as the number of emails sent. Some products have a combination of license and usage fees. Once you learn your product pricing, review a few client agreements to understand how the costs were calculated.

It's also important to understand your customers' average annual contract value (ACV). This gives you a sense of how much money each customer pays you on average. The higher the ACV, the more effort is typically required for each customer and the more valuable they are. All this knowledge helps improve your overall business acumen.

How do customers purchase your products? Your customer's buying process may be as simple as a direct purchase from your website, or it may require extensive marketing and sales efforts to influence the decision. A more complex scenario may involve a reseller partner that sells your product on your behalf. Familiarizing yourself with how your prospects make buying decisions and the various contributors to the sales process will provide a deeper understanding of customer origins and potential challenges that may emerge in the future. For instance, you might discover that customers who go through a trial adopt your product faster than those who don't. The key takeaway here is to not focus solely on the post-sales journey but consider the entire buying process, as it significantly influences your ability to retain and grow customers.

How do you differ from your competitors? Take the time to learn the competitive landscape that you play in. You may be the three-hundred-pound gorilla in your space, owning the majority of the market share in your category. Salesforce.com is one such example in the CRM space. Or you may be a young start-up trying to dethrone the established players. Know where you stand and who you're up against. Ask for any available competitive information your company provides to learn who your competitors are and how your company distinguishes itself. For example, you may have a unique approach or set of features that differentiates you from your competitors. How you price your products may be what sets you apart from the pack.

Expert tip: Start preparing before your first day

Start preparing for your new CSM role before your official start date. Sure, your company probably has an onboarding process—but it's rarely as thorough as you need. If you have some extra time before your new role starts, use it to get ahead so you can hit the ground running.

Review any recent webinars your new company offers—especially ones that feature your customers—as well as any case studies. You'll learn about your customers' challenges, how your product helped them address those challenges, and the metrics that are meaningful to them. In addition, you'll start to become acquainted with the terminology your company and your customers use, which will speed up your learning in your first few weeks.

Next, go to online review sites such as G2 and take note of what customers love about your company and what they don't. Do they mention issues with your product, your service, or both? Is there a specific industry or size of company that may be experiencing more issues? You can then further discuss with your colleagues as to how truthful these statements are.

In addition, check out the competitor comparisons highlighted in G2 to understand who you're competing against and how your company is perceived compared with others. It will also highlight your company's strengths and weaknesses.

Learn the industry your company operates in

Being a product expert will only get you so far as a CSM. It's essential to grasp the bigger picture of the market your product belongs to, allowing you to see how it connects with other similar products. This typically means learning the industry or industries that your company operates in. Some examples of relevant industries for CSMs may be health care technology, financial technology (FinTech), ecommerce, or marketing technology (MarTech). Spend time understanding the terminology used in your industry, as it will improve how you communicate within your company and with your customers. This also includes the metrics that are important to your customers and the emerging trends that are driving change. Your company may have its own studies and reports, or there may be third-party analysts such as Gartner or Forrester who can provide additional insights. Knowing how to walk the walk and talk the talk of your customers will increase their faith in your ability to assist them with their business needs.

Some of this information will be covered within your onboarding training, but it's best to ask your colleagues how they keep up to date on industry trends. Are there resources that they recommend subscribing to? Podcasts they listen to? Are there industry influencers they follow? Carve out time within onboarding and beyond to learn from these resources.

Which market segments does your company play in (horizontal versus vertical)?

Companies typically focus on a specific vertical, or they serve multiple industries—a strategy often referred to as a horizontal play. For instance, if your product only serves ecommerce customers, then it's a vertical play. If your products serve multiple verticals such as ecommerce, travel and hospitality, finance, and entertainment, then it would be referred to as a horizontal play. Have a sense of whether your company sells to a specific market segment (vertical play) or to multiple market segments (horizontal play), as you'll want to know if you will be supporting one or more of these markets.

Learn and embody your culture

Your company's culture is immensely powerful. To thrive in your role, learn how to adapt to it. To accomplish this, align your behaviors, attitudes, and actions with it. As a starting point, learn your company's vision, mission, and values. Review these carefully and ensure that you comprehend their true meaning. Try to discern which values are the most important to the company.

A company's culture reveals itself as you meet with colleagues from within your team and from other teams and departments. But to get started, ask your colleagues:

- Which company values are the most important? Your company may have several values listed on its website, but which are the ones that are most talked about or celebrated? If your company has employee awards, schedule coffee dates with the previous winners so you can better understand what separated them from the pack.

- What are the company's unwritten rules? Every company operates by certain unwritten rules that you must get a handle on. Some of these rituals and practices are very apparent, but others just exist without people even realizing it. For example, at one company I worked for, there was the "old guard" of employees who had been there for several years and tended to stick together. Another company I worked at had a cliquey high school atmosphere that was very political. Some of these cultural norms change over time as the company evolves, but some persist. The better you understand these secret codes, tribes, and practices, the easier it will be to find your footing and get things done.

- Which department or function drives the company? Is your company sales-driven, customer-driven, or product-driven? This typically determines which function gets the most attention and the most resources. The background of the company's founders tends to influence the answer to this question. Of course, this can change over time and may shift due to your company's priorities.

There are no right or wrong answers here. Knowing your organization's most important values, the unwritten rules, and where the center of power lies will give you the knowledge to focus your actions and avoid potential landmines. You'll gain insight into what drove these decisions.

As renowned author Peter Drucker said, "Culture eats strategy for breakfast."[21] This means that your company's culture will dictate the direction of the company. Get to know your organization's culture and what it values the most to maximize your effectiveness. Pushing for change that con-

---

21 Jacob M. Engel, "Why Does Culture 'Eat Strategy for Breakfast'?," Forbes, November 20, 2018, https://www.forbes.com/councils/forbescoachescouncil/2018/11/20/why-does-culture-eat-strategy-for-breakfast/.

tradicts your company culture can be career-ending, so beware. Change can happen, but it's easier when you're paddling in the same direction as the rest of the company.

Get to know the customers who buy your products

During your onboarding, learn about the types of customers your product serves before you're assigned specific clients. You may have never worked in this industry, so the better you know your customers, the greater the chance you can earn their trust and help them achieve value.

To assist you in getting to know your customers, ask your colleagues:

- What are the typical customer roles/personas that you would work with? In which departments do your customer contacts work? What are their various titles? What are the distinct characteristics of these people? It's important to distinguish the different roles and personas of customers you work with to assist you in building closer relationships with them and to determine whether you are connecting with the right people.

- What terminology do your customers use? Review recorded customer calls, case studies, webinars, industry reports, and case study blog posts to learn the common terminology your customers use. For example, at Kustomer, our customers would mention the terms customer satisfaction, workforce management, and omnichannel, as they were in the customer experience space. As you start to hear the same terms over and over again, jot them down, along with the context in which they were used. This is worth the investment: The faster you learn the standard terms your customers use, the faster things will start to click for you, and the quicker you can jump into your role and start managing customers with greater confidence.

In the book *The Challenger Sale*, Matthew Dixon and Brent Adamson found that the best-performing sales reps "win not by understanding their customers' world as well as the customers know it themselves, but by actually knowing their customers' world better than their customers know it themselves, teaching them what they don't know but should."[22] CSMs who want to transform into SCSMs should follow this sage advice. To accomplish this, find out how your customers keep up to date on industry trends and hang out in the communities that they are members of. Put in this extra effort to immerse yourself in their world; it will pay off in the long run.

- What types of metrics are important to your customers? Track the specific metrics your customers consider to be proof of real impact. These metrics may include increases in sales, decreases in workplace accidents, increases in leads generated, or decreases in dollars spent. It's your job to become familiar with what they track, where this data is stored, and how it impacts their organization.

- Who are the customers mentioned the most by your sales team in their pitches, and whose logos are plastered all over your site? Get to know your most important customers and what makes them the poster children for your company. Why are they so special? How are they uniquely using your products? What benefits are they achieving? How is their team structured to leverage your product (if applicable)? The answers to these questions can provide clues to how to best manage your own book of business.

- How are your customers segmented? Most businesses divide their customers into specific segments. This can depend on several elements, including how much your customers are paying you or the

22 Matthew Dixon and Brent Adamson, *The Challenger Sale: How to Take Control of the Customer Conversation* (Penguin UK, 2013), 45.

number of employees they have. More sophisticated segmentation models factor in aspects like customer growth potential, their strategic value, the complexity of their needs, and how well they adopt the product. At this point in your onboarding journey, familiarize yourself with how your company categorizes segments and identify which ones your role is centered around.

- Which areas of your product cause customers the most problems, if any? Most products have strengths and weaknesses. Find out where customers struggle the most with your products so you can determine how best to assist them and whether their challenge is a one-off or a common occurrence. For the known issues, inquire within your company about plans to address these shortfalls.

- What product features do they value the most? Identify the features your customers use and actions they engage in that will most profoundly impact their ability to realize value from your products. This will guide you on what you should focus on with your customers.

Expert tip: Meet up with a few members of your team before you start

Once you sign your job offer, begin bonding with your new colleagues. These people will be your go-to resources for understanding your product, learning the hidden tricks only seasoned employees know, and navigating the nuances of your company's operations.

While you may have met some of them during the interview process, you've only scratched the surface in understanding who they are and what's expected of you. Reach out to a few of them and ask for a brief meeting or ask if they can suggest someone else to meet with.

Aim to meet with two to three people before you start. Besides providing you with inside information to help you hit the ground running, you'll begin to form closer connections with your teammates, which is critical for your success. Make sure to open up to them too. The more vulnerable you are at the outset, the deeper the level of trust and intimacy. You will depend on these relationships once you get into the thick of your role.

To get to know them, consider asking and sharing in return:

- Where did you grow up, and how did you end up in this role? This is an icebreaker question to help you learn more about your teammates on a personal level.

- What are you most excited about right now in the company and outside of work?

- What are the characteristics of a successful customer? Can you give me a few customer examples and any reading material, videos, or recorded calls that I should review?

- Tell me about some of your at-risk customers and customers that have churned. What makes them at risk or want to churn, and what led to this situation? Be mindful to listen more than speak and resist the urge to solve their issues immediately. You're new, and your colleagues have been in the trenches for much longer—you must respect that.

- What are your biggest challenges day to day? Probe into where your peers get bogged down and which teams, individuals, processes, or systems are problematic. Your goal is to watch out for any pitfalls as you commence your onboarding.

- What advice do you have for me as I start my onboarding process? What should I focus on, and who do you recommend I meet with?

You can end the discussion with questions such as what someone can expect on the first day or the expected attire (if that even matters). Don't overwhelm your peers with questions; remember that you can continue the conversation once you start onboarding.

Get hands-on with your product

I can't emphasize enough how important it is that you fully immerse yourself in understanding how your products operate when you start your new CSM role. Knowing how to use your products will secure the trust of your clients because you can devise solutions to achieve their business needs. It will also earn you much-needed respect from your colleagues—especially the product and engineering teams. For example, if you can demonstrate the steps you've taken to recreate a bug or outline the technical gaps in your product, you'll be perceived as someone who is knowledgeable and wants to collaborate to solve problems.

There should never be an expectation that you can answer every product question, but by the ninety-day mark in your onboarding, you should have a firm grasp of the core aspects of your product. But how do you achieve product mastery? Your company may provide you with live or recorded training, but you must take it up a level to be a strategic CSM. The most successful CSMs I've managed didn't just watch training videos. They experimented on their own by trying out features and tinkering with the product in their own demo environments.

In several of my own CSM roles, I spent countless hours outside of the typical business day trying to grasp various aspects of the products I managed. Is this a requirement for your role? No, but it will take you much longer to hone the product skills required to be successful in your role if you don't do it. You shouldn't expect your onboarding to provide you with all the necessary knowledge and practice to get up to speed on your products. Take the initiative and put in the time required to learn your product.

Another approach to hone your product skills is to partner with your support team and field support tickets for a few hours each week when you first start. You'll put your new product skills to the test by investigating client product issues and determining the best solution needed.

You can also tag along with your onboarding or professional services team. And look for opportunities to assist in configuring new customers or contribute to postlaunch service projects. As a new CSM at Eloqua, I launched a few marketing campaigns and found the experience invaluable. By being hands-on with our products, I better understood how everything fit together and how my actions impacted the results.

Applying your skills is part of what author Daniel Coyle calls *deep practice* in his book *The Talent Code*. Getting your hands dirty with how your products operate provides you with crucial experience that will pay off in the long run. And don't worry if you make a few mistakes along the way. I certainly made a few memorable ones myself as a new CSM at Eloqua. Mistakes are part of the learning process. Don't beat yourself up too much when they happen; just learn from them and move on.

The key to the learning process is applying your knowledge and getting out of your comfort zone. If you consistently do this, your product knowledge will be accelerated, and your product proficiency will increase. It should also help you ideate on possible solutions to your customers' challenges that no one may have ever considered. The long-term benefits of deep practice will compound over time as your knowledge grows and you develop even more robust solutions for your customers.

Just remember to limit how much direct product work you perform for your clients. If you immerse yourself too much in issue triaging or service work, you'll reduce the time available to deliver on your customers' business outcomes. Know when to draw the line and bring in your professional services team, service partners, or support team at the appropriate times. Avoid being a fixer or firefighter so you can focus on the strategic aspects of your role.

Putting this into practice

Go to strategiccustomersuccess.com and download "The Strategic CSM 90-Day Onboarding Plan: Company, Customers, Products." Even if you have been in your current role for several months, see how much of the plan you can complete.

Summary and key takeaways

During onboarding you need to acquire general knowledge about your company, your customers, and how to operate your product to set you up for success in your CSM role.

- A strategic CSM's onboarding goes beyond product functionalities. It should cover how your offerings align with your customers' needs and how they surpass your competitors' offerings.
- Learn to improve your understanding of your company's market positioning by delivering elevator pitches about your company, ranging from succinct one-liners to a version your parents would understand.
- You should thoroughly understand your complete product lineup, the typical customer purchase process, customer motivations, and pricing strategies.
- Dive into your company's industry and understand the terminology, metrics, and emerging trends.
- Company culture is a powerful force. Align your behaviors with your company's vision, mission, and values. Uncover the most celebrated values, understand unwritten rules, and identify the driving force within the company to integrate seamlessly and contribute effectively.

- Get a comprehensive view of your customer base by identifying roles, personas, the industries, and the vertical market segments they represent.

- Immerse yourself in your customers' world by accessing industry resources, participating in industry communities, and staying current on emerging trends.

- Learn your company's customer segmentation model and the factors influencing customer focus, such as growth potential, complexity, and strategic importance.

- Identify the product features most valued by customers and understand how they extract value from your offering. In addition, be aware of the areas where customers encounter challenges with your product.

- Actively experiment and tinker with your product as part of your training and spend extra time outside regular hours to grasp various aspects of the products you manage.

CHAPTER 5

Beyond the Basics: The Customer Journey, Processes, and Tech

Ever find yourself thrown into a job with insufficient training and little guidance? This happens all too often with CSMs, and I'm guilty of doing it myself as a CS leader. Even companies with a strong employee onboarding program still might fail to fully define your role and leave gaping enablement holes, leaving you unclear on your daily responsibilities and how to accomplish them. Never expect your company to provide you with all the tools and knowledge you need to be successful—this is on you. The good news is that you have the power to make the best of your onboarding experience and ensure you are on the right track.

Knowing the customer journey

What happens to your customers once they sign on to start using your products? How do the different teams in your organization work together to make the customer successful, and where do you fit in? This is all part of the customer journey, "the complete sum of experiences that customers go through when interacting with your company and brand. Instead of looking at just a part of a transaction or experience, the customer journey documents the full experience of being a customer."[23]

In the world of customer success, this is usually divided into phases that include presales, onboarding, optimization, and renewal, although this varies from company to company. While CSMs sometimes interact with prospects during the sales process, their primary journey with customers begins after purchase.

Your company's engagement strategy should adapt to match where customers are in their journey. For example, during the onboarding phase, you may send a welcome message and conduct a kickoff call. In subsequent phases, you may perform QBRs or send product updates. Many customer journeys also track key milestones when customers achieve moments of value. For example, one milestone typically occurs when your client achieves their first significant sign of value, such as saving time, cutting costs, or generating additional revenue, or when they officially launch your product.

Even if your customer journey isn't fully fleshed out, you should have a general understanding of how different teams engage with customers—including the cadence and communication channels they use. You should focus primarily on your core responsibilities and key areas like keeping clients informed about new product features. The better you understand these touchpoints and milestones, the clearer your role and responsibilities will be.

For example, you need clarity on when and how to engage clients during the onboarding phase. Do you manage the onboarding process? If another team owns it, when do you get involved—before the client launches, after launch, or at a specific milestone? CSMs should engage early in the customer journey to begin building a trusted relationship, though the timing may vary depending on the company's structure, roles, and available resources.

---

23 Aura Sorman, "The Best Way to Map the Customer Journey: Take a Walk in Their Shoes," SurveyMonkey, last modified December 23, 2024, https://www.surveymonkey.com/curiosity/map-customer-journey-keep-customers-happy.

Renewals and expansions are another important part of the customer journey that require their own playbooks. For example, if the sales team owns upsells, what role do CSMs play in uncovering these opportunities? How do you collaborate with the other teams? Familiarize yourself with where your role fits in, even if you're not leading the effort. We'll return to the topic of renewals and expansions in chapter 20.

Your customer journeys may be slightly different depending on your segments. For example, small-to-midsize customers may undergo self-onboarding or have a much more streamlined onboarding experience. But your enterprise customers may receive a high-touch experience with a dedicated onboarding manager and CSM. Understanding the varying service levels by segment and how your role fits into this is important.

Keep these questions in mind regarding the customer journey as you go through your own onboarding journey:

- What are the different customer touchpoints for which CSMs are responsible? For example, how often do CSMs need to conduct business reviews (QBRs—covered more in chapter 19)? What is the expected meeting cadence that CSMs should have with their clients? How is this determined?
- How are customers onboarded? What are the different components of the onboarding journey? When are customers considered to be launched?
- When do customers achieve the *first value*? In other words, when do your customers start to see a return on their investment in your product? What are the different milestones in the journey when customers expect to achieve value based on using your products?
- What resources are available for customers seeking help with product-related issues or inquiries? This is a critical question because if

you constantly troubleshoot issues or answer basic questions, you won't be effective in your role.

- Who owns renewals? Who owns upsells/expansions? Know who owns the customer commercial responsibilities within your organization. Are there shared responsibilities between CSMs, renewal managers, and sales? How do you ensure a smooth customer experience? This may impact your compensation, so clarify your role responsibilities and how you collaborate with other teams.

- What is the product training experience like for customers, and who is responsible for it? What training resources do customers have access to? How do they get access to training? How often are training resources updated? Your customers will only be effective if they know how to use your product. Knowing what training and education is available will help you determine what resources you can point customers to versus what training you may need to perform yourself to fill any gaps.

- What are the various types of communications customers receive? For example, does marketing send customers regular product updates? Are there automated messages sent to customers based on where they are in the customer journey? Are customers asked to regularly complete Net Promoter Score (NPS) surveys or other surveys? Is there a customer community? Are there customer webinars or a customer newsletter? What are the various channels used to communicate with customers—email, in-app messaging, or other methods? These insights will help guide you when you need to intervene.

Your CS teammates can answer many of these questions, but don't stop there. Engage with your marketing, sales, and product colleagues for their perspectives (see chapter 6 for guidance with having these conversations).

Getting out of your bubble and speaking to other functions is essential. No matter how much information you gather as part of this initiative, you'll only truly understand the customer journey when you start directly working with customers.

You may find that your customer journey is a complete mess. For example, there are very few written processes, and it's unclear which team should do what, and when. You may also find that no one follows the existing processes, so there is no consistency. Take a deep breath. I can guarantee that no organization has a perfect customer journey, so you're not alone. On a positive note, no matter the current state of affairs, you have the power to initiate positive changes. Just be patient and concentrate on first learning the lay of the land.

One misstep I've seen some CSMs make is that they believe they own the customer relationship. No one owns the customer except for the customer. As noted in chapter 1, understanding who owns the current moment in the customer journey is more important. You may want to control the experience for the customer, but you'll soon realize that you don't have the bandwidth to handle every client interaction, nor can you completely control anything regarding customer success. Knowing who the owners are across the customer journey is even more critical. This requires documented processes, which we'll cover next.

Expert tip: Leave your baggage at the door

Sometimes, new CSMs let ghosts from their past roles negatively impact their new ones. A history of challenging relationships with managers or sales teams can create unnecessary barriers to success. You must toss out any baggage from your former roles and come into your new role with a fresh perspective.

If you allow these feelings to persist, you will be in a perpetual state of unease and not allow others to see the real you. This will hurt your chances of forming the strong and trusted relationships that you'll need to succeed in your role. Immerse yourself in your new company. Be humble. Be curious. Be open. Press your internal reset button and start afresh.

Dig into the processes that will help you succeed

I have a saying that I often use: "If it's not written down, it's not a process." Unfortunately, many organizations, primarily young start-ups, haven't taken the time to write out their processes. It's either in someone's head, or stashed away in a place that people can't find. You can get away with this when you're a small team, but things will break down as your company starts to grow beyond fifty people.

This situation is quite normal and part of the maturing process that start-ups go through. When I started at Kustomer and Siena, we didn't have much written down within our CS teams. If you're at a small start-up, don't expect to have every process written out or easily available. You need to lower those expectations and be patient.

Ideally, you have playbooks for specific scenarios in your customer journey. If you're lucky, you have a functioning CS platform or similar technology that has automated many of these processes for you or notifies you when you need to step in. For example, a CSP will create specific tasks to complete a QBR or inform you of a potential churn risk.

You may also find yourself in situations where processes are outdated or nonexistent. This is why building relationships with your colleagues is so important, as they'll outline how they navigate through this fogginess. Whatever situation you find yourself in, take it upon yourself to learn these processes (both written and unwritten).

You should have a handle on these processes:

- What do regular customer meetings consist of? What works best to engage customers?
- How do CSMs track customer health, and what is the at-risk process? Every company scores customer health differently, but typically, a health score indicates a client's current state.
- How are feature requests submitted to the product and engineering teams?
- How are QBRs conducted, and how often do these occur? What are the other types of regular customer engagements, such as success plans or health checks?
- How are customer meetings, activities (such as calls and emails), and other customer engagements recorded?
- What is the handoff process (if any) between sales and onboarding/ CSMs? What is the handoff process between services/onboarding and CSMs?
- What is the handoff process from one CSM to another?
- How do CSMs get assistance when they have complex product questions?
- How are clients billed, and how is the CSM involved if at all?
- Are there any regulatory laws that you should be aware of that could impact certain processes such as how information is shared and stored?

These are just some of the processes you will want to familiarize yourself with when you start your role. You should also keep track of instances where the information you need isn't well defined. Once you have completed your onboarding, you can return to that list to help improve the experience for future newbies.

Leveraging the technology available to you

"Thank goodness we only have to work with this one tool," said no CS professional anywhere. Salesforce, Gong, Gainsight, Gmail, Guru, HubSpot, Jira, Linear, Asana, Zendesk, Zoom, Tableau—need I go on? One of the biggest headaches for CSMs is that they have to use at least thirty different tools to get their jobs done. I want to apologize on behalf of all customer success leaders out there. We're sorry that we put you through this torture every day.

CS teams tend to use a hodge-podge of tools because customer success is forced to borrow from its more established siblings: sales and marketing. Historically, customer success has been overlooked in technology budgets, but this trend is reversing as its significance and the need for efficient customer management and revenue growth are acknowledged. This change will take time, so for now, you're at a disadvantage as long as CS is still the newer kid on the block.

And even then, we won't entirely overcome it in the foreseeable future, so it's best to come to grips with the fact that you'll need to work with and leverage several applications. More mature CS organizations tend to have more sophisticated tools that are better integrated and have CS or revenue operations that assist with this. While this problem won't go away, it should improve—especially with the continued investment in CS technology and rapid development of AI products.

Initially, I planned to dedicate an entire chapter to CS technology, but it would become obsolete within a year or two. Instead, I'll suggest some tools to focus on during your onboarding that will assist you in becoming more strategic in your role. I also offer some CS technology recommendations on strategiccustomersuccess.com.

CRMs and CSPs

The most important, and probably most frustrating, technologies you'll leverage in your day-to-day are your CRM system, which may be Salesforce or HubSpot, among others, and your CS platform, such as Gainsight, ChurnZero, Vitally, ClientSuccess, or Totango/Catalyst. Some CS teams operate directly in their CS platform, while others work in their CRM or a combination of the two. Other CS teams just use their CRM with a combination of different tools to manage their customers. It's still the Wild West regarding customer success tools, with new technologies coming to market regularly—especially with the recent AI boom.

Ask your teammates how they leverage your CRM and/or CS platform to accomplish their daily activities. For example, does your CS platform automatically generate QBR-related tasks that require your attention? Where should meeting notes be stored, and in what format? Be sure to clarify with your manager how these tools track your progress toward your goals.

If you have a CS platform, dive deeper into areas such as the health score and usage data. Ask your colleagues how they leverage this data in their day-to-day client interactions. For example, your fellow CSMs may have customized their dashboards and views to easily detect when a client is struggling based on their usage data or other factors, such as their support interactions. They may also have a way of organizing their tasks so they focus on the most essential items. The best CS pros have a go-to approach to quickly determine where to focus their time.

CS platforms can also be overwhelming—especially when you have a long list of tasks screaming at you to be completed. Ask the more experienced people on your team how they keep on top of these and which ones they prioritize. Don't let the tech distract you from your core role—helping clients achieve value. Technology should aid you in achieving your goals but should never be the goal. Make sure you grasp the *why* behind the instructions you're expected to carry out. If you aren't sure, ask your manager.

Analyzing your customer's data

Three major types of data are generated by your product that are important to CSMs: product adoption metrics like user counts and feature utilization; platform-generated analytics, such as email engagement rates and case resolution times; and—crucially—your customers' own success indicators, such as revenue growth, employee engagement, customer satisfaction (CSAT) scores, or operational efficiencies. The challenge for CSMs is how they access the data and leverage it to drive value for clients.

Some CS teams must log in to each client's instance of your product to view their clients' data. Other user data may be stored in your CRM or CS platform. More sophisticated and data-driven companies have amalgamated their data in a data warehouse and leveraged business intelligence tools such as Looker, Tableau, Domo, or other similar products to make data available to other teams. Early-stage start-ups that lack these tools and analytical expertise may require CSMs to know basic SQL to query their customers' data. It all depends on the tooling and data resources that are available to you.

Regardless of how you access the data, improving your data analytics skills, such as creating pivot tables and charts in spreadsheets, can be crucial to your success. Your ability to mine your clients' data for insights, demonstrate the value they have achieved, and provide recommendations to help them gain more value are key components of being a strategic CSM.

You may need to take a data analytics course or sharpen your spreadsheet skills. Over the years, I've taken several inexpensive online courses on Excel and Google Sheets, which have been extremely helpful. You should also consider improving your AI prompt engineering skills with a specific emphasis on data analysis. Spend time exploring your customers' data and how your colleagues leverage it in their daily customer interactions, and determine what skill gaps you need to fill to feel comfortable analyzing and reporting on data.

Project management and knowledge management tools

Most CS pros should have access to a project management tool such as Asana, Monday.com, or ClickUp, among many others. These tools can be used for multiple purposes, such as client onboarding, success plans, account plans, customer service projects, general client management, managing internal projects, or simply to keep yourself organized. There are even project management tools such as Rocketlane and GuideCX that have been developed specifically for onboarding new clients. Many CS platforms also have a project management component to help you manage your clients.

Beyond the technology, it's essential to understand the basics of project management. If you've never taken courses on project management, I recommend taking an introductory course or reading an overview of project management, such as *Project Management for the Unofficial Project Manager*. These efforts will improve how you manage your clients and yourself. The best CSMs have developed a systematic way to keep track of their clients' most pressing items and keep them accountable.

Besides relying on project management tools, you'll frequently engage with various knowledge portals that store product and process information. This data can be challenging to locate because it is usually scattered across different systems, including your customer-facing knowledge base, internal knowledge base, online community, learning management system, Slack and other messaging tools, and other knowledge portals, not to mention the data repositories each person uses to stash all their personal notes.

And as always, you can keep a close eye on what top-performing employees are doing. Most CSMs have standard processes to address their questions—find out what your colleagues do or create your own. Last, emerging

AI technology should drastically improve these data silo issues by amalgamating disparate data and allowing more customers to access the information they need in the most helpful format.

Engaging your customers at scale

Customer success has evolved beyond the traditional one-to-one relationship between a client and a CSM. While the one-to-one relationship remains crucial for some client segments, the advance of technology and the increasing demand for CS teams to achieve more with fewer resources has prompted a greater emphasis on scaled approaches to customer success.

Scaled customer success includes leveraging technology to automate communication and deliver the right message to the right customer at the right time in their journey via the right channel, such as email. For example, you may have an automated series of emails sent to new customers or messages sent directly in your application. Community software, learning management systems, and webinar software are also key components in a scaled CS strategy, as they allow customers to self-serve and interact with your company without necessarily relying on the CSM. This creates a richer and more engaging customer experience while freeing up some CSMs to work on more critical tasks.

So what does this mean for you? Understanding how these scaled approaches to customer success are currently implemented in your organization, if at all, is crucial. These initiatives can save you hours each week. For example, when a customer asks to speak to similar customers, encourage them to ask their question in your online community, if you have one. You may have digital or scaled CSMs on your team (and you may be one of them) who have created campaigns you can leverage. This may also fall under the marketing team and require close coordination with CS. Find out if your organization has implemented a similar approach.

Even if you are more of a traditional CSM or account manager who has a large book of business, you can look for ways to leverage technology to improve how you communicate with your clients. You can create your own group within your community tool to encourage your customers to converse with each other and use it to engage them. You can even host a monthly webinar with your clients to discuss specific topics or best practices. Recording short videos for your customers highlighting new features may also be an option.

Know what technology is available to you so, when you're ready, you can experiment with different approaches to engage your customers. Don't worry about what's been done before—think outside the box and pave your own path to driving value for your customers. This is just the tip of the iceberg of scaled customer success approaches. Expect vast advances in this area in the next several years with the rise of AI which should allow for a more personalized client experience.

AI tools to increase impact and improve productivity

It would be remiss of me not to include something specific about AI tools, as this is a crucial and emerging component of the CSM role. Unfortunately, anything I write about AI tooling will soon be out of date. My advice is to determine which AI applications your company uses, such as ChatGPT, and pair up with the people who are most well-versed in this area. Tools like ChatGPT and others with AI baked into them will make every part of your role easier, so be sure to keep up to speed on the latest advancements and how they can improve your efficiency and effectiveness. I would also encourage you to experiment with building new tools using AI technology that can assist your entire team. Just make sure you're up to date on any regulations your company has on what data can be shared with these types of applications.

Drawing on your understanding of the customer journey and the expected processes for CSMs, start to envision your daily tasks and how technology will support these efforts. Don't dismiss tools like your CS platform—even if they seem daunting and tedious. When properly configured and utilized, these tools can address your blind spots, providing insights into areas you might have overlooked. They can also help you scale your efforts to ensure you spend time on the most impactful activities.

Putting this into practice

Go to strategiccustomersuccess.com to access "The Strategic CSM 90-Day Onboarding Plan: Customer Journey, Processes, and Technology." Review this to confirm if the elements in your own organization are clear to ensure you can make the transition to an SCSM.

Summary and key takeaways

You need to understand your customer journey, key CSM processes, and the technology available to you as part of your employee onboarding:

- Learn what the customer journey is and what roles you will play within it.
- Confirm some key moments in the customer journey, such as *first value*.
- Understand who owns the renewal motion and what your role is.
- Remember that you don't own the customer—you own a moment in the customer journey.
- Determine the key processes critical to your role, such as how to conduct QBRs, track client health, and submit feature requests.
- Look for gaps in the process and attempt to clarify what the expectations are for ill-defined areas.

- Get up to speed on how your team uses your CRM and CS platform and observe how the high performers leverage them.

- There are three major types of data generated by your product that are important to CSMs: usage data, reporting data, and most importantly, the data that your customers deem as equating to value. Determine how to access the data you need and how to analyze it so you can demonstrate value to your customers.

- Project management tools can assist you in keeping you and your clients organized.

- Find out where the information you need to address customers' questions is stored and how best to access it.

- Look for ways to leverage technology to deliver CS at scale. This includes sending communication en masse via email or in-app, video conferencing, short videos, and community software.

CHAPTER 6

How Best to Align Yourself with Other Teams, Departments and Partners

I just didn't understand it. The client was renewing within three days, and the sales rep hadn't made much progress on it. We were in jeopardy of missing the renewal deadline. This was the real-life fire drill we faced at one of my start-ups. It turned out that the sales team who owned renewals was compensated significantly less for renewals than for new deals. No wonder this wasn't a high priority for them.

I was still new to my role and had no clue how and when the sales team was compensated or how this could directly impact my role. I should have understood this better, but it wasn't covered in the fluffy departmental overviews I received during onboarding. I could have avoided this mess if I'd done my homework ahead of time.

To prepare you for success as a strategic CSM, I want to help you collect the information you need from the teams and departments crucial to achieving your goals. While it may seem daunting to seek out and meet team members from across your company, this exercise will give you the clarity you need to perform at your best. You don't need to gather this information all at once. Set weekly goals for who you plan to meet with, and break this up over your first ninety days. I also recommend sending some or all of your questions ahead of time, so people come to meetings prepared. Yes, this is time-consuming, but your efforts will quickly pay off.

Working with support

A strong support team can significantly enhance your effectiveness. They can shield you from having to tackle product questions and issues, and they can take on escalations that would normally drain your time. This lets you focus on proactive client engagements to drive more customer value. You can ask the support team:

- What are the different ways customers can access support, and what is the preferred method? Support teams typically offer a few options for customers to engage them. This can include email, chat, Slack, or voice support. It can also include a support community, or you may even have an AI-powered agent. The level of access to support channels often depends on the specific products a customer has purchased and the tier they are on. Knowing your support team's preferred support channel can expedite issue resolution and create better ties between your teams. For example, they may prefer that you drive customers to a chatbot or a web form.

- What is the support team's structure? Are there different support tiers? Some support teams categorize issues by type or complexity. For example, some companies have a basic tier or "tier 0" to triage problems. Then, depending on the expertise needed to solve the problem, they may escalate items to higher tiers.
  If you work with larger and more complex companies, you typically have a premier or dedicated support option. If applicable to your role, learn about what this service includes and the costs involved.

- How do support and CSMs generally work together? How should CSMs forward issues to the support team? How can CSMs escalate issues? How are escalated issues handled? Of all the questions, these are the most important in building a trusted relationship with support, and where most of the challenges lie. Support may expect CSMs to provide client issues in a particular format with a specific level of detail, but this may not be consistently executed or adequately communicated. When I've found misalignment between these teams, it's usually due to poorly documented and communicated joint processes. Be sure that you understand the expectations when working with support. How is the support team measured? Does the support team have service level agreements (SLAs) on how quickly they respond to new issues and responses in general? Their metrics may include first response time (FRT), average resolution time (ART), CSAT, or customer effort scores (CES). You'll want to see a support team that balances responsiveness with customer satisfaction. If they only measure their ability to respond within the defined SLAs, this could be problematic, as the actual responses may not be adequate, which can drive down customer satisfaction. It's essential to know these metrics and how they're trending. For instance, if the FRT and ART are increasing, it takes longer to address client issues. This could lead to lower customer satisfaction scores and put more pressure on CSMs to make up for a slower response time, which impacts a CSM's overall productivity (see chapter 12). Having a sense of these metrics and how they are trending will give you an indication of the strength of the support team and where they may need to improve.

- Are specific customers supported differently based on their segment, customer journey stage, or health? Some support teams will pay more attention to customers in the renewal stage of the customer journey or those who are at risk.

- What are the support team's business hours? Do they operate on weekends? What are their holiday hours? Familiarizing yourself with your support team's working hours and time zone coverage is essential for managing customer expectations and understanding when your intervention might be necessary. For instance, if your support team doesn't have proper holiday coverage and you have a mission-critical product issue, you may need to make yourself available during off-hours.

- Which languages are supported? If you serve a global market, you may require multilingual support. Learn about the different languages your support team can handle and where the gaps are.

Working with professional services/onboarding/training

Many organizations have separated onboarding and professional services from the CSM role. It's important to examine their roles and responsibilities to ensure they align with yours. This will ensure a smooth customer experience. So make sure to ask:

- How are clients onboarded? What are the key metrics for onboarding new clients? In one of my CS leadership roles, I discovered that the onboarding team didn't configure reports for clients, which caused a lot of friction in the handoff process between onboarding and CSMs. When I dug deeper into this, it turned out this was skipped because the onboarding team was measured on the time required to move clients live. The issue was that the onboarding team was optimizing for a metric and not optimizing for clients to achieve value and build trust. When this issue was uncovered, we modified the metrics to ensure that reporting was covered during onboarding.

- Do all customers receive onboarding assistance or can clients self-on-board? How does onboarding differ based on the size or complexity of the customer? What's the estimated timeline for customer on-boarding? This can differ based on the complexity of your client's requirements.

- When are CSMs introduced to clients? In many companies, CSMs are part of the new client kickoff process or even part of the presales process. Clarify how this works at your company.

- How are clients transitioned from sales to onboarding? Once on-boarding is completed, how are clients transitioned to CSMs? Tran-sition points in the customer journey are critical moments in deter-mining the customer's long-term success. Any change in the client relationship can degrade the trust that was previously established, so these handoffs should be as smooth and seamless as possible.

- What type of training options are available for customers? Are these live or just recorded? Are there specialized training services available that can be tailored for specific customers? Be aware of the training and education options available as they can be valuable tools to en-sure your clients achieve their goals.

- What other types of services are available to clients after onboard-ing? Your clients may need additional paid services after the on-boarding phase, and you need to know what options are available. In addition, be aware of the typical costs for these services and pos-sible discounts. Professional services teams usually have a standard list of services and custom service options. You may also have service partners that can carry out similar tasks and projects (which we'll cover later in this chapter).

Let me share something I've seen play out countless times in my CS ca-reer: There's often an interesting gap between what gets discussed during the sales process and what actually lands on the CS team's plate. Review those early onboarding experiences carefully. Any unresolved issues can snowball if they aren't addressed. As I mentioned in chapter 2, don't take on a client unless you have been fully briefed or have no other choice. The first impression you make with your client is critical in securing your client's trust—don't screw it up, or you'll be playing catch-up right out of the gate.

Working with sales

The sales/CS relationship is probably the most contentious relationship of them all. Much of this comes down to not taking the time to clearly understand each other's priorities. Ask your sales counterparts:

- What are the responsibilities of the sales team? Are they solely focused on new business, or are they responsible for upsells and renewals? Find out if there are any overlapping responsibilities, such as upsells, and make sure your duties are clear. I've typically seen role confusion between CS and sales in younger organizations that are growing quickly and don't have all their processes mapped out. If there are gaps in existing processes or overlapping responsibilities, raise these with your manager.

- What is the structure of the sales team? How are they segmented— by geography, product, industry, or a combination? Who are the sales leaders, and how are items escalated when there are problems? Sales leaders are usually tied to the sales segments. Get familiar with the sales org chart so you know who to go to and when. Don't wait for a crisis to figure out which sales leader needs to be informed.

- How does sales interact with the CS team? Are sales reps aligned with CS by geography or by segment? Do the sales and CS teams regularly meet with each other? Alignment with sales can make or break how well a CS team performs. Figure out how sales and CS collaborate so you can maximize your impact. For example, you may have a few clients with the same sales reps. Get to know those reps, as their expertise and connections can be highly beneficial.

- How are sales reps compensated? This is the most underrated question on this list and is not often considered by the CS team. The sales compensation breakdown is critical in determining how collaboratively sales and CS will work together and may be an underlying cause of churn. At the beginning of the chapter, I shared an example where sales earned less commission on renewals than on new deals and the impact this had. I'd also ask whether there's a commission clawback if the client defaults on payments or cancels within the first year. This links a sales rep's earnings to the client's long-term success—not just the initial contract.

- How are client requirements gathered in the presales process? Different companies handle requirements-gathering differently. In some situations, this process is skipped, as clients can purchase products without any assistance. In other situations, a scope of work (SOW), which details what services are included, is attached to the main agreement. This tends to occur for more complex products.

  You'll want to know the scoping process and who is involved. For example, you may have solution engineers/consultants who are in charge of the requirements-gathering process. Being aware of the stages when customer success or professional services get involved may help you anticipate possible scope issues you will face when you start to work with your clients. The earlier CS is involved in the sales process, the better.

- Can CS veto specific deals? If a prospect is a borderline fit for your product, is there a process for CS to review these deals before the deal closes? It's essential to understand the decision-making process in these situations, as it will provide more significant insights into the culture of your organization. If CS can prevent risky deals, customer success will have a more prominent seat at the executive table.

Swallow your pride and make nice with sales. When sales is successful, you will be successful, and more importantly, your company will be successful.

Working with marketing

Your marketing team can be a difference maker for CS. From delivering timely customer communications to sending customers cool company swag, marketing can significantly improve the customer experience and influence customer retention. They can also assist you by providing you with ideas and resources to engage and educate your customers, such as customer webinars and special campaigns to celebrate customer milestones such as launching. Many of these responsibilities fall within a subset of the marketing team called customer marketing, but every company is structured slightly differently. Some CS teams have even taken over many of these tasks. To get more familiar with your marketing team's responsibilities and priorities, ask them:

- How does marketing support customer success? Their purview depends on the maturity and size of the marketing organization and its focus. Get a feel for the types of communication marketing sends and the cadence. You can then determine if there are any communication gaps that you need to fill to ensure you keep your customers informed.

- How is the marketing team measured? The answer to this question will drive everything. If marketing is solely focused on generating leads and opportunities for new business, then there may be few, if any, resources for customer marketing efforts. This just means that customer success may need to take on more of the load that marketing usually covers, such as running customer events, capturing customer case studies, and owning customer communications.

    When marketing's success is gauged by the number of referenceable customers, customer reviews, and case studies they provide, their objectives are more closely aligned with those of customer success. In an ideal situation, your marketing team is assessed, at least partially, based on client retention and growth. This creates proper alignment between marketing and customer success. In these circumstances, marketing is aware of the value that can be generated by existing customers and understands the influence of customer advocates in producing additional leads through referrals and positive word-of-mouth efforts.

- How does customer success interact with marketing? This could simply mean having a joint Slack channel, but there should be more formal ties between marketing and customer success. For example, there may be a regular joint meeting to share customer stories and other positive customer experiences as well as challenges that CS needs help with.

Working with product and engineering

Besides sales, the departments that can be the most challenging for CS to work with are product and engineering. At the heart of the issue is how much input CS has on the product roadmap—a complex problem for the product team, given their many priorities and limited capacity. This means that some features will get tossed out or deprioritized. To get more acquainted with your product and engineering colleagues, ask:

- What drives the product roadmap? The product roadmap is a sacred document for customer success teams. What gets into the roadmap and what falls out can determine whether some clients will continue to stick it out with your company or decide that they can't wait any longer and look at your competition.

  The construction of your product roadmap is primarily driven by your organization's vision and priorities, which are influenced by customer success and sales. You'll want to know how much influence the CS team has on the roadmap and how they're consulted as part of the roadmap creation process. Understanding this will give you an indication of how customer-centric the organization is.

  You'll also want to know how often your roadmap is updated and where these updates are stored so you can highlight where your product is headed when interacting with customers. I've found the product roadmap to be a magnet in attracting customer decision-makers to meetings as they want to ensure their priorities are aligned with the future of your product.

- How are customer feature requests prioritized? Ask the product team to provide the criteria they use to prioritize feature development. Some companies leverage customer feedback tools or community software packages that allow customers to submit and upvote features. They may also consider criteria such as the number of customers and potential revenue impacted or the need to fill a competitive gap. For example, if a certain number of customers may be saved if a feature is built, the product team may move that feature into their immediate roadmap. Know what the criteria are so that when you submit your features, you can stress all the important points to ensure they are prioritized.

- How are the product and engineering teams measured? You'll know that the product and CS teams are aligned if you see that the product team has shared goals with CS. This will also provide another indication that you've joined a more customer-centric organization. The joint metrics usually consist of product adoption goals, and even customer retention and growth. Product teams that are measured just on delivering features can be more challenging to work with, as their objectives are not directly tied to yours (see chapter 11).

  It's music to my ears when I hear that the engineering teams are measured on quality and platform stability. That tells me that quality is a core metric that will ensure that bugs are minimized and risks are mitigated. Platform issues such as downtime and latency, as well as product bugs, can destroy client trust.

- How many resources are dedicated to quality assurance (QA), and how are features tested before being released? You can also request to see product uptime data, usually widely available via products such as status.io, to let you know how stable your systems are.

- How often are features released—weekly, monthly, or ad hoc? Are they phased releases or are features released when mostly complete? Do all clients receive updates at once, or are releases staggered to catch potential issues? These questions will tell you a lot about the culture of a company. Frequent ad hoc releases may prioritize speed over quality, benefiting engineers eager to see their work in action but potentially frustrating customers with constant changes and bugs. While rapid iteration helps companies stay competitive and address issues, it can lead to chaos if quality controls are lacking.

A strong release process with built-in quality measures mitigates risks. However, if there's no retrospective analysis for poor releases, no bug reduction goals, and no commitment to quality improvement, that's a red flag. As a company scales, weak quality practices erode customer trust, leading to churn and overburdened support teams—what I call churn and burn. Prioritizing product quality ensures long-term success for both your clients and your business.

- What is the beta process for new features? Product teams will regularly have clients test out new features before they are more broadly released. This should help squash major bugs and ensure that no critical capabilities are overlooked. Having your customers included in a product beta can also be a customer perk you can leverage, as many customers like to test out the shiny new objects they have been pleading for. This makes customers feel more included in your company's success.

- How are product updates communicated to customers? How is the product roadmap communicated to customers? Find out how the product team contributes to this process and the potential gaps.

- Does your company provide a regular roadmap webinar? Your customers haven't just bought your company's product for its existing features. They've bought into your vision, so it's essential to keep them informed not only of past product releases but also of what the future holds.

- How are bugs logged, and is there a prioritization process to ensure that the most critical bugs are addressed quickly? How are product issues and bugs escalated? Most product and engineering organizations will have a method for classifying bugs and specific steps to address them based on their level of severity. For example, a *P0* (priority 0) issue usually means that the system is down and the engineering team needs to do everything possible to get it back online. There may be other processes, such as an escalation process, to ensure that there are eyes on the most pressing issues.

- How are critical bugs communicated to clients? It can be a hot mess when your system goes down. Having a defined process, so each team knows their role in addressing the issue and providing client communications, can make all the difference. Tools such as status. io can display the status of an issue as well as communicate with clients—even when your own platform is out of commission. This makes it easy to keep customers in the loop.

  Bugs will happen. Systems go down. Just expect it. What's important is knowing how your company responds when crap hits the fan. Make sure that the processes for addressing issues are appropriately defined and that you fully understand them. The last thing you want to do is improperly classify a critical bug and have your system down longer than it should be.

- How and when can a CSM have a product manager (PM) or engineer join a client meeting? At times, it may be appropriate to have a PM speak to a client to outline a new feature or to gather client feedback. You may also need a PM to communicate some tough love, such as a product limitation or a decision not to build a particular feature. Similarly, you may need an engineer to help troubleshoot an issue, due to their specialized knowledge. The process for requesting a PM or engineer's time may be very informal, such as through a Slack conversation, or via an official request form. Get to know this process so you can leverage these resources when needed.

Working with customer success/revenue operations

Customer success operations (CS ops) is still in its infancy compared with sales and marketing operations but is growing quickly. It's a critical function, as it can improve your productivity by providing you with the tools and insights needed to be successful in your role. CS ops may sit directly within customer success or it may reside under a more centralized operations function, typically called revenue operations, but have an indirect (dotted-line) reporting relationship with CS. Dedicated CS ops isn't typically found in smaller organizations, but this trend is changing with a greater focus on scaled approaches to customer success.[24] Below are some recommended questions to ask the CS operations team:

- How does CS/revenue operations support CSMs? If you have a CS ops or revenue operations (rev ops) team in your organization, that is a great starting point! Find out from them what their mandate is and what their responsibilities are. If you don't have a CS or rev ops team, ask your manager how these responsibilities are being handled today.

- Does CS/rev ops provide data insights or access to data? How else can they help you be more effective in your role? Apart from supporting CS technology, some operations teams assist by providing data insights or facilitating easy access to the data necessary for your role. For example, they may create reports for you in your business intelligence tools that provide insights into product usage or supply benchmark data that you can include in your customer business reviews. They may even introduce new tools to help you better understand the state of your customers or automate the QBR process. You need to determine how they can best support you and what you

---

24 Scott Salkin, "Customer Success Operations: The Hottest Career in the Customer Service Space," Gainsight, May 10, 2022, https://www.gainsight.com/blog/customer-success-operations-career-advantages/.

need to do on your own. CS ops can be a game changer for CSMs, so be sure to leverage this resource if you can.

Working with finance

Your finance team can play a key role on the customer billing side, which is a critical part of the customer journey. If your customers are billed incorrectly or if they don't pay their bills on time, these problems may land in your lap. To foster a better working relationship and stay ahead of potential issues, try asking your finance colleagues:

- How does the finance team interact with customers? What types of billing communications are sent to clients and when? What happens when a client doesn't pay their bills on time? No CSM ever wants to send out payment reminders to their customers, but there may be times when you need to step in. As you may have the closest relationship with your customers, you can try to find out why a customer may not have paid their bills and why they've been unresponsive. I've found that most of these issues are due to communication breakdowns that can be easily solved by contacting the right person.

- What happens if a company doesn't pay their bills? Some companies have a shutdown process for businesses that fail to pay their outstanding bills after a specific period. If this happened to one of your clients, it could be catastrophic for the relationship. Trust me on this—I've been there. Familiarize yourself with the billing procedures and the different communication methods your finance team employs when dealing with delinquent customers. This will save you a lot of frustration and potential issues later on.

- What's the process for securing budget to visit your customers? This is more of a question for your direct manager but understanding your company's customer travel process can be helpful when needing to go see a customer in person.

Working with partners

Some companies rely on established partnerships to grow and scale their business. Most CSMs focus on their direct clients and don't fully understand that their company may be part of a more extensive network of companies that form an ecosystem. Take the time to familiarize yourself with your organization's partner network so you can identify opportunities for effective collaboration. Partners can offer significant value to your company and customers and furnish you with valuable insights.

A *partner* can mean a few different things, so let's break down the four distinct types of partnerships:

- Referral partners contribute to your company's growth by referring potential customers to you.
- Reseller partners are a form of indirect or *channel* sales. They sell your product directly to their clients.
- Service partners can help onboard your customers or provide ongoing consulting and services.
- Technical partners are partners whose product is somehow integrated with yours to create a better customer experience and increased value.

Where it can get confusing is that certain partners can wear multiple hats. For instance, a referral partner can also be a technical partner. At Kustomer, Aircall was both a referral partner and a technical partner. They integrated their voice solutions with our product and resold Kustomer to their customer base.

Another complexity of partner relationships is that some of your closest partners can also compete directly with your products. We sometimes call these partners "frenemies." A good example of this is how intertwined Google apps such as Google Maps are on Apple iPhones. Google's Android operating system is a direct competitor to Apple, but Apple permits the Google Maps app on iPhones because it's a superior product at the moment and customers demand it.

Seek out your head of partnerships or your colleagues who manage partner relationships so you can learn more about your partner ecosystem. Find out which of the four types of partners your organization relies on and which are the most important to the success of your business, then ask them where they plan on expanding their partner relationships.

Once you understand the partnership landscape within your company, inquire into how your partnership team is measured. They might need to hit a defined percentage of revenue goals over a month or quarter. According to a Forrester survey, companies with mature partnership ecosystems derive around 28 percent of their total revenue from partnerships, whereas those with less mature ecosystems garner approximately 18 percent of their revenue from partnerships.[25] Knowing your company's targets gives you a sense of how important partners are to the business.

Depending on the type of partners your company utilizes, you may ask:

Referral partners

- How are referral partners compensated? When a deal that was sourced by a referral partner is closed, they will get some sort of compensation. This is usually a certain percentage of the total price the customer pays. Referral fees can vary between 5 percent and 25

25 Jaime Singson, "Research Shows Companies with Mature Partnerships Grow Revenue Nearly 2x Faster," impact.com, accessed May 21, 2024, https://impact.com/partnerships/research-shows-companies-with-mature-partnerships-grow-revenue-nearly-2x-faster/.

percent of the total sale, depending on the type of transaction.[26] Knowing how partners are compensated will give you an indication of how motivated partners are to bring in new business for your organization.

- Who are the top referral partners, and why? By determining which referral partners your partnerships team values most, you can prioritize them accordingly. It's equally helpful to ask your CS counterparts which referral partners have a bad reputation and refer poorly performing customers. These partners may lack the right knowledge or may not reflect your culture. The customers they refer may require more handholding and are more likely to churn.

The sales and partnership teams have specific new business revenue targets and may favor certain partners based on the money they bring in versus worrying about how these new customers align with your value proposition. Be aware of these nuances and act accordingly.

Reseller partners

- How do reseller partners coordinate with your sales and CS teams? Reseller partners resell your products to their clients directly, but customer success is typically involved in managing the reseller relationship, servicing the customer directly in some way, or both.
- What is the customer journey for these types of partner-led clients and what does your involvement entail? For example, your company may still provide direct support for some reseller customers while not for others.

---

26 Emma Kimmerly, "Paying Referral Fees to Individuals: How Much and How Do They Work?," Friendbuy, January 29, 2023, https://www.friendbuy.com/blog/paying-referral-fees-to-individuals.

Resellers who manage the client relationship directly can be both a blessing and a curse. These arrangements typically ease the workload for CSMs, as the partner handles the majority of the customer interactions, but this can also be a CSM's worst nightmare. I've worked with reseller partners that excelled at signing up new customers, but when things became too complex, they lobbed the clients over to customer success to clean up their mess. Some didn't raise red flags at all and let clients churn out. These poor customer experiences can catch up to you and lead to higher levels of churn.

If you are responsible for managing partner-sold revenue, you need to have a keen eye on these customers and be as proactive as possible. Work with your manager to shore up any broken or incomplete processes to avoid future issues. Look for ways you can improve reseller training to prevent as many of these situations as possible. In addition, clarify your internal escalation process so you know who to go to when issues crop up.

Service partners

What types of services do your service partners provide? Service partners can be invaluable assets for CSMs, offering additional support for onboarding new customers or tackling your customer's most important tasks. The challenge is finding a service partner that embodies the same culture as your company, so you ensure customers are being provided with an experience that matches your own company's.

In the past, I've seen many flavors of service partners. Some service partners were attentive but lacked certain product skills and, ultimately, did more harm than good. Other partners may charge higher fees, which can lead to ill feelings from your customers as they see the total costs of your products and services as being too high. Other partners lack the customer centricity that you would expect and can hurt overall customer satisfaction. Ask your fellow CSMs if they prefer certain partners and which ones they avoid.

Well-trained service partners can be lifesavers for CSMs. They're capable of independently driving product success and turning around struggling accounts while you focus on other priorities. If you see issues with service partners, raise them to the appropriate people in your organization and do your part to guide them in the right direction where it makes sense.

Technical partners

- Which technical partners are part of your partner ecosystem?
- Which product add-ons or apps are the most popular with your customers?
- Most software products integrate with other systems. Salesforce. com's AppExchange is one of the best examples of creating a technical partner ecosystem as you can find hundreds of apps that integrate with the core products.

When it comes to technical partnerships, it's important to know who your company's most critical partners are and why. For example, in Eloqua's early days Salesforce.com was one of its main lead generators making it a critical partner for us. Make sure you understand the technical partner ecosystem, how other products can integrate with yours, and which technical partners are the most critical for your company and your customers.

Know the lay of the land in your organization

One of the mistakes I made early in my career was believing that if I worked hard enough, I could make any customer successful all on my own. This was so completely wrong. I needed to engage with other departments in my organization and my partner ecosystem to be successful in my role. It's the only way I could level up in my role and be able to take on a more strategic outlook.

Your success is also dependent on the relationships you establish with people across your organization. Enhance your relationships with your co-workers by meeting with them and asking them questions, as suggested in this chapter. At the very least, you will gain insights into how these teams operate and their perception of customer success. This may result in some surprises—both positive and negative. At the end of the day, your organization needs to work together to keep the promises made during the buying process. The only way to do this is to have everyone operating on the same page.

No company is perfect, and all companies have some form of dysfunction. Having triggered some of the known landmines as part of your meet and greets, you can now determine how to avoid them, correct them, or work around them. There will be opportunities to make improvements as you get to the end of your ninety days. Keep a list of challenges you've found so you can come back to them once you have a better perspective.

As you're expanding your internal network, keep track of those colleagues who really inspired you and figure out how you can partner with them in the future. In chapter 11, we'll dive into how best to work with other teams so you can build off what you learned from the meetings outlined in this chapter. Relationships within your company matter—make an effort early on to get to know your teammates, as it's more challenging to do so once the work starts piling on.

Expert tip: Look for the unwritten rules and go above and beyond

When you're new to an organization, your main focus is on picking up the established processes and codes of conduct. But keep an eye out for the cultural elements of your organization that others are aware of but that aren't necessarily written down. For instance, you may have an established process to log feature requests, but you notice that the veteran CSMs provide additional details to the product team and set up a time to discuss the feature with them. Discovering these hidden secrets and performing these same actions sends a clear message to your team and others that you are committed to performing at the highest level and that you're immersing yourself in the culture of your organization.

Listen for the common sayings your team uses, the rituals they follow, and the idiosyncrasies of the top performers. Look for ways to get noticed by your colleagues so you create a solid first impression. Taking the time to meet with people is a good start. Don't blindly follow processes and what's always been done. Find out the *why* behind existing processes so you can potentially look for improvements.

Putting this into practice

Go to strategiccustomersuccess.com and access "The Strategic CSM 90-Day Onboarding Plan: Cross-Team Alignment." Even if you've been at your company for several months, consider leveraging this as a way to reconnect with your colleagues, confirm your understanding of their processes, and determine where improvements can be made.

Summary and key takeaways

You need to gather information from the various departments in your company so you can learn how best to leverage them as well as your partner network:

- Take the time in your first ninety days to get to know your teammates, so you have a better sense of their responsibilities and how you'll interact with them. Forming these relationships now will pay off in the long run.

- Get to know support's processes so you can best work together—especially when there is a crisis.

- Learn about how clients are onboarded and how they are transitioned to CSMs. Get a sense of the issues that customers may go through as part of the onboarding process and what gaps may exist that CSMs will need to step into once they take over.

- Learn about how you can impact the product roadmap and how features are released. Find out what metrics the product and engineering teams are accountable for to see how their objectives stack up against yours.

- Get to know what the sales team focuses on, the team structure, and how they are compensated. Learn about how new deals are scoped before the deal is signed.

- Determine how your marketing team will assist you through customer communications, events, and other activities. Marketing can be a difference maker in creating customer advocates if they are aligned with CS.

- CS/revenue operations are still establishing themselves in organizations and can take many forms. Confirm the mandate of this team and how they can assist you in your role.

- Learn about how your finance team bills clients and the communications they send out.

- Partners come in many forms and can play a large role in your day-to-day. Determine what types of partners your company leverages: reseller partners, referral partners, service partners, technical partners, or a combination. Learn which partners will be the most impactful to your success.

CHAPTER 7

A Detailed Plan for Your First Ninety Days and the Road Ahead

"Hey, Linda. Sorry to bother you, but can I ask you a question?" Linda David, a customer success manager on my team at Eloqua, sat beside me when I began my journey there as a CSM. In those first few weeks, I asked Linda at least ten questions a day, and they always started with "Sorry to bother you . . ." (as a good Canadian would phrase things). Linda was patient and kind and always answered my questions thoroughly. I was very lucky.

When I first started as a CSM at Eloqua, I had no idea how to prepare myself properly. I was told to watch some training videos, given some clients to manage, and expected to figure things out by myself. Thank goodness I had Linda and my other teammates to help me out.

Unfortunately, I was, and still am, a little shy. If I were to do things over, I would've taken more time to get to know my entire team early on. This would have sped up my onboarding and ensured that I tapped into the collective knowledge of those around me.

With what I know now, here's how I would approach the ninety-day onboarding—broken down into thirty-day increments. Completing these tasks in your first ninety days will ensure that you've covered all of your bases and set yourself up for success. As a word of caution, don't try to cram three months of onboarding into your first two weeks. You must pace yourself because there is a lot to learn. Conserve your energy—you'll need it.

Four primary actions to stay on the right path

You'll be pulled in many directions in your first ninety days. Consider these four primary actions to ensure you're on the right path in your new role:

- Clarify your role expectations and what you are being measured on.
- Get to know your manager on a personal level.
- Track your progress and share your results.
- Make an immediate impact.

Clarify expectations

One of the items that held me back at times as a CSM was that I didn't level set with my manager on what they expected of me. I assumed I knew what they wanted and that my results spoke for themselves. When it came to performance review time, I would be dumbfounded that I hadn't performed as expected in some areas.

The problem was that I wasn't clear on what the expectations were. You could argue that it's the manager's responsibility to communicate this, but it's a two-way street between you and your manager. You need to manage and guide them, just as they need to do the same for you. Think of your career as a car. You, and only you, are the driver of your career. Your manager is the passenger. You must look out for your interests and find what will make you successful in your role and your career.

In your first few weeks in your new position, sit down with your manager and clarify what their exact expectations of you are and how you're being evaluated. Have them walk you through your role and responsibilities. Ask about their goals and key performance indicators (KPIs) to better understand how your actions impact their performance. Be sure to clarify what you're being measured on, how those metrics are calculated, how often those metrics are reviewed, and where those metrics are stored, so you can keep track of your progress.

Getting it done and doing it right. I've borrowed a 2 × 2 matrix that the former chief revenue officer at Eloqua, Alex Shootman, called Getting it Done and Doing it Right, or GID/DIR. I've found it applicable at every company I've worked at—regardless of their approach to performance management. I'm sharing it with you because it can help you visualize how you should perceive your performance and will aid you when speaking to your manager (see Figure 4). GID is all about the results you need to accomplish. DIR is about the behaviors you need to exhibit. These two concepts are closely tied together because if you are demonstrating the right behaviors, you should accomplish the expected results. Let's break this down.

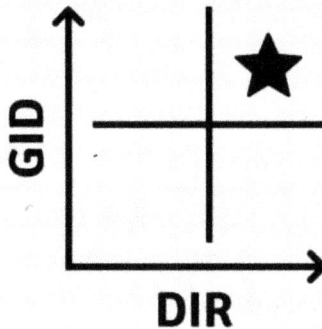

Figure 4.[27] The "Getting it done and doing it right" 2 x 2 matrix.

The results you are expected to achieve can include achieving retention and growth targets, identifying customer advocates, achieving key adoption

---

27 Scott Ingram, *Sales Success Stories*, podcast, book sample episodes, "Getting It Done & Doing It Right—Recipe for a Great Sales Culture," August 7, 2018, https://top1.fm/getting-it-done-doing-it-right-recipe-for-a-great-sales-culture-sales-success-stories-book-sample-story-5/.

or client health goals, completing a required number of QBRs, or uncovering a specific amount of upsell opportunities. This ensures you are *getting it done*. The behaviors you are expected to exhibit as part of *doing it right* can be a combination of the behaviors we identified in chapter 3.

Ask your manager for:

- the explicit results you are being evaluated on and which behaviors are required
- the definitions of those behaviors to reduce any ambiguity
- examples if there are no written definitions

You want to see yourself in the top right quadrant of the GID/DIR framework. This will take time, as you need to prove yourself, but you'll never get there unless you clarify what's expected of you.

To further clarify expectations, ask:

- What are your overall expectations of me in my role, and what should I prioritize?
- What are the results you expect of me, and by what date?
- Where are these metrics captured, and how often are they updated? This allows you to track your performance.
- What behaviors do you want me to emulate, and what are some examples?
- What is the promotion process, and what do I need to do to be considered for a promotion?
- How do you want me to update you on my activities, and how often? For example, I could send these via a weekly email/Slack message or discuss them in our 1:1 meetings.
- What is the format for our 1:1 meetings, and what am I expected to prepare for those meetings?

Once you get these questions clarified, write up your notes, send a message to your manager, and ask them to confirm what was discussed. This gives your manager the opportunity to clarify any misconceptions. It also demonstrates your organizational skills, which are important to *DIR*.

Get to know your manager

In your first ninety days, build a personal connection with your manager—just as you would with your colleagues. Trusted relationships are built on transparency and vulnerability. Learn what is important to them outside of work. What makes them tick? What are they passionate about? Ideally, your manager will reciprocate and learn more about you, but not every manager has the desire or capacity to do this. If you initiate this, you can present yourself in a better light and start the relationship off on the right foot.

Track your progress and communicate your accomplishments

You may be thinking, "Why do I have to broadcast my recent big renewal or the progress I made on a key project to the whole company? My manager knows, and that's enough." That is the wrong attitude. While your manager is aware of your achievements, they don't see the full extent of your efforts.

As Fern Mallis, the founder of New York Fashion Week, has said, "Your work won't be recognized unless you champion it."[28] Leverage platforms such as Slack, Teams, Notion, and other internal communication channels to share your achievements and the insights you've gained. For instance, my CSM teams would often share short clips from their call recordings that highlighted positive customer exchanges.

These self-promotional efforts not only reinforce your value but also ensure you have a documented record of your progress and accomplishments. You might be surprised how much knowledge you've acquired and how little

---

28 Meredith Fineman, *Brag Better: Master the Art of Fearless Self-Promotion* (Penguin, 2020), 13.

others know about what you do on a day-to-day basis. Don't downplay your accomplishments—your insights are valuable gifts to be shared.

Make an immediate impact

Your primary goal during the onboarding phase is to get yourself up to speed so you can start contributing. Your colleagues will also be observing you closely, so push yourself to complete your training and advance to the next phase of your development. Once you have the basics down, start racking up some wins, such as delivering a QBR, helping a client adopt a new feature, or uncovering an upsell opportunity. Be sure to chat up your accomplishments and start to make a name for yourself.

As I've stressed, customer success isn't just about demonstrating value to your customers. You also need to create value for your teammates. While you don't want to come in with an I-know-everything attitude and start suggesting major changes, find opportunities to make an impact. This can be a small thing, such as documenting a process that has not been written down or doing some competitive analysis that can help the product team determine where they should focus. As a newbie, you see things with a fresh set of eyes—use that to your advantage.

In summary, take the time to clarify your roles and responsibilities, develop a more personal relationship with your manager, track your progress, broadcast your results, and make an immediate impact. Doing this will establish the right foundation for you to be a valued and trusted contributor and set you up for continued career growth.

The first month: The honeymoon

The first thirty days in your role will seem like a whirlwind. You'll be bombarded with information, making it easy to feel overwhelmed. At the same time, this period is filled with optimism and anticipation. You just signed your offer, received some company swag, and powered up your new laptop.

As you go through your company's standard onboarding process, don't get too distracted by these niceties or feel you can sit back and relax. Beyond the onboarding basics, there are some key actions you should take now to set yourself up for long-term success as a strategic CSM.

I've already touched on the need to master your product skills in chapter 4. That should be your primary focus in your first thirty days, as it will be the foundation for everything else. Beyond that, do the following:

- Meet your team.
- Identify people in other teams to meet.
- Shadow customer calls.
- Get familiar with the critical tools and processes required for your role.

Meeting with your team and other key colleagues

In your first thirty days, it's critical to establish specific allies on your team that will help you get up to speed. You need someone like Linda David, someone to turn to when you get stuck or need encouragement. But don't stop with one person. Make it a goal to meet with everyone on your immediate team in your first thirty days. These can be formal meetings, but they can also be informal, such as a virtual coffee date which implies that it's more of a get-to-know-you meeting. Leverage the same questions outlined in the expert tip section on meeting up with a few members of your team before you start, as well as the company culture questions from chapter 4.

Are you a bit shy? Here's me being real with you: I've always had a tougher time developing personal relationships. Over time I've learned that I need to be very deliberate in getting to know people. One strategy I use is asking specific questions in my initial meetings with colleagues, such as where they grew up, how many siblings they have, and how they ended up in their current roles. I then write all of their answers down so I can refer to them in future conversations.

If you dig deep enough, you'll uncover fascinating stories about your coworkers that you might never have known otherwise. I make a point to share information about my life in return—something that wasn't natural for me at first. I used to believe my life was boring and that no one would care to know anything about me. But I learned that if you want to bond with others, you need to give them a glimpse into who you are as well. Strengthening personal connections fosters trust. As Professor Paul J. Zak said in his article on the neuroscience of trust, "When people care about one another, they perform better because they don't want to let their teammates down."[29]

Beyond your immediate team, it's crucial to begin building relationships with coworkers across various teams and functions. Make a list of people outside your team that others have suggested you meet. Prioritize those within your department, such as onboarding/professional services, support, and CS/revenue operations, and then include those in sales, marketing, and product/engineering. Refer to the questions I suggested in chapter 6 to learn how to best collaborate with these teams. Take the time to meet with these individuals now to lay the groundwork for essential relationships that will serve you well as you delve deeper into your role.

Use this time to learn about how customers are onboarded and when and how CSMs are introduced. If you can, spend some time shadowing your support team toward the end of your first thirty days so you can start putting your product knowledge to work and learn about how they assist customers. This provides more context on your role and how the various teams support and service your customers.

---

29 Paul J. Zak, "The Neuroscience of Trust," *Harvard Business Review* 95, no. 1 (2017): 84–90, https://hbr.org/2017/01/the-neuroscience-of-trust.

Expert tip: Seek out the high performers
During your onboarding period, look for the high performers, the go-to people that everyone reaches out to when they have questions, and people who have won company awards. Try to uncover what makes them stand out so you can emulate those attributes. While not essential, this will expedite your ability to impact your organization.

Shadowing customer calls

The most important action you can take to supplement your training is to shadow customer calls. This includes joining live calls or listening to recorded ones. While most of the calls will be customer calls led by the CS team, I also recommend shadowing prospect calls led by your sales team.

Observing a variety of calls will help you understand the structure of customer meetings, what customers expect from you and your company, and the typical challenges customers experience. To get the full picture, pay attention to the communication exchange with a client before and after the meeting—this will give you insight into the overall interaction.

As you shadow different team members, compare their approaches and identify the most effective strategies.

To maximize the learning opportunities from these shadow sessions, complete the following exercise before each customer call:

- List out the key contract details:

  o MRR or ARR
  o Contract end date
  o Customer segment
  o Products they use

- Examine who is joining the meeting:

  - List the customers' names and roles. This is useful information to give you more context on who is on the call and what they may be expecting. It's important to start to understand the different types of customer personas you will be working with.
  - List the people from your company and their roles. This provides context on how people within your company work together to support the customer and the different parts they play.

- Follow the 3C framework:

  - Write down what the company does and how it makes money.
  - Provide a summary of who their customers are.
  - Document any known challenges that the business is facing or any other pertinent challenges.

- Take note of any other relevant information that provides useful context:

  - Where are they in the customer journey? Are they still in onboarding or closer to their renewal?
  - What is the client's current health? Are they at risk?

- During the call, write down your observations. Use these questions to assist you:

- o What was covered on the call? Was there a particular structure?
- o Were any challenges brought forward by the client?
- o How were those challenges addressed?
- o What are the client's most important priorities right now?
- o Were there any specific goals that they mentioned? Were there certain metrics mentioned that would support those goals?
- o What areas of your products were mentioned? Why are they important to the customer?
- o When did the client seem excited during the call? What did they like or appreciate?
- o When was the client upset or agitated? How did your colleague(s) handle that?
- o What was the outcome of the call? Did it end on a positive note? What are the next steps?

Keeping these questions at the forefront of your mind will keep you present and attentive during these shadow sessions. After the call, take some time to reflect on your notes and fill in any additional details. Was there anything discussed that you need further clarification on? Were there any moments of particular interest? Review your notes with your manager or someone who was on the call to get their perspective on how the call went.

The second month: The messy middle

You should start hitting your groove within the first thirty to sixty days of your onboarding. You've completed your basic training, shadowed several client calls, researched your customers, begun to forge strong connections within your company, and grounded yourself in your company, the product, and the culture. You've also started to familiarize yourself with key processes, such as customer onboarding.

While you should use this period to keep developing internal relationships with your colleagues, you're now ready to take on more responsibilities and cut your teeth with some clients of your own. You're that player at the end of the bench yelling, "Put me in, coach!" Based on my experience, your wish will be granted—and then some. Most CSMs take on a significant portion of their client responsibilities by the sixty-day mark.

The only thing that may be holding you back is you. You may have a fear of taking on clients. Your internal voice may be saying, "What if they ask me something I don't know?" or "What if I make an ass of myself?" As I mentioned in chapter 4, it's OK if you make a mistake. Just own it and move on.

Put your skills to the test

You've been diligent in learning about your products, your industry, and your processes, and it's time to put this training to the test. You'll never fully understand your knowledge gaps unless you start to leverage what you've learned. You should be assigned your own clients in your second month at the latest, as it will force you to better understand your customers, your processes, your tools, the data accessible to you, and your products.

Have someone, such as your manager or a mentor, review your meetings and communications to ensure you're not committing any glaring errors. Schedule time with that person so you can hear their valuable feedback on where you can improve—don't wait for them to do it. Do some practice runs by role-playing some of these meetings to improve your confidence and get some of the kinks out of your delivery.

At this stage, you've removed the training wheels and are cruising on your own. Leverage your new skills and knowledge, and remember from chapter 2 that you know more than you think you do. You were hired for a reason, and your company needs you. Your customers need you. Most importantly, your team needs you.

The third month: You're getting the hang of things

Congrats! You're just about through your onboarding and have started becoming a productive member of your team. By the end of your first ninety days, you should be assigned a full book of business or a client segment. While you may not feel fully comfortable with all aspects of your role, you're getting there. It will still take you longer than your more tenured teammates to respond to clients, as everything is still very new to you.

At this stage, you can take several actions to gain control of your situation and better organize yourself.

First, leverage your CS platform or CRM, as it will help you manage your clients. It can list your clients by their ARR, renewal date, client health, and growth potential. You can also segment clients based on factors like product usage, the length of time they've used your product, and their industry. If configured properly, the system will also create alerts about upcoming renewals, QBRs, potential upsell opportunities, and important product usage issues. This will help you prioritize your outreach. Your CRM should allow you to create reports and dashboards that can mimic some of this functionality.

If you don't have a CS platform or a CRM, or would like more flexibility, create a client tracker to manage your clients. You can keep this simple—just be sure to have at least this information:

- Client name
- Contract start date
- Contract end date
- MRR/ARR
- Client health (red/yellow/green)
- At-risk reason (product gaps, implementation delays, financial issues, etc.)
- A description of why the client may be at risk

- The main contacts and what their roles are
- Their business outcomes (see chapter 17 on defining business outcomes)
- Client pulse. This is the latest client update, including recent wins and overall sentiment.
- Their growth potential (high, medium, or low). This indicates whether they have the potential to spend significantly more with you in the next ninety days

This tracker allows you to easily sort your clients by their upcoming renewal date, health status, or growth potential. Review this weekly to determine where you should focus your time. I also recommend that you build account plans for your most important clients. Please refer back to chapter 2 for more details on account plans. To download client management and account plan templates, go to strategiccustomersuccess.com.

These exercises will help you prioritize your time so you're spending it on the most impactful activities. It's very easy to get caught up in the whirlwind of your day-to-day activities. You need to quickly assess where your focus is most needed and dig in. For more tips on productivity see chapter 12, and for managing client health see chapter 8.

Beyond the first ninety days

Making it through the first ninety days of your customer success role is no easy feat. You've demonstrated your ability and your commitment to get up to speed and contribute toward your team and company goals. Besides performing your core duties, look for ways to deepen your connections with clients and with your colleagues, which will be covered further in the upcoming chapters. As you spread your wings and fly past the ninety-day mark, here are key principles to keep in mind:

- **Product mastery never ends:** You're never done learning about your products. Keep up to date on any new product releases and feature changes. Keep experimenting with your products in your demo environment (if you have one) to increase your product expertise. Think about new use cases and how new features can be adapted to meet your customers' needs. Ask your colleagues how they've used certain features to drive value for their customers. Provide feedback on product gaps to your product team based on customer feedback.

- **Look for ways to improve your processes:** You've now had enough time in your role to reflect on your experience so far, and you should start to suggest improvements to current processes. This could mean changes to how you onboard new team members, broader changes to renewals, improvements to playbooks, or new ways to share information. My only advice is that if you're bringing the ideas, be prepared to do the work. Don't just complain and expect that things will magically change.

- **Keep learning about your industry:** The industry or industries that your company operates in are always changing. It's important to identify what the emerging trends are and if any outside factors may drastically impact your company. As an example, the advent of generative AI has resulted in major disruptions in the technology sector. To stay ahead of the curve, carve out time to review research reports, industry analyses, and insights from recognized experts in your field. Read what your customers are reading and listen to what they are listening to.

- **Stay up to date on your competitors and your competitive differentiators:** It's easy to get caught up in your own products, but don't lose sight of what's happening with your competitors. Have any of your major competitors shifted their strategy? Have they launched any game-changing features that may outflank your offerings? Are any of them struggling to keep up with the rest of the pack? Are there new players that have joined the field, and do they have a competitive edge over you? If they've gained any type of advantage, they could use it to lure your customers away. Don't wait for anyone else to sound the alarm—take the lead.

Don't look now, but you are well on your way to becoming a strategic CSM. After you've survived your first ninety days, you should feel more confident about the base of knowledge you've acquired; the solid internal relationships you've formed; and the initial impact you've started to make, especially with your customers. Follow the recommendations in this chapter to begin your new role with positive steps, and even get a leg up on your colleagues. If you feel overwhelmed at times or even defeated at others, just know that every CSM has felt this way at some point. Believe in yourself. You've got this.

Putting this into practice

Go to strategiccustomersuccess.com and access "The Strategic CSM 90-Day Onboarding Plan Cheat Sheet."

On this site you'll also be able to access helpful tools such as "The Strategic CSM Shadow Session" template, which can be helpful for both novice and veteran CSMs.

Optional: Download "The Client Tracker" template from strategiccustomersuccess.com

Summary and key takeaways

To start off strong, complete key activities during your first ninety days.

- During your employee onboarding, focus on setting a strong foundation: clarify your role and expectations with your manager, build a personal connection with them, proactively track and communicate your achievements, and find ways to make an impact early.

- In your first thirty days, your main focus should be attaining product proficiency and understanding the basic processes and tools required for your role. It's also recommended that you spend time meeting and getting to know your immediate team, identifying people in other teams to connect with, shadowing customer calls, and learning about how customers are onboarded.

- In the second month of your CSM role, you need to put your newfound skills to the test. Lead a QBR or similar strategic meeting to expose you to many distinct aspects of your role. You should have a solid set of clients that you're working with.

- With the groundwork laid for managing your client portfolio, focus the third month of your onboarding on refining your approach and maximizing your impact. By leveraging available resources and seeking support from your colleagues, you'll be well positioned to navigate the challenges and opportunities that lie ahead in your customer success journey.

- Beyond your first ninety days, continue to hone your product and industry skills and deepen relationships with your customers, colleagues, and manager.

CHAPTER 8

Building a Proactive Client Risk Management Strategy

"**H**ey, Chad! Did you see who just sent a churn notice?" One of my CSMs sent me this Slack message at the end of the day. My first reaction was, *Ah @#(%)*. A wave of anxiety washed over me as my thoughts scattered in all directions. I learned it was one of our high-profile customers that was prominent in our marketing materials. Needless to say, I didn't sleep well that evening.

This news hit when the tech sector started cooling off after the COVID-19 pandemic boom. We were already walking a tightrope with client retention—losing this account was not an option. Even worse, they were planning to move to our biggest competitor. "That wasn't on our at-risk list. What happened?" I asked my CSM. I was trying to keep my cool, but I could feel my face going completely white as reality slowly sank in. How could we not have seen this coming?

After the initial shock had worn off, it was time to act. Our client's unhappiness stemmed from our inability to integrate with a crucial technology partner, while our competitors could. Our customer champion had lost faith in us and was pushing to move to our competitor. This didn't look good.

While I had a decent relationship with the decision-maker, our CEO had a better one. I helped broker a conversation to see if we could save them. Luckily, they hadn't yet signed with our competitor and were willing to work with us to rectify the situation. Our CEO reassured them that we would do our best to act quickly and address their integration request.

I led the efforts to get things back on track. Working with our talented services team, I broke the integration work into phases and got something up and running for them within a few weeks to demonstrate our seriousness in winning back their business. We delivered on our promise and, after a few rounds of negotiation, secured a two-year renewal. We even uncovered an expansion opportunity that we would explore after we completed the second phase of integration work.

While I was ecstatic with the result, it wasn't a cause for celebration. It was clear that our processes had suffered a major breakdown. Why hadn't we detected this churn risk? How could we have almost lost one of our "can't lose" customers? This experience underscores the importance of identifying renewal risks early—especially as you take on clients in your first 90 days.

The importance of tracking client risk and general approaches to handling at-risk customers

One key difference between a CSM and a strategic CSM is that the latter has a clear view of their customers' health. SCSMs know which of their clients will most likely renew, which have the best chance to grow, which are at risk and may renew but at a lower fee (downsell), and which will probably churn.

This data feeds into the renewal forecast, determines how much revenue your business will preserve, and can evaluate future growth opportunities. The daily grind of being a CSM can consume your attention, making it challenging to spot what could derail your clients from achieving their business outcomes. That's precisely why surfacing possible client health risks has to be woven into your DNA.

Even with robust customer health tracking, you will still be surprised by some that churn. Your clients may be secretly testing a competitor's product or have plans for a complete strategy overhaul that doesn't include your product.

So what can you do? Strategic CSMs don't shrug their shoulders or blame their organization's ineptitude. OK, maybe they vent a little, but they quickly realize that this doesn't solve anything. You need to work through these challenges because, ultimately, you will be responsible for renewing your clients. A key part of this is flagging at-risk clients' risks early to deal with them while there is time.

AI technologies will make this process more manageable and reliable, but you will still need a general approach for monitoring client health. After years in the trenches, I've developed a solid radar to spot early warning signs. Let me walk you through what works so you can leverage this regardless of the technology you have supporting your efforts.

How to track at-risk clients

The truth is that you'll never have all the data you need to fully understand the health of your customers, even if you have an accurate client health score. To stay on top of the health of your clients regardless of your situation, follow these tips:

- **Start small.** You can still monitor and manage your at-risk clients even if you don't have a fully formed at-risk process. Simply use a spreadsheet and assign a red, yellow, or green color to your clients. Green means that there is a greater than 90 percent chance the client will renew. Yellow means that there is a 50–90 percent chance the client will renew. Red means that the chance the client will renew is below 50 percent (this strategy was mentioned in chapter 2 as part of the health score on an account plan). You can download the client tracker template on strategiccustomersuccess.com to keep track of the health of your customers.

If you're uncertain about a client's health status, take proactive steps, such as arranging a strategic conversation (see part IV). Classifying your clients into these three buckets can also help you determine where to spend your limited time (see chapter 12 on productivity).

- **Categorize the risks.** After pinpointing potentially risky clients, sort them into distinct at-risk categories. This will allow you to decide on the most effective course of action and identify emerging trends within your customer base. Most customer success organizations have at-risk playbooks to guide you. If none exist, you can take the lead in creating one by leveraging what we'll cover in this section.

  When creating an at-risk playbook, consider the at-risk categories below. You may have additional categories based on the nuances of your business:

  o Product gaps: This usually means your product lacks key features that customers need to achieve their business outcomes.

  o Product issues: Your customer may be experiencing a high number of bugs or product instability that is impacting their ability to use your product.

  o Low customer engagement: Your customers may frequently cancel meetings or ignore communications from you and others in your company. You may also recognize that you don't have solid connections with key client stakeholders such as the decision-maker.

  o Key client stakeholder turnover: Your primary contacts or decision-makers have left their roles.

  o Low product adoption: Your customers' use of your product is below the minimum threshold you've defined. This usually has two elements: breadth and depth of usage. Breadth refers to how many features clients are actively using within your products. Depth measures the intensity of their usage, including feature engagement or the number of licenses in use. It also usually refers to using key features that create product stickiness, which is critical to achieving value.

o   Low value achieved: This category is all about your customers achieving their business outcomes—the jobs they need your product to fulfill. Low adoption relates to this category, but even a client with high product usage may struggle to achieve meaningful value.

   This category is also tied to low customer engagement. You might have a strong rapport with your main point of contact, only to discover that the decision-maker you haven't engaged opts to cancel due to low perceived value.

o   Financial instability/acquisition: Due to financial difficulties in their business, you may have clients who are behind on their payments or unable to pay their bills. They may also have gone bankrupt or been acquired. These situations may present an opportunity to work with the acquirer but usually results in customer churn.

o   Delayed or poor onboarding: If your customers' onboarding is off track or stalled, it will hinder their ability to achieve their business outcomes and could jeopardize the entire relationship.

o   Low customer satisfaction: This is a bit of a catch-all, but it is usually used when the client has expressed their dissatisfaction or mentioned they will churn, and you've yet to designate a more accurate at-risk reason.

- **Mine for issues.** It's your responsibility to monitor your client's product usage, stay alert to any changes in key stakeholders, track shifts in their business, and identify if they're encountering any obstacles with your products or services. As AppsFlyer's Chief Customer Officer Ziv Peled says, "Embrace data," which includes monitoring your customer's usage trends but can simply be reviewing how quickly they are responding to you.[30] Mining for issues also means posing difficult questions to your clients, particularly when you notice negative patterns like canceled meetings, a decline in product usage, or an interest in your competitors. For example, ask them, "On a scale from one to ten, with ten being the most likely, if your renewal date is tomorrow, how likely are you to renew with us?" Your customers can't shy away from this question, as they need to give you an explicit answer. You then need to follow up to understand why they gave you that number.

- **Don't be complacent with your customers**—be proactive and seek out problems.

How to turn around at-risk clients

Now that you have identified your at-risk clients, determine how to right the ship. Admittedly, I don't have any magic tricks or secret potions to save your clients. The reality is that when clients have lost faith in your company, it will be tough to turn things around. Additionally, Greg Daines, a.k.a. the churn doctor, has found from his research that it may not even be worth saving these clients as "the majority of rescued customers will not renew again."[31]

30   Ziv Peled, "Decoding Success: The 10 Daily Rituals of High-Performing CSMs," LinkedIn, June 27, 2023, https://www.linkedin.com/posts/zivpeled_customersuccess-productivity-strategy-activity-7079299070116175872-XCkZ/.

31   Greg Daines, "The Cardinal Sin of Customer Success Is Not Churn. It's Unexpected Churn!," LinkedIn, November 28, 2018, https://www.linkedin.com/pulse/cardinal-sin-customer-success-churn-its-unexpected-greg-daines/.

So, what do we do? Here is a hard truth: You can't save everyone—you have neither the time nor the resources. Align with your manager on which at-risk clients are worth pursuing and which you'll take off life support and let nature take its course.

Once you've determined it's worth investing your energy in, ask others in your organization for help, focus on the root issue, fill the value gap, and envision the future.

Ask for help. When your client may be on the verge of churning, it can seem as if the entire problem rests on your shoulders. This is your client, so you feel it's all on you. You're most likely measured on retention, so it's natural to take this to heart. But you shouldn't feel you have to handle the burden alone. Seek out people within your organization who can assist you. You could leverage the sales rep who originally sold the deal, one of your executives who may have a connection with a senior client stakeholder, or anyone else in your organization who can lend a hand. Not sure where to go? Reach out to your manager; don't hide this type of news. They can help you brainstorm next steps—this is when you'll need all the help you can get.

And that doesn't just mean within your organization. Scout your customers' LinkedIn relationships for allies you can tap into. Leverage your customer advocates, former colleagues, and joint partners. I've turned around several customers by simply matching them with another customer they were familiar with. Partners can also be invaluable—especially technology partners. If your renewal is uncertain, chances are theirs is too. By exchanging insights, you can piece together the complete picture and develop an effective strategy to mitigate a churn risk.

You may feel uncomfortable connecting with people you don't know. You have to get over your fears. Your customer's contract end date is like a ticking time bomb. Trust me, things will get much worse if a significant client churns, and you haven't done everything you could to save them. There is never any harm in asking for help. The worst someone could do is say no.

You'll be surprised by how many people are willing to step up when you need them most. You just need to ask. And when you don't hear back the first time, ask again. Be persistent, but be polite.

In my second week as head of CS at Kustomer, Brad Birnbaum, the CEO, jokingly told me that I could never let a particular luggage brand churn. I was a little freaked out at that point, but I had my marching orders. Luckily, my CSM determined that one of our designers had gone to school with one of our key client stakeholders. Our designer led an in-person workshop with the client, which helped rebuild the relationship. You never know who is in a position to help you unless you ask.

Find the root issue. When categorizing your at-risk clients, focus on the underlying problems, not just the obvious ones. I'm referring to a concept that Gainsight CEO Nick Mehta and former Gainsight CCO Allison Pickens expounded on in the book *The Customer Success Economy*. They suggest prioritizing the root causes of risk over the surface-level issues.[32] Just as roots form a tree's critical support system for survival, discovering your customer's essential pain points allows you to implement solutions that drive meaningful change.

Quick fixes such as rushing out a feature request or providing heavy discounts seem like solutions to prevent customer churn, but they're Band-Aids if you haven't solved the underlying problem. I've suffered through multiple situations where clients were categorized as at risk due to low usage, but the challenge was that they didn't achieve measurable results. When facing a possible churn situation, use the OARS framework, the SOON funnel, and other strategic conversation techniques covered in part IV to get to the root issue. You can then put together a success plan to repair the damage and work toward the renewal. Similar to an iceberg, where the majority of it resides underwater, you need to dive down and get to the heart of the issue.

---

32 Nick Mehta and Allison Pickens, *The Customer Success Economy: Why Every Aspect of Your Business Model Needs a Paradigm Shift*, (Wiley, 2020), 50–51, Kindle.

Fill the value gap. Most churn I've experienced has been due to customers not achieving or fully realizing value. It wasn't due to a stakeholder change or our products being too expensive. When value recognition is at the heart of the matter, your initial focus should be on how the client defines and measures success. Once aligned with your client, you may discover opportunities to bridge the perceived value gap and assist your customers with their business objectives.

To fill the value gap, provide something meaningful to your client—even if it's different from what they originally anticipated. For example, let's say that your client is upset because they expected your product to work in a certain way, and they're now waiting for you to build a new feature to fulfill this need. But it could take months to roll out this product request and their renewal is right around the corner. What are some creative ways you can fill the value gap?

- Provide them with additional services that will give them the functionality they need in the interim
- Provide a greater discount that will make up for the disruption to their business
- Offer them free access to advanced features or additional licenses
- Offer additional data such as benchmarks or in-depth analysis that will help them to make better decisions

Consider what your clients deem valuable and try to use that as leverage to repair the damage so you can fill the value gap and buy yourself some time. **Paint a picture of the future.** We all suffer from nearsightedness at times. I'm not referring to my terrible eyesight but rather to our tendency to get tangled in our thoughts when we're in the thick of a problem. Our clients fall prey to this as well. They could be looking to leave you due to underwhelming results, frustration from significant product defects, the lure of cost savings, or perceived benefits from a competitive solution.

Despite your clients' challenges, most aren't looking to change their technology stack. They purchased your product for a specific job and don't want to expend additional resources to replace you if it's unnecessary. Many are in search of a reason to restore their confidence in you and will give you a chance for redemption.

So lift the fog from your client's eyes and paint a brighter picture by focusing on the future:

- **Present your product roadmap**. To reassure your client that you're in alignment, show them your product roadmap and outline how it matches their goals and priorities. By demonstrating your company's planned innovation, you can defend against competitors trying to lure your customers away. Too often, companies hide their roadmap because they don't want to overpromise. If that's the case, keep it at a high level. It is better to show something than keep it hidden and allow your competitors to paint a better picture.

  Your roadmap doesn't need to focus solely on product features. It can also include scheduled process improvements, key hires, and other breakthrough solutions to address your clients' needs. For instance, investing in your quality assurance processes and speeding up your product's processing time may alleviate your clients' pains.

- **Assess their maturity**. When your customers suffer from nearsightedness, they are caught in their echo chamber and lose sight of how their situation compares to that of their industry peers. A customer maturity model can give your customers the clarity they need to better understand their present situation.

  These models establish a clear baseline for your customers and highlight the path to their desired future state. Once clients see how they measure up against peers, they often acknowledge needed changes and look to you for strategic direction. You can also include your at-risk clients on your customer advisory board, where they can compare their progress with their peers and broaden their perspectives. This is risky, as they could be detractors, but what do you have to lose? It's time to pull out all the stops.

- **Calculate future value**. Leading a QBR or a renewal conversation with an underperforming client can be particularly stressful. Several factors could have gotten you to this point, but here you are. Some client relationships are beyond repair due to not being the right fit for your products, but others have a chance to improve. How do you get these clients on a better path in these situations?

    A helpful strategy when working with struggling clients is to develop a value calculator that forecasts potential outcomes based on specific client actions. Value or ROI calculators can generate predictions for future outcomes by entering specified variables. For example, at Influitive we created a value calculator that showed how our customers could achieve more customer advocacy if they increased certain activities. Consider how you could replicate this concept in your own organization. How can you paint a future success path for your clients that can spur them to action?

Recovering from a near-churn situation can be challenging. When your clients' trust has been broken or they feel they have wasted their resources, it can be extremely difficult to turn things around. Some clients may not be worth saving based on their risk factors—but if you believe a client is salvageable, you owe it to them (and yourself) to try.

Putting this into practice

Go to strategiccustomersuccess.com and access "The Client Risk Management Cheat Sheet."

Optional: Download "The Client Tracker" template from strategiccustomersuccess.com

Summary and key takeaways

Managing client risk requires a proactive, strategic approach.

- Focus on early detection and proactive management of at-risk clients by consistently monitoring client health and addressing issues before they escalate.
- When churn risks arise, ask for help, uncover root causes, and close value gaps to rebuild customer trust.
- To retain at-risk customers, shift the focus to the future by showcasing your roadmap, highlighting growth opportunities, and demonstrating measurable value.

PART III

Navigating Your Professional Growth

CHAPTER 9

How to Create Unbreakable Customer Relationships

I was having one of those days—you know, the kind where you can't do anything right. I was leading a customer success team at Influitive while managing a few direct customers—a typical position at an early-stage start-up.

Just as I was feeling at my lowest, a package arrived at our front desk. To my surprise, it contained two large boxes of donuts. I ripped open the card and read it out loud: "FAME donuts for all your hard work behind the scenes that made our launch a success." It was signed by Bo Bandy, the head of marketing at ReadyTalk, the client I recently onboarded. I was in complete shock. What had I done to deserve this? Before I could finish this thought, my colleagues were crowding around me and chanting, "Donuts! Donuts!" We all started to chow down on this sugary goodness.

You see, these weren't just regular donuts. These were some of the most delicious donuts I've ever had in my life. Some were covered with melted marshmallows, while others had bacon crumbs. I was in donut heaven. I was proud of this achievement because I had worked my ass off to get to this point. I also became the office hero as we all enjoyed those sweet treats.

Years later, I still think back to that moment. I see it as a milestone in my CS career, as it demonstrated that my efforts in building strong relationships and focusing on business outcomes had paid off. I took the time to understand this particular client's needs and set proper expectations for their launch. I kept them on track and proactively shared advice. I didn't just blindly carry out whatever they asked. I pushed back respectfully, practicing what I call *radical customer candor*.

Figure 5.³³ Donut celebration at Influitive. Photo by Chad Horenfeldt. November, 2013.

I'll dive deeper into this concept and more in this chapter, where we'll cover how to solidify long-term relationships with your customers and continue your transformation into an SCSM. To achieve this, I've pulled together my top ten most impactful recommendations that have guided me in my career, as well as additional tips:

- Provide value in every interaction.
- Don't just show value, sell it.
- Practice *extreme ownership*.

---

33 Chad Horenfeldt, *Donut Day at Influitive, Nov.* 2013, Author's personal collection.

- Be responsive.
- Set the right expectations.
- Communicate with clarity and purpose.
- Give clients access to internal resources.
- Recognize your clients' achievements.
- Teach your customers—don't just talk at them.
- Practice *radical customer candor*.

I will go into each of these items in detail and provide practical examples that you can start using with your clients. The key to success is to perform these actions consistently.

Provide value in every interaction

No more check-ins

A mistake I see CSMs make consistently is sending a check-in email to their customers—you know, the ones that begin with "Just checking in" or "How can I help?". This mistake inevitably leads to customer disengagement, as there is no compelling reason for them to respond. The antidote? Ensure every interaction delivers meaningful value. It's time to ditch the "check-in" language, which only serves your needs, and give your customers something of value that demonstrates you care about theirs.

Proactively designing specialized reports that uncovered hidden insights in my clients' information was a successful strategy. This created a moment of surprise and delight for my customers. Another successful approach was to send a personalized product release update to certain clients that described how the new features would help them achieve their business outcomes. When possible, personalize what you send to your customers and explain why it's important to them.

Don't let important information get lost in the marketing shuffle. Share customized updates that speak directly to your customers' needs. And don't hesitate to resend it—they might have missed your first one. Just be mindful not to inundate them with too much noise, as they'll tune you out. For scaled CSMs who serve higher volumes of customers, segment your customers by industry, product, persona, or use case, and tailor your updates to these segments so you can deliver relevant updates en masse.

The golden nugget

A valuable strategy I learned from Paul Teshima during my time at Eloqua involved keeping an insightful *golden nugget* that I could share during client conversations or through personal outreach. A golden nugget is like a hidden gem—it provides your clients with fresh knowledge they hadn't considered, establishing you as a trusted advisor.

That golden nugget could be product best practices that your clients can immediately leverage and benefit from. It could be a recently released product feature that's flying under the radar but could significantly impact their operations. Whether drawn from their own product analytics or from emerging market research, any meaningful intelligence that adds value can serve this purpose. It can even be a relevant client story that could inspire your client to take action.

Since you want to have two or three of these nuggets at the ready to inject into client conversations, work with your colleagues to create a list of possible golden nuggets, so you keep replenishing and refreshing your nugget stockpile. Try to generate weekly or monthly nuggets that everyone can use, and you can even create a goal for yourself to communicate it to a certain number of customers.

What sets this approach apart is its proactive nature, which provides customers with unexpected benefits. The key is customizing these insights for each client's unique context, for instance by distilling relevant articles or research findings in a way that directly connects to their business outcomes, making them more likely to act on and value your expertise. This creates a better overall experience and separates you from your competitors. You can also consider delivering these tips at scale by crafting these messages for specific segments and leveraging technology such as in-app messaging.

By adopting a mentality of *no more check-ins* and focusing on always providing value, you'll strengthen your client relationships.

Don't just show value, sell it

When clients abruptly churn, it's frequently not because your solution isn't working—it's because you haven't successfully demonstrated its impact to the key customer stakeholders. It's all about selling the value.

Don't assume that your day-to-day contacts relay your product's impact to their boss who is typically the decision-maker. They may not know how to convey the value of your products, or they may never have realized the importance of doing this. You must maintain a clear understanding of your clients' business outcomes, track their forward momentum, and consistently update important stakeholders on their journey.

Either communicate key moments of value directly to the decision-maker or arm your customer champions with the information they need to keep the right stakeholders informed. It's best to do this as part of a meeting, such as a QBR, so you can confirm that they're on track. These types of messages can also be delivered via other channels, such as email—especially where it's impossible to connect directly with every client.

Given the growing challenge of securing face time with executives, explore creative ways to showcase value. A succinct video update or streamlined message focusing on goal progress and roadblocks can cut through the noise.

Since most decision-makers step away from your product's day-to-day operations and are not kept informed of the progress made, you must start this habit early in the relationship and convey the wins that have been gained as well as any issues. Doing this early on can make customers feel more comfortable with their purchase and open up a line of communication that can be beneficial down the line, especially when there are challenges.

Practice extreme ownership

As an SCSM, you have to face the reality that unexpected challenges will arise. How you respond in those situations is what separates strategic CSMs from regular CSMs. In their book *Extreme Ownership*, authors Jocko Willink and Leif Babin define the idea of extreme ownership: "The leader must own everything in his or her world. There is no one else to blame."[34] This is how you should go about your business as well. Did you drop the ball on a customer request? Take ownership of it. Did an unexpected product issue bring your customer's work to a standstill? Take ownership of it. Is there a disconnect between the customer's expectations from sales discussions and their actual experience? Take ownership of it.

You may be saying, "Wait a minute, Chad. Do you want me to take the heat for sales overpromising something? No way." While you shouldn't take the blame for another team's actions, your role as the customer's primary point of contact in that moment means stepping up and owning the situation, regardless of where the issue originated.

When things go wrong, your customers don't care about who caused the problem. What they want is someone to be accountable and help them resolve the issue. Don't blame the engineering team for releasing code without properly testing it. Don't blame the sales team for overselling. Don't blame the billing team for sending the wrong invoice. Focus on addressing the immediate problem.

---

34 Jocko Willink and Leif Babin, *Extreme Ownership: How U.S. Navy SEALs Lead and Win* (Macmillan, 2015), 124.

Though it may be tempting to point fingers at other departments, doing so in front of customers diminishes your company's reputation and trust-worthiness. Furthermore, badmouthing your colleagues will negatively impact how your peers perceive you and their willingness to collaborate with you.

You can also practice extreme ownership when you directly screw up. Acknowledge that you made a mistake and move on. Trying to defend yourself or make excuses for your actions will only make the situation worse and generate mistrust between you and your customers. Put your ego aside, fall on your sword, and apologize. You'll most likely be forgiven and permitted to move past this.

Finally, extreme ownership includes being accountable for the overall health of your client base and ensuring that you're doing everything in your power to help them achieve their business outcomes. Taking ownership of your clients' success will also pave the way for career growth and advancement.

Be responsive

You have so much coming at you that it can be hard to keep up. I get it; I've been there. But you can't let your customer correspondence slip through the cracks. You must respond within a reasonable timeframe.

Letting customer messages go unanswered undermines customer trust. Even when you're pressed for time, a quick "received and will respond by . . ." message sets clear expectations. Better yet, help them find answers without relying on you. This can include your documentation, training portal, AI chatbot, or online community, if you have one.

If you're having trouble keeping up with your customers' requests, reach out to your manager or colleagues for advice. Don't be afraid to seek help. Having another person's perspective can be invaluable—especially when your client is being unreasonable. One of the worst outcomes is your client messaging your boss, saying that you've been unresponsive. Don't let this happen to you. To avoid it, you must not only be responsive but also set the right expectations.

> **Expert tip: The "non-update"**
>
> When a customer is waiting on a specific feature or bug fix, I make every effort to share the current status with them regularly so they don't feel I've forgotten about it, even if there is no fresh information. I call this the "non-update." I simply let them know that we're still working on their request and provide an updated timeline if necessary.
>
> I know this can seem strange, but let's consider it from the customer's perspective. Your company is a big black box to them, and not providing updates on their important items can lead to distrust and a feeling of neglect. This can be easily avoided.
>
> Just set a reminder in your calendar to send a quick update about their high-priority items, even if progress hasn't been made. This will also remind you to regularly review their pressing requests. If your company has determined that they can't fulfill the customer's product request, let the client know. You don't want your customers to feel like you're leaving them hanging.

Set the right expectations

The root of customer disappointment frequently traces back to unclear or improperly set expectations. Your customer may have been promised a certain product feature or capability that doesn't exist. You may have a customer who complains that they can never get a hold of you when they message you at 10:00 p.m. Both situations require an examination of the client's assumptions.

Take proactive measures to set proper ground rules with your clients. Always specify the following:

- Your company's support ecosystem for customers, clearly indicating how to get assistance when needed—especially during critical situations that require immediate attention. Let your clients know if you use another system for communicating system outages.

- The channels, such as email or Slack, through which clients can contact you.

- Your availability, based on your time zone and how often you'll meet.

- Your typical response time. For example, you can specify that you aim to respond to customers within twenty-four business hours. Use this as another reason to nudge your customers to the other resources you have available so they aren't asking you support-related questions.

- Whom to contact when you're out of the office. Reduce potential issues by setting up the proper notifications or letting customers know ahead of time. When you're taking more than three consecutive days off, give your clients a heads-up.

Some of the expectations previously set are out of your control such as the sales team downplaying the level of effort needed to configure your product. In these situations you need to rip off the Band-Aid and reset these with your customer. I may offer a concession such as a reduced or free product add-on or some other type of discount when this has caused a severe rift with the client. Your goal is to make things right so you can restore trust and reboot the relationship. In chapter 11, we'll cover how to work with the sales team to limit these issues from happening.

Communicate with clarity and purpose

When I discuss with my CSMs why they haven't engaged with their customers recently, they often say, "They never responded to me." When we dive into their client correspondence, I often see long-winded emails from CSMs that contain a lot of our jargon and don't have a clear message or call to action.

Your clients are inundated with emails, Slack messages, text messages, notifications, and more. You must be as succinct as possible and clearly convey why your message is important. This is especially true when communicating with senior client stakeholders (see chapter 17).

When communicating with your clients, ask:

- What outcome am I trying to achieve? What do I want from the client?

- What message am I trying to convey? Am I conveying it?

- Are the actions I want my customers to take clearly laid out?

- Does this sound like it will benefit my customer, or does it come off as a selfish request that will only serve my company's interests? What benefit does the customer achieve?

- Do I have the relevant information to persuade my customer to act? This could include relevant data or similar customer examples that can support your points.

- What is the right channel? Should I use email, in-app messaging, or text messages? Or is it better to discuss this in a live meeting?

- Will my target audience be able to easily understand the terminology I'm using, or do I need to simplify it?

- Can I tighten up my sentences to make them crisper? Is there superfluous information that doesn't need to be communicated at this time? Have I pared the message down to the bare minimum?

AI technology now makes it easy to review your emails for clarity and brevity so you have no excuses. Communicating with clarity is a skill that takes time to learn, but it's unbelievably valuable. It will also help you advance your career, as the same skills are needed to communicate with your manager and other senior leaders within your organization.

Expert tip: When emotions are running high, pick up the phone

Reflecting on the many renewal negotiations I've been a part of, one stands out in particular. While I was at Kustomer, I sent one of our long-standing customers an email outlining what I felt were fair renewal terms. Unfortunately, the client didn't feel the same. They sent a heated reply that asked for greater discounts. I realized my mistake right away: I hadn't effectively communicated the reasoning behind the pricing proposal, so my message got lost in translation.

You have to assume that some part of any email, text, Slack, WhatsApp, or other message will be misunderstood. Those few minutes you thought you were saving by sending an email instead of calling when you knew the subject would be a sensitive one will usually cost you in the long run. These episodes can cause irreparable damage to your client relationships.

My former boss and mentor at Kustomer, Vikas Bhambri, used to always say, "Pick up the phone." This doesn't just mean dialing your customer. It means having a direct, two-way conversation with them. This will help you solve problems faster, avoid additional issues, foster an environment of trust, and save yourself headaches.

If you find yourself in a lengthy and unproductive email or Slack exchange, or if you need to convey a message with emotional nuance, arrange a meeting instead. Drop your client a quick note suggesting a meeting to save time going back and forth and prevent any misunderstandings. It's also good advice to follow when you seem to be stuck in an ongoing Slack thread with colleagues or notice a hint of anger or passive-aggressiveness in their messages. Don't let this fester: Pick up the phone.

Give clients access to internal resources

One of the biggest mistakes CSMs make is that they are too protective of their clients and don't allow other teams to communicate with them directly. It's natural to feel anxious about your colleagues saying the wrong thing to your customers because they lack your historical context. Many of you may have been burned by sales pushing an upsell on the wrong customer at the wrong time. Rise above territorial instincts and facilitate open connections between your customers and other valuable team members—after all, this direct access is exactly what they're seeking.

Your customers want to speak to your product team to give their feedback. They may want to speak to your customer marketing team to provide a testimonial and increase their personal brand. They want to speak to your industry or product expert who can provide them with unique best practices. Avoid being the bottleneck that limits your customers' access to other team members in your organization and prevents opportunities for your customers to build stronger bonds that will make them customers for life.

Another reason to be less concerned about others conversing directly with your customers is your sheer lack of time to oversee every customer interaction. You have enough to focus on with all your responsibilities. You should welcome any assistance from your teammates, as they can provide cover for you while you focus on other pressing items.

Should you completely ignore the conversations that other teams are having with your customers? Of course not! You need to stay informed of any ongoing discussions and developments. However, you should direct your efforts toward facilitating connections between your customers and different teams within your organization rather than limiting access or impeding their ability to interact. Share customer summaries with other teams so they know what to focus on and what to avoid bringing up.

Match senior leaders from across your organization to your larger customers' senior stakeholders. This is typically accomplished as part of an executive sponsor program. The main goal of these programs is to ensure that you create multithreaded connections between your client and your company. Giving your customers access to your executives makes them feel more valued and helps address small fires before they become uncontrollable infernos. They can also help you sell the value to your key customer stakeholders. In addition, these programs build company-wide customer empathy as you have representatives from multiple functions, such as sales, marketing, product, and engineering, participating. This helps bring everyone into the realm of customer success.

Including select customers as part of a customer advisory board can increase the connection they feel with your company. CABs provide your customers the opportunity to learn about your company's vision, hear from your leadership, and share their feedback on challenges they are experiencing. They can also shape your future product strategy. Your most strategic customers (those that are paying the most, growing the fastest, or have the most potential to grow) expect that their voices will be heard and listened to. They are hooking their wagons to your company and demand assurances that your product vision is aligned with their desired outcomes. CABs help facilitate the access they are looking for.

One more way to help your customers feel more connected with your company is to connect them with other customers. This works extremely well because your customers are typically more receptive to advice from their peers than from you—especially when you don't have a strong relationship. As a CSM, you can play the role of matchmaker and introduce your customers to other customers so they can learn from their peers. This can also be accomplished with an online community. I've found that many customers are very open to networking with their peers and welcome the chance to meet others. This tactic can also be helpful when trying to reengage a dormant customer.

Recognize your clients' achievements

You have a secret power that you may not realize: The power to brighten your customer's day by recognizing their achievements. This is your opportunity to show them some love by:

- Sending a message to your point of contact's boss, letting them know about hitting a major milestone, such as a key goal, and highlighting your customers' achievements—even the small ones
- Calling out their accomplishments in front of their boss at a QBR or other high-level meeting
- Showing appreciation by sending gifts when they achieve small victories, like experimenting with a new product feature (The gift doesn't have to be extravagant. It could be company swag, an industry-related book, or a gift card.)
- Suggesting them for speaking gigs at conferences or on webinars (Your clients will be honored that you asked them. Many see this as a way to build their personal brands.)
- Trying to help them win industry awards (Why not nominate your top-performing customers for awards? Winning an industry award is a major honor that can elevate their status and your relationship.)

One of the most successful customer appreciation activities we did at Eloqua was to start the Markie Awards for the top B2B marketers around the globe. To help motivate my customers to do more with our products, I would present a slide of the Markie Award at key meetings such as QBRs. They were crafted to look and feel like an Emmy award. Who wouldn't want something like that sitting on their desk or on a shelf behind them? The Markie Awards are legit and are still going as of the date this book was published but have been renamed the Customer Excellence Awards.[35]

---

35 They were renamed the Customer Excellence Awards in 2024.

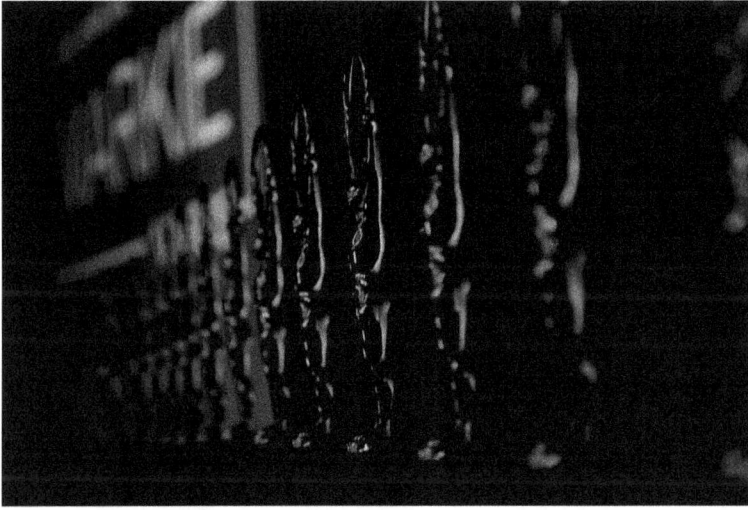

Figure 6.[36] The Markie Awards. Photo by Aaron Rothschild. October 7, 2008.

You need to be your customers' biggest cheerleader. Push them. Encourage them. Reward them. Assume they don't get any recognition within their company and highlight their achievements. At the very least, send key clients some swag or a small holiday gift. Some vendors out there make this a snap so you can easily surprise and delight them (see strategiccustomersuccess.com for some suggestions). Recognizing your clients will deepen your client relationship because it's a form of reciprocity, which is another one of Robert Cialdini's core principles of psychological influence. Follow these practices with your clients, and you'll create customers for life.[37]

Teach your customers—don't just talk at them

One of the best ways to position yourself as a strategic advisor is to teach your customers something of value rather than just talking at them. For instance, don't just describe new product capabilities to your customers; bring them

---

36 Aaron Rothschild, The Markie Awards, October 7, 2008, https://www.smugmug.com/gallery/n-G2vXx/i-t43Ksmn/A.
37 Raluca Budiu, "The Reciprocity Principle: Give Before You Take in Web Design," Nielsen Norman Group, February 16, 2014, https://www.nngroup.com/articles/reciprocity-principle/.

to life through interactive screen-sharing sessions that walk them through the functionality. Have them share their screens so they can practice using your product with your guidance. Highlight a relevant use case so they can easily grasp the feature's value.

Teaching involves tailoring the message and ensuring the customer understands what you discussed. Asking questions such as "How will you leverage what we discussed today?" can gauge how well the customer comprehended what was covered and lead to more in-depth discussions.

Expert tip: Increasing vulnerability

To deepen your customer relationship, be more open and share how you're feeling with your customers. While you don't want to complain about being overly busy or overshare about office politics, they should see your human side and not perceive you as an AI bot. Let them know about an allergy issue that has kept you up at night, a new trick you taught your pet, or that you're excited for an upcoming vacation. You decide what your comfort level is. Just use discretion as to what you divulge and to whom.

It can feel uncomfortable to share personal information, but it's a tried and tested way of building trust and rapport, according to the renowned author Brené Brown. In her book *The Gifts of Imperfection*, she explains that "Staying vulnerable is a risk we have to take if we want to experience connection."[38] The more you can humanize your relationship with your customers, the greater bond you'll create, and the more trust will be formed. Be real to your clients, and they will do the same in return.

Practice radical customer candor

Recognizing your customers and investing time to guide them shows you care—but earning their loyalty sometimes takes the courage to deliver tough

---

38 Brené Brown, *The Gifts of Imperfection: Let Go of Who You Think You're Supposed to Be and Embrace Who You Are* (Hazelden Publishing, 2010), 39.

love. This involves being frank with them and questioning their actions. As a CSM, you need to practice what author Kim Scott calls *radical candor* in her book of the same name.

Scott describes radical candor as "caring personally while challenging directly."[39] Being an effective CSM requires you to boldly help clients examine their conventional wisdom and standard practices. You can't be a doormat who lets customers walk all over you and gives in to every demand. As I said earlier, you're not a waiter who simply takes orders and your goal isn't to make customers happy. You need to have your own opinion on what is best for your customers. You also can't be complacent and accept it at face value when your client says that "everything is going OK." Trust me—it usually isn't.

Your clients may be trapped in their own bubbles, completely isolated from what is happening around them. You have the power to give them the gift of perspective and help them see their situations from a different angle. This is what I call *radical customer candor*, and it is a central part of being an SCSM.

For instance, I've seen numerous examples of clients demanding that CSMs recreate outdated and inefficient processes during onboarding. When faced with such clients, I stood my ground as best I could instead of acquiescing to their requests. I pointed out how other similar clients had made measurable advancements in their business by implementing our software, following our recommended approach, and moving away from legacy processes. I also reassured them that we would be there with them every step of the way so we could help them through this transformation.

I stood up to them, but I did so in a respectful way that took into account the vast amount of experience my client had in this space and their reluctance to change. I also had this conversation after I had already estab-

---

39 Kim Malone Scott, *Radical Candor: How to Get What You Want by Saying What You Mean* (Macmillan, 2017), 82.

lished a trusted relationship that embodied many of the recommendations covered in this book. The client knew I cared about them and their interests, and I had earned the right to challenge them. This is what radical customer candor is all about.

At times, you will need to take control of the situation. The good news is that most of your customers will welcome this with open arms. Authors Matthew Dixon and Brent Adamson, in their book *The Challenger Sale*, conclude that buyers want sales reps who can help them avoid landmines and offer a unique perspective. This is no different in the world of customer success.

Dixon and Adamson claim that your customers are secretly saying, "Challenge me. Teach me something new."[40] They don't want to be pampered—they want you to be real with them. They need and want to be challenged. As previously noted, an effective means of engaging your customers involves educating rather than lecturing. People yearn to learn, so don't worry about standing up to your customers or disagreeing with their views.

Being a challenger is a central component of radical customer candor. It may mean asking your customers tough questions, questioning their motivation to act, or confronting them with a completely different approach. If this approach feels daunting, take heart—the upcoming chapters will provide frameworks to help you master this vital competency.

> **Expert tip: Sometimes the answer is no**
>
> As a former CSM, I understand that no one likes to say no to their clients. But sometimes you have no other choice—you must be OK with pushing back on your customers. For instance, your customer may demand a product feature that only they require or unreasonable discounts. Being a people pleaser all the time will not ensure that your client renews. You must accept that your customers aren't always right.

---

40 Dixon and Adamson, *The Challenger Sale*, 53.

You set yourself up for failure when you continue to cater to your customers' extravagant requests. While I maintain that you should assume the best of people, the reality is that some clients will take advantage of your generosity—whether they do this consciously or not. They'll continue to ask for more because you've demonstrated a propensity to cave to their demands. This creates a cycle of unattainable expectations, which can damage the trust between you and your customer and impact your long-term relationship. There are times when it's necessary to firmly say no and feel confident about standing your ground.

The mistake many CS professionals make is that they skate around the issue and don't definitively shut down their customers' requests. If a feature request clearly conflicts with your product's direction, be direct rather than letting clients believe it might materialize down the line. Be straight with them so they can determine what their next possible action is. They will respect you more when you're clear on what you can and can't do. The issue comes when you set the wrong expectations, leading to miscommunication and an eventual breakdown of trust. In chapter 18, I'll cover in greater depth how to discuss feature requests with your clients.

When you have to give a hard "no," provide as much detail as you can about how the decision was made and why their request is being denied. For instance, when I had to turn down a deep discount request from one of my clients, For instance, when I had to turn down a deep discount request from one of my clients, I let them know that their pricing was in line with that of similar customers and I couldn't do any better. I also outlined what my discounting limitations were and explored other ways to assist them if they had budget issues. When you have to say "no," look for ways that you can offset their disappointment and show you care.

Bonus: Be proactive

A common theme throughout this chapter revolves around having a proactive mindset. It's probably the most overused term in customer success but with good reason. Yesterday's wins don't guarantee tomorrow's success—constant vigilance in monitoring client health is essential. You must continually mine for possible issues and opportunities that could impact your client's current predicament.

To improve your proactiveness, ask yourself these questions:

- Based on the data available to me, which of my clients are struggling or having issues? What can I do to help them improve?
- Based on what I know about my clients, what is something I could do to increase the value they're receiving? What information or data could I provide to help them be more successful?
- Which of my clients has not engaged with our company for some time? What value can I provide to reengage them?
- Do I know all the key stakeholders at my client's organization? How can I improve my relationships?
- Which of my clients require a QBR or similar strategic engagement?
- Are any of my clients facing obstacles to achieving their business outcomes? What actions could be taken to assist them? Have I let the right people in my organization know of these issues so I can get the help I need?
- Which of my clients is ripe for an expansion opportunity? What are the products they could take advantage of, based on their desired business outcomes? Which teams could start using our product that have yet to leverage it?
- Which product features are my clients requesting, and have I effectively communicated their needs to my product and engineering teams? How have these features been prioritized, and are they on

the roadmap? Has the client been updated recently on the progress or lack of progress?

- What new product features have been released or will be released soon? Have I effectively communicated to my clients the significance of the product updates, conveying not only what the features entail but also their importance?

- Are there any current product issues that could impact my clients' productivity? Have I ensured they're being addressed, and have the clients been updated?

At the end of the day, most of your customers will renew. If they didn't, your company wouldn't last very long. That said, you can be the difference maker. You can increase their propensity to renew, open up revenue growth opportunities, and create customers for life. The key to this is having a proactive mindset.

You're probably saying, "I would love to be more proactive, but my role doesn't allow for it." As a former CSM, I understand that you only have so much time in the day. Your ability to be proactive will depend on your team structure and the amount of work on your plate. That said, your overall attitude and the way you spend your time can impact your actions (see chapter 12 on productivity).

Another approach to being proactive is to segment your customers. Instead of treating all your customers the same, you can categorize them into buckets such as low engagement, low product adoption, their stage in the customer journey, and potential to grow, to name just a few examples. This can assist you in prioritizing your proactive strategy. You can also automate and streamline your communication by segment, saving you time and maximizing your efforts. AI tools should also simplify this by pointing out possible issues and opportunities.

Expert tip: Build personal relationships

Go beyond monotonous business communication and nurture authentic relationships with your customers. One of my relationship-building tactics is connecting with customers on LinkedIn. This adds another dimension to our professional communication. It allows me to monitor what is important to them and keeps me connected with them if either of our roles change.

Sending an occasional personal message to your customers is a simple gesture that lets them know that you're thinking about them on a human level. One approach I use is to send a text message that starts with "No need to respond." As an example, if my client is sick and has missed a few days of work, I may send a simple message such as, "No need to respond, but I just want to say that I hope you're feeling better." Showing you care matters.

During the most recent tech meltdown, which saw massive layoffs in the tech industry, I used this technique to send several messages of support to customers. As their companies suffered from large layoffs, I wanted to let them know that I was there for them, but they were not obligated to respond to me at that moment. Your customers are human, just like you—build relationships for the long run.

Putting this into practice

Go to strategiccustomersuccess.com and complete the "How to Create Unbreakable Customer Relationships Exercise."

Summary and key takeaways

In this chapter, we covered how strategic CSMs deepen their relationships with their customers:

- Always impart something of value in your customer interactions. Create a list of golden nuggets to share with your customers.

- You can't just provide value; you need to sell it. Make sure you communicate your product's value to the right stakeholders.

- Practice extreme ownership. When you or your company screws up, take responsibility for it. Be accountable for your clients' success.

- No matter how busy you are, you need to be responsive to your customers. If you can't respond in detail right away, send them a quick reply and indicate when they can expect a thorough response.

- Set the right expectations with your customers. This extends to setting clear timelines for feature releases and establishing optimal channels for communicating with your clients.

- Keep your customer communications clear and concise—especially with customer decision-makers and other senior stakeholders.

- Stop being so protective and give your clients access to others in your organization, such as product and marketing. Connect your customers to senior leaders within your organization and look for ways to match them up with other customers.

- Show your customers some love by recognizing them. This might mean highlighting their accomplishments to their leadership or celebrating their milestones with branded swag.

- Teach your customers something of value—don't just talk at them.

- Practice radical customer candor by challenging your customers when necessary but ensuring that they know that you care deeply for them.

- Always have a proactive mindset.

CHAPTER 10

How to Cultivate Strong Connections With Your Colleagues

"Why did you promise that feature when it's clear that we wouldn't have that until next year? We're now screwed." That was the gist of an email that a former CSM on my team had sent to a sales rep. The client had just ripped the CSM to shreds, and his immediate reaction was to blame the rep who sold the deal. He didn't just send that email to the rep. He cc'd me, my boss, and the sales rep's boss. Long story short: This didn't turn out well for the CSM, and he soon exited the company.

Do I blame my CSM for being angry at sales? No. He had a right to be angry, but judging the rep without speaking to them first and publicly criticizing them was wrong. This behavior is the opposite of what I described as *Doing It Right* in chapter 7, as it doesn't demonstrate a collaborative spirit.

It's critical to build relationships across your organization and to do this based on the foundational elements of customer success I mentioned in chapter 1—trust and value. These words take on a slightly different meaning when the focus is within your company. If you want to develop a solid foundation of trust with the product or support teams, you need to provide them with value. To do this, SCSMs embody ten core concepts designed to strengthen internal connections and foster a more cohesive company culture:

- Be a giver
- Ask for help
- Assume the best of others
- Demonstrate gratitude
- Cheer on your colleagues
- Give direct feedback
- Have your colleagues' backs
- Share your knowledge
- Attend informal work events
- Cultivate a mindset shift for long-term success

Be a giver

I often get asked this question: "What is one piece of advice that you recommend to those wanting to advance their careers?" Jeff Pedowitz, a former colleague of mine from Eloqua who led the professional services team at the time, once shared some sage advice with me. Many years ago, Jeff sat me down to discuss a disagreement I had with someone on his team. I was upset with how this person had handled one of our customers, but Jeff cautioned me to demonstrate more empathy. I needed to be more mindful of the constraints that my colleagues were under.

As Jeff got up, he left me with a final thought: "If you want to grow in your career, ask people on other teams how you can help them." I had to let that one sink in for a while, as it seemed strange to me at the time. I had plenty to deal with on my own. Why do I need to help them? Shouldn't sales, marketing, and product focus on getting their own houses in order? After reflecting on my talk with Jeff, I realized my thinking was flawed.

What I didn't appreciate up to that point was how interconnected everyone was and how much I needed other teams if I wanted to be successful. I decided to try out Jeff's advice. At the next company event, I sat down with one of our account executives and asked her, "How can I help you?"

She was pleasantly surprised by the question and a bit taken aback. "Well, I could really use some more customer stories to round out my sales calls." It dawned on me that I had the power to help others, improve the perception of customer success within our organization, and improve my stature within the company—all with that one question and a change in attitude.

That conversation with Jeff led to many groundbreaking ideas and opportunities. I started to look for gaps across the company and fill them. Instead of just thinking about my customers, I thought about how I could improve our overall business. But it's more than just wanting to help others—you need to do so without expecting an immediate payoff. You need to be a *giver*.

Renowned author and social psychologist Adam Grant defines givers as "the rare breed of people who contribute to others without expecting anything in return."[41] For instance, helping your marketing team find reference-able customers is being a giver. You are helping your colleagues in marketing by leveraging your customer relationships. In contrast, a *taker* is someone who takes advantage of others and expects reciprocation.

Being a giver means you need to be patient. You shouldn't expect to see any immediate benefits from your actions, but they will come. You're like a farmer planting seeds across your organization that will grow over time. If you keep performing as a giver, new opportunities will present themselves and you'll gain cross-functional support for that promotion. This doesn't happen by waiting for your manager to give you a juicy opportunity. Seek out opportunities to help others. Be a giver.

---

41   Adam Grant, "Give and Take," adamgrant.net, January 3, 2021, https://adamgrant.net/book/give-and-take/.

Ask for help

I'm not sure why, but earlier in my career, I feared asking for help. My ego seemed to get in my way, as I equated asking for assistance with weakness. That couldn't be further from the truth. Asking for help is normal and leads to stronger relationships with your colleagues.[42] That's right: People will respect you more when you seek their advice, as you're giving them an opportunity to feel needed. I also had this fear that I would annoy my colleagues if I asked for their help. I would rather spin my wheels on a problem for hours than bug someone. If you have a similar mentality, you need to do a one-eighty and start to leverage those around you.

If you've followed my recommendations from chapter 7 as part of your ninety-day onboarding plan, you should have a solid network of people you can turn to. Just be mindful of how often you go to the same person for help—spread out your requests to various people as best you can. You'll also get to meet more people along the way.

Assume the best of others

Remember the story at the beginning of this chapter where the CSM blamed the sales rep? That's an example of assuming the worst of others. Instead of trying to get all the facts, the CSM's first inclination was to place blame. Unfortunately, it's a common reaction—and one I've been guilty of many times.

The good news is you can prevent your emotions from getting the best of you: assume the best of others. This requires a complete shift in your mindset if your first inclination is to blame others. Use these four methods:

1. **Visualize the world through the other person's eyes.** In situations where I feel slighted, I try to step into the other person's shoes

---

42 Adam Grant, *Give and Take: Why Helping Others Drives Our Success* (Penguin, 2014), 699.

and consider the motives behind their actions or words. It's rarely the case that someone wants to deliberately harm you. They are trying to do their best—just like you. I've learned that if I lead with my empathetic self, I'll usually get to the heart of the issue.

2. **Before you lay blame, get all the facts.** How often have you passed judgment on a coworker before you spoke to them? Take the time to gather the facts before you get on your high horse. I've found that mistakes are usually due to unclear processes, poor communications, or temporary lapses in judgment. In many cases, a small process shift is all that's required to prevent the situation from reoccurring.

3. **Ask yourself what role you played in the problem.** Several years ago, I scolded a colleague for botching an upsell campaign they ran, which upset many clients. Instead of criticizing my colleague, I should have considered what I could have done to prevent the mess we found ourselves in. Instead of pointing fingers, take a moment to reflect on your actions and explore what you could have done differently to achieve a more positive outcome.

4. **Respond, don't react.** We've all experienced instances where we feel unfairly accused or strongly object to remarks that have been made. When you feel rage building inside, take a deep breath. Don't immediately reply to that Slack message or raise your voice in a meeting. That will make the situation worse. Shut your laptop. Put your phone away. Go for a walk. Respond when you've calmed down and have a clear mind. Stay curious and seek out the facts. Don't react based on your gut instincts; respond with your head.

Demonstrate gratitude

Did a colleague recently help you either directly or indirectly? They could have answered a technical question for you, provided a summary of a competitor, or covered for you while you were on vacation. If so, show them some love! This can be as simple as posting a message of gratitude where others can see it or giving someone a shout-out during a team meeting. When giving kudos, be specific about what they did rather than being generic. Letting others know about their heroic feat is the easiest and most often overlooked action you can take to build bonds within your organization.

To make this easier, create a habit of keeping track of anyone who goes out of their way to help you or does something you immensely benefit from. For example, did a PM jump on a last-minute client call with you? Did the IT team send you a new laptop right away after you spilled water all over your old one? Give them both some love by expressing your gratitude.

Schedule ten minutes on your calendar each week to send your messages of thanks. Either message them directly, post a message on Slack, or publicly acknowledge their efforts on LinkedIn. Share your appreciation for your colleagues today. They'll be in a much happier mood, and you'll also get all the feels.

Cheer on your colleagues

Be a cheerleader who cheers on your teammates. Did the product team release an awesome feature? Show them how happy and appreciative you are. Did sales close a massive deal? Give the people involved a cool emoji in Slack or an in-person high five. Did someone win a company award? Send them a personalized message congratulating them. Even if you were passed over for a promotion or you didn't get that award you felt you deserved, swallow your pride and cheer your colleagues on.

Give direct feedback

When a colleague does or says something that offends you, the easiest thing to do is to tell your boss and ask them to deal with it. The problem is that this can actually make the situation worse. Your colleague may not have realized they caused you harm, but now they'll have their guard up when working with you. A better approach to resolving conflict with your coworkers is to have a direct conversation with them.

The challenge lies in our natural aversion to difficult conversations. We often struggle to find the right words for fear of making an uncomfortable situation even worse. But if we don't deal with it, or if we blow it out of proportion, it will get worse. Follow these three steps to engage in those difficult conversations with your colleagues:

1. Ask for permission. When you feel slighted, don't put it off—even if it's your boss who did the slighting. Ask the other person right away if they have a few minutes to speak and if it's OK to share some feedback. If they agree, pull them into a meeting and proceed to step 2.

2. Start with the facts and discuss the impact. Repeat back to them exactly what they said or did and the impact their words or actions had. For example: "You said you were going to help me, and then you never showed up to our meeting or responded to my messages. This led to me missing my deadline and putting our team behind."

3. Work on a solution together. Ask your colleague for their input on the situation and discuss how you can work together to prevent this from happening again. For example: "What was your take on this, and how can we work better together to avoid this situation happening again?"

That's it. The biggest hurdle in these situations is usually you sweeping it under the rug and hoping it doesn't happen again, which leads to ill feelings, negatively impacting your working relationship. Take the high road instead of defaulting to complaining to your boss, engaging in harmful workplace gossip, or dropping passive-aggressive hints. If you go that route, it could negatively affect your long-term relationship with that person and your reputation.

When you have an issue with a teammate, only go to your boss when you've exhausted all other avenues. While it can be awkward, it's always best to handle these situations head-on and right after they happen. Although some people can get defensive in these situations, most will value honest communication and respond with increased trust.

Have your colleagues' backs

Keep an eye out for teammates who may be struggling or having a bad day. It could be that your marketing colleague launched a campaign with a big typo, an engineer released a feature with a major bug, or a deal fell through for a sales rep at the last moment. Send a quick message of support and ask them if they want to talk about it. Never ever kick anyone when they're down—no matter how badly the mess-up impacted you. We all make mistakes. You will want the same type of support when your difficult day comes along, and it will.

Share your knowledge

Share your knowledge. Share your knowledge. Share your knowledge. It bears repeating and reinforcing. Your efforts may have led to a stellar net dollar retention rate and customers who love you, yet all that success only gets you so far when it's locked up inside your head.

By sharing your knowledge, you empower others and amplify your influence. It also unlocks your full career potential because, as you share your expertise with both colleagues and customers, you further accelerate your learning curve. My former boss at Eloqua, Nadia DeVilla, imparted a piece of wisdom to me that has forever changed my career trajectory: You'll only get so far on your own, but when you share what you learn with others, everyone can leverage your collective knowledge. In this way, you can help your team and company ascend to greater heights. This helped me in my own career and contributed to the multiple Eloqua employee awards I won including the Customer Excellence Award in Figure 7. It's another example of being a giver. Impart your wisdom to others—it will pay off for you and for everyone.

Figure 7.[43] Eloqua Annual Employee Awards. Pictured here is Eloqua CEO Joe Payne and the author receiving the 2008 Customer Excellence Award. January 7, 2009.

Attend informal work events

Amid packed schedules and back-to-back meetings, the notion of attending an in-person or virtual event with work colleagues might seem like a waste of

---

43 Aaron Rothschild, Eloqua QSR Employee Awards, January 7, 2009, https://www. smugmug.com/gallery/n-vxB83/i-4BMdCHx/A.

time. But it's not. By skipping these events, you're forfeiting valuable chances to bond with your teammates, as it's in these casual settings that individuals often feel most at ease, sharing more of their genuine selves. Having some fun can also relieve some of your daily stress.

At one point, I stopped hanging out with my coworkers at social events. I had a good excuse, as I was busy raising my young family, but this was a mistake. While it was challenging to juggle everything, I still should have prioritized these informal get-togethers, as it's in these casual conversations that you learn more about each other. If you can't attend based on your schedule, let your manager know why you can't attend and ask whether changes can be made to accommodate you.

In addition, don't let being an introvert hold you back. As a self-declared introvert, I realize that it's important to get out of my comfort zone and socialize with my coworkers. As you attend more informal get-togethers, you'll feel more comfortable, and you'll start to notice a positive change in your day-to-day interactions with your teammates.

Cultivating a mindset shift for long-term success

You don't need to begin following all these recommendations at once though. They will take time to implement and master. Start by taking one small step, such as sharing an interesting customer story with your colleagues. You'll be surprised how impactful one tiny action can be in the minds of your teammates.

Will you face obstacles on this journey? Of course! You may be at your wit's end with your colleagues some days. We've all been there. You may ask, "How do you expect me to have my teammates' backs when I keep getting dumped on due to other people's mistakes?"

In these situations turn to Alex Shootman's words: "See the truth, but not for worse than it is."[44] The essence of his message is to focus on the facts

---

44 Charlie Katz, "Alex Shootman of Workfront: Five Things You Need to Be a Highly Effective Leader During Turbulent Times," *Authority Magazine*, February 23, 2021, https://medium.com/authority-magazine/alex-shootman-of-workfront-five-things-you-need-to-be-a-highly-effective-leader-during-turbulent-37b60d0bb79b.

but not blow things out of proportion. Keep cool in times of crisis and gain some perspective by talking it out with a friend or loved one. Try to see beyond the current problems and look to the future. Instead of dwelling on the problem, take action. When my team is in a crisis, I like to say, "No one died." I do this to remind my team to take a breath and just focus on the immediate next step. Don't get too caught up in the bullshit that is forming in your head.

Once you address the most pressing issue, consider what improvements can be made to prevent the same predicament from reoccurring. In most situations, you have the power to enact change, but you can't do it alone—you need to work with colleagues from other teams. Get over any animosity you may have. Stop blaming other teams. If you feel slighted, give them direct feedback in a respectful way. Put your trust in others, and they will do the same for you. This will create mutual value, leading to improved working relationships across your company and a positive long-term impact on your career.

> **Expert tip: Don't accept the status quo—act like an undercover agent**
>
> "But that's how we've always done it."
>
> "We've never had to do that in the past."
>
> "The feature is working as designed."
>
> "Don't worry about that. It's not our problem."
>
> If you've heard at least one of these statements from a teammate, raise your hand. It's natural to feel discouraged by such statements, but you have the power to challenge the current state. You represent the voice of the customer and must ensure that their interests are represented. But you also want to be a good teammate. How do you push for change but do so in a respectful way?
>
> In these scenarios, it might be wise to operate like a covert agent who bends the usual rules. This may mean testing a workaround that hasn't been proven or devising a new process to address a pres-

ent need. Whatever the case, don't accept the status quo. Push the boundaries if need be. Follow the *do first, ask for forgiveness later* mentality, but do it in a way that limits potential issues. That way, you can experiment with an unproven method but not risk a major catastrophe if things don't go as planned. If you can demonstrate positive results, you'll be in a strong position to recommend further investment in your approach.

Putting this into practice

Go to strategiccustomersuccess.com and complete the "How to Cultivate Strong Connections with Your Colleagues: Cheat Sheet and Exercises."

Summary and key takeaways

If you want to build trustworthy relationships within your company, you need to follow these tips:

- Ask your colleagues how you can help them without expecting anything in return. Be a giver, not a taker.
- Don't try to go at it alone. Swallow your pride and ask your teammates for help.
- Don't criticize your teammates without getting the facts. Assume the best of others.
- Take the time to thank your colleagues who have positively impacted you.
- Cheer on your colleagues and celebrate their successes.
- Give your teammates direct feedback when needed—don't sweep issues under the rug.
- Identify coworkers who might be facing challenges, and reach out to them with a message of encouragement.
- Share your knowledge with your colleagues—don't hoard it.

- Don't skip social events with your colleagues. They will foster closer connections with the people you rely on most.
- At times, you may need to bend the rules. You can always ask for forgiveness later.

CHAPTER 11

How to Forge Internal Relationships with Key Cross-Functional Teams

One moment from my time as a CSM is unforgettable: The VP of marketing at Aon, one of Eloqua's largest clients, summoned me and other senior leaders from Eloqua to a meeting in NYC. When we arrived, there were no pleasantries. The VP stood up, said a few choice words that I won't repeat here, and fired us on the spot. And then it got worse—for me.

As we were reeling from the shock of being dumped, the person I thought was my customer champion pointed their finger at me and said, "This was all your fault." It's what I refer to as the "red wedding" of my CSM career for all you *Game of Thrones* fans out there.

I learned a painful lesson that day, and I want you to avoid my mistake. Let me start by providing some context and background information. I was a senior CSM at Eloqua at the time, and my role included managing some of our largest and most strategic clients, one of which was Aon. Aon is a multinational financial services firm that had been using Eloqua for several years. Because of their size, they had challenges coordinating all the marketing campaigns they launched in Eloqua across their various global teams. Moreover, they were also looking to improve how they attributed marketing's impact on revenue, which is the holy grail for B2B marketing.

Lo and behold, Eloqua had the answer. We debuted a cutting-edge campaign management product that offered a holistic approach to tracking marketing campaign performance but unfortunately had significant usability issues upon its initial release. I eagerly pushed Aon toward early adoption to help them create a more consistent approach across their large user base and improve their campaign tracking abilities. Things didn't work out as hoped.

It wasn't long before my day-to-day contact at Aon complained about all the product issues they were experiencing. After a few weeks of hearing their concerns, I knew I was in trouble. We couldn't address all their issues quickly enough. Aon escalated this to our senior leadership, which resulted in that fateful NYC meeting.

Despite that meeting, we salvaged the relationship and kept Aon.[45] After that decisive meeting, we devised a strategy to implement the necessary product enhancements and focused on rebuilding our overall relationship.

My main takeaway from that debacle was that I shouldn't have blindly trusted our product team and should have actively participated in the initial testing phases. This product release meant a massive process change for Aon. It reminded me that CSMs are the stewards of our customers, and we must proactively identify potential dangers. I realized that too late at the time.

While I recovered from that incident, it did leave some lasting scars. Afterward, I was more mindful of the products and features I suggested to clients—especially when they were brand new. In addition, I made a more concerted effort to strengthen my cross-functional ties with specific departments within Eloqua.

This and the previous chapter reflect key lessons from my early CSM career. It took me years to really appreciate that it wasn't just the relationships I formed with my customers but also the relationships with my colleagues that would make or break me as a CS professional and leader.

---

45 Remarkably, Aon is still an Oracle (Eloqua) client as of 2025—more than eighteen years after I first started working with them.

Instead of playing the victim card and saying that no one cared about customer success, I took ownership of how customer success was perceived and took it upon myself to start these conversations. Once I made that mindset shift as a strategic CSM, I focused on the most impactful teams to collaborate with: sales, product, marketing, support, services, and finance.

How best to work with sales

As mentioned earlier, the sales-CS relationship is both the most critical and often the most contentious cross-functional partnership. Your organizational culture heavily influences how these two departments get along. When leadership favors the sales team over CS, it fosters an environment where sales may treat CS as subservient. If sales continuously closes bad-fit customers or mismanages client needs, CS won't trust them. This lack of trust can lead to animosity and a communication breakdown.

The challenge is that there is a fundamental constraint that both sales and CS must contend with. There will always be short-term revenue numbers the company needs to hit—usually quarterly or even monthly. If sales reps aren't consistently hitting their numbers, they'll eventually lose their jobs. It's that simple. This is why new customers land in your lap with requirements that haven't been properly scoped or product requirements that don't quite match up with your product's capabilities. Learning more about how the sales team operates, as recommended in chapter 6, will help you understand the environment they live in, the culture of your organization, and what drives them.

Unfortunately, as a CSM, much of this is outside your direct control. You can't control how a sales rep is compensated. You can't control what senior leadership tolerates in terms of closing wrong-fit deals. Many of the changes needed will have to be driven by your CS leader, including demonstrating the impact CS has on revenue growth and the negative impact of bad-fit customers. The good news is that there's a lot you can control and influence.

You can control your attitude and actions when it comes to making customers successful. You can bring forward examples of poor-fit clients that either churned or required an inordinate amount of effort to turn around. You can expose and fix broken processes between sales and CS. You can share client stories and wins that the sales team can leverage. You can uncover expansion opportunities and push to formalize new processes. You can even advocate for changes to your compensation that provide you with better incentives for driving additional customer revenue. By setting a positive example and suggesting new ideas, you can change the perception that sales may have of CS, and possibly improve your team's performance.

Work with your CS leader to expose bad-fit customers and those where expectations were misaligned. This might involve conducting a retrospective on certain clients with team members from both sales and CS to identify what's gone well and pinpoint areas for improvement. This can also include reviewing the reasons clients churned. The objective is to identify where mistakes occurred and establish procedural changes to prevent future occurrences.

These exercises also help identify both positive and negative trends. For example, you may find that too many new customers fall outside your ICP. An ICP "describes the characteristics or attributes (e.g., industry, location) of a prospective company that is most likely to buy what you're selling and become a loyal and profitable customer."[46] Customers falling outside of your ICP tend to struggle and demand disproportionate resources from your CS team. It's normal for this to happen from time to time. But if it becomes a trend or if there is a common thread, such as a particular sales rep who keeps bringing in deals that are problematic, you need to sound the alarm.

---

46 Amita Jain, "How to Define Your Ideal Customer Profile (ICP) for Precision Targeting," Gartner, January 16, 2024, https://www.gartner.com/en/digital-markets/insights/b2b-ideal-customer-profile.

Like it or not, your sales team is critical to the success of your business, so let go of any resentment you have toward them and embrace a collaborative approach to focus on making improvements where needed. Not only are they revenue growth engines for your company, but they also play a key role in solidifying customer relationships based on their connections. It's in your best interest to improve how sales and CS work together.

How you can help sales

To build stronger bonds with the sales team, take these steps:

- **Share your client stories—both good and bad.** Sales relies on client stories to pitch prospects. They prefer high-level summaries of how customers of a specific size and industry have used specific features to address a challenge and attain measurable results. For example, a clothing retailer had a low average customer satisfaction rating with a previous provider. When they switched to Kustomer, they leveraged our advanced routing and AI chatbot capabilities to speed up the distribution of customer inquiries. This improved their first response time to their client inquiries by 20 percent and improved their CSAT scores by 30 percent. This is what the sales team is looking for. The more stories you can share that cover various industries and flavors of companies you serve, the easier it is for reps to facilitate the buying process for prospects.

- **Share positive feedback on your client's experience with your company**—especially if they mention how much better that experience has been than with your competition. You can also provide sales with tips on how to best position your products and what most resonates with customers. This can help them overcome objections in the sales process. Share client stories and wins in a dedicated Slack channel, present them at a company kickoff or town hall, or share them at regular sales meetings.

- **Uncover expansion and cross-sell opportunities.** Expansions and upsells are all about generating additional revenue from your customers. No matter who owns this stage, CS plays a critical role in pinpointing such opportunities. This includes uncovering customers who are ripe for additional products as well as identifying new customer divisions that want to leverage your product.

- **Share information on competitors.** Whether you like it or not, your competitors are actively engaging with your customers to try to win their business. This provides you with an opportunity to gather competitive intelligence from customers and pass that on to the sales team. Your customer champions will often willingly divulge what they like and dislike about your competitors—you just need to ask them.

- **Reduce the friction points.** Friction is inevitable because CS and sales have different goals, and things around you keep changing whether you like it or not. However, much of the hostility between CS and sales is unintended and can be avoided. For instance, an account executive might misrepresent a feature to a customer due to a lack of updated training. Similarly, sales might promise a thirty-day product launch without realizing that the onboarding team recently extended the timeline to forty-five days. These issues can be addressed by raising a red flag to your manager or sales leadership when they occur. When you see a gap or a broken process, don't just complain—document the problems and escalate them.

Another flash point between these departments is when responsibilities overlap. For example, sales may contact your client for an expansion opportunity without consulting you. This can lead to communication breakdowns between your teams, which can confuse the client. Refining processes so that both sales and CS notify each other before engaging with the customer can resolve these problems.

You can set an example by proactively informing your sales partner if you have a QBR or other important meeting coming up. Then, you can demand that your sales counterpart do the same. Be the individual who fosters harmony by leading the charge and aiding in the resolution of issues instead of exacerbating divisions.

How best to work with the product team

Beyond sales, your biggest source of friction is the product team. I can't count the number of times I've said, "If only the product team would build this one feature . . ." If only it were that simple. Unfortunately, we tend to view situations only from our perspective without considering the hundreds to thousands of feature requests the product team faces.

They're juggling input from CS, sales, customer feedback, internal research, and executive directives—all while managing limited engineering resources. Betting on the wrong feature can derail the entire business.

So with that understanding, you can improve how you work together. Their role is to prioritize what truly benefits the company, preventing feature creep and bloated designs. They try to keep the company focused on the existing product roadmap.

Product also needs to prevent overcomplicated monstrosities from being green-lighted (Simpsons fans may remember Homer's ridiculous car with tail fins and a bubble dome). Product needs to be the voice of reason. Once a feature is released, removing it is far harder than blocking it in the first place.

Your job, on the other hand, is to figure out how to solve the customer's problems and help them achieve value so you'll retain and grow them. This leads to CSMs naturally saying yes to customer requests more often than not. When your customer proposes a product idea, you may hear yourself saying, "That's a great idea. I'll put that forward to our product team." The problem is, this can set the wrong expectations with your customers, as your product team may have a very large backlog of features they've already committed to.

Demanding immediate attention for a feature that benefits only a few customers can infuriate your product colleagues. They only have so many resources they can tap into. The good news? You can encourage more effective collaboration.

How you can help the product team

To assist the product team, take these steps:

- **Dig into customer requests and question them**. Just accepting customer feature requests without doing some additional discovery will erode your product team's trust. First, gather the details and level of importance of your customer's requests. Once you understand what they're asking for, question whether it's really necessary. You may be able to achieve what they're requesting using existing product functionality. Or maybe what they're asking for is well outside the realm of what your company does (see chapter 18 for guidance on how to lead these types of strategic conversations).

- **Create a feature prioritization process**. CS and product should have a jointly defined process for submitting feature requests and bugs so CS captures the necessary degree of granularity. Few things are more frustrating to the product team than vague and unclear feature requests. Work with your product team to solidify the level of detail they need so there are no muddled expectations between the two groups.

    Any product enhancement submission process should include a specified service level agreement by the product team for reviewing feature submissions and addressing issues. In addition, there should be an explicit process for prioritizing certain feature requests over others.

A feature prioritization process may include the following criteria: the number of customers and prospects impacted, the amount of customer revenue impacted (measured by total ARR), the impact on upcoming renewals, and whether the request is a current gap compared to competitors. Representatives from product and CS should meet regularly to review the prioritized list and determine which items should go to the top and which items are no longer relevant.

- **Back up your requests with data**. "If we have data, let's look at data. If all we have are opinions, let's go with mine." Peter Johnson, the former head of product at Kustomer, often repeated this famous quote from James Love Barksdale, the former CEO of Netscape. You shouldn't expect that the feature request you submitted will be put on the roadmap just because one customer requested it. Seek out input from across customer success and sales to indicate how many clients and prospects would benefit from your desired enhancement and how much potential revenue this feature would impact. In addition, you should include details, such as the number of at-risk clients that would benefit from this feature, and supplement your request with data from other data sources, such as churn data, support ticket data, and customer survey data. You could also highlight any additional benefits. For example, saving CSMs just one hour a week might result in substantial cost savings.

- **Be flexible**. Try to be as flexible as you can with the product team. This may mean that the first version of a new feature may not have all the bells and whistles you want, or that one feature is deprioritized in favor of another one that will have a higher benefit. Explaining your company's strategic choices directly to customers can be challenging, but demonstrating flexibility can help forge a more resilient and trust-based relationship with the product team.

- **Share the positive feedback—not just the negative.** CSMs often take our daily access to customers for granted. Product and engineering teams, on the other hand, rarely speak to customers and don't receive direct feedback on their hard work. They typically hear customer complaints rather than anything positive. That needs to change.

  You can ask customers this simple question: "Which product features have you really enjoyed lately?" This usually leads to some positive insights that you would never have captured if you hadn't asked. Share that feedback with the product and engineering teams so they can celebrate their achievements. With call recording tools, it's so easy to share a snippet of a call on Slack so those involved in building the feature can be properly recognized. Don't underestimate the power of hearing the customer describe their admiration for your product. This can instantly create tighter bonds with your product and engineering teams.

Help product in any way that you can. You need the product team on your side, so when they ask for your help, do your best to accommodate them. This can include identifying customer beta testers, piloting new features, and finding suitable customers for them to interview. If I could go back in time, I would've partnered more closely with my product teams to ensure that their newly built features would hit the mark.

How best to work with the marketing team

As I highlighted in chapter 6, marketing plays a pivotal role in enhancing customer success. From managing customer communications to organizing events and distributing your company swag, marketing teams fulfill multiple customer-facing roles. These various activities can strengthen the trust and affinity that customers have toward your organization, which is why they are so critical to your success. Set up recurring touchpoints and direct communication channels with marketing—a shared Slack space can facilitate quick, efficient exchanges.

A customer communication calendar should also be established to help CS and marketing align more effectively and avoid overwhelming customers with too many messages. A strong CS-marketing relationship forms the foundation of an exceptional customer experience. Even when organizational goals differ, these departments remain intrinsically linked.

How you can help marketing

To assist the marketing team, follow these approaches:

- **Identify customer advocates**. Marketing typically handles the creation of social proof—from case studies to testimonials and references—but CSMs can serve as vital scouts sourcing potential customer advocates who can contribute to these efforts. Customer advocates are those "willing to publicly support, endorse, or recommend your company, products, or services."[47] By identifying and activating advocates, you can extend your impact within your organization by influencing topline revenue growth.

  While you might hesitate to approach your customers for a case study or webinar for fear of overburdening them, many clients actively welcome these opportunities. Beyond supporting your organization's brand and sales efforts, being an advocate can raise

---

47 "Advocate Marketing Dictionary," Influitive, accessed September 21, 2022, https://influitive.com/dictionary/.

their stature and accelerate their career growth as they become more widely known in their respective industries.

Advocates can also receive additional benefits such as regular access to your executive team, being added to your customer advisory board, or being invited to exclusive dinners and social events. Gainsight, Salesforce.com, and HubSpot are examples of companies that have built phenomenal customer advocate communities. They recognize that nurturing a robust network of advocates strengthens customer relationships and increases business opportunities.

- **Recruit customers to provide case studies and reviews**. You can play a pivotal role in encouraging customers to take part in case studies and provide online product reviews due to the close connection you have with your customers.

- **Amplify marketing campaigns**. This typically involves informing customers directly about upcoming webinars, events, surveys, product updates, and other marketing messages. While much of this can be automated, you'll get a higher response rate due to the trusted relationship you've formed with your customers. Just make sure that you vet what you send or mention, as you don't want to erode trust by sending irrelevant content.

- **Pass on customer feedback and value points**. The marketing team is always looking for unique ways to position your products to customers and prospects. Being on the front lines, you have firsthand experience observing what your customers find the most beneficial about your product and your competitive differentiators. Don't hoard that information! Marketing will also appreciate any positive tidbits you hear from customers—especially with newly released products. They can package these up as part of future marketing campaigns.

- **Generate content**. Whether you realize it or not, you have collected some valuable product insights, even if you've only been at your present company for a few months. These insights can become valuable pieces of content that can be shared with a broader audience. This content can be a blog post, a video, a webinar—whatever. Additionally, creating content helps deepen your understanding of the subject. And don't worry if you aren't the best writer—if your content is insightful, it won't matter. I mean, I convinced you somehow to read this book! In all seriousness, your subject matter expertise and experience are invaluable. Just like I had a great editor to make this book a half-decent read, your marketing team can help clean up your content and make it shine.

Working with support

Working in support is one of the most stressful jobs you can have. Support reps find themselves trying to solve complex issues as quickly as possible, with little context and few details. They do their best to resolve issues but rarely receive the recognition they deserve. They also take the brunt of your customers' frustrations. In short, this team has it rough. Given these challenges, it's wise to invest time in finding ways to collaborate effectively. When they resolve issues efficiently, it reduces escalations, strengthens customer relationships, and allows you to focus on strategy rather than firefighting.

How you can help support

To make their job easier—and yours too—you can:

- **Provide clear and accurate details.** If you want support to quickly address your client issues, you need to provide them with as many relevant details as possible and any necessary background information. If you forward items to them, include the severity of the issue, how it's impacting the use of your platform, and the priority of the issue based on such factors as an upcoming renewal. Take those extra few minutes to give support the right context and details, and you'll gain some much-needed street cred with them and get your issues addressed more quickly.

- **Treat support as equals and with respect**. Support team members are usually more junior than CSMs in terms of experience and compensation, but that should never mean that they are treated subserviently. Never talk down to the support team, and always assume the best. This isn't a team you want to get on your bad side.

- **Streamline communication during escalations**. When the crap hits the fan, and your customer is freaking out, tensions can run high. This isn't the time to put your head in the sand and let support deal with the client's wrath. Partner with support and act as an air traffic controller to streamline communication between your support team and the customer to ensure that issues are addressed. If you have a client who submits all their support items as escalations, you need to step in, guide the customer regarding what truly is a high-priority item, and ensure they understand your support processes. Try to get ahead of clients who abuse support by proactively handling them. For example, additional training, new product features, or an improved onboarding experience could reduce the need for customers to reach out for support.

- **Protect your support team**. Doing so strengthens relationships and improves the customer experience. One way to do this is to monitor the customers who submit the most support issues and their categories. Then, leverage that data to make a case for change with your customers.

- **Avoid going escalation crazy**. A pet peeve of support is when you escalate a ticket without reviewing the progress that has already been made. This typically happens when your client complains to you directly about a ticket they filed. In most cases, the issue is already being worked on. In addition, avoid being that person who escalates the majority of your issues or the most trivial items. This can create animosity with your support team as it will require them to drop what they are doing and look at your issue. If this happens too frequently, you'll become the person who cried wolf, and your client's items will be put at the back of the support queue.

Even when you're following best practices, challenges are bound to arise. If you're consistently running into roadblocks with support, bring it up to your manager or to the support team directly. If it's a particular individual you have an issue with, use the guidance on providing direct feedback outlined in chapter 10. Be the person who helps resolve these gaps rather than create larger ones. You will not be able to perform as a strategic CSM and be proactive in your role without a solid support team at your side. Ally with them, and you will be more successful in your role.

Other teams that need you

While we've focused on sales, product, marketing, and support, other teams need your help too.

Give professional services the context they need

Many companies have a professional services or technical account management team that handles onboarding, ongoing services, and technical assistance. When working with these teams, be sure to provide them with as much context as possible to meet your customers' business needs.

Before involving them in post-onboarding work, confirm client requirements, budget, and timeline. Service teams hate scoping projects only to have customers back out due to budget or time constraints.

Help finance connect with the right customer

Many companies have a finance or billing team that oversees collecting the cash from your customers. To create a better relationship with this team and a better customer experience, help the billing team connect with the right customer contact when they aren't getting a response. Lend a hand when you can. This is a team that you want on your side—especially when you need their help to resolve a contract issue.

Putting this into practice

For more approaches to building relationships with key cross-functional teams, visit strategiccustomersuccess.com and download the "How to Work with Different Teams: Cheat Sheet & Exercise." Then, complete the exercises provided.

Summary and key takeaways

You need to deepen your relationships with specific departments by establishing trust and providing additional value.

- Focus on what you can control rather than what you can't: You can provide insights on poor-fit customers, trends you're seeing within your customer base, and other valuable insights.
- You can help the sales team by sharing your client stories, uncovering expansion and cross-sell opportunities, sharing information on competitors, and searching for ways to reduce friction points.
- You can help the product team by pushing back on customer requests, creating a feature prioritization process, being flexible about feature timing, sharing positive feedback, and assisting with feature development.

- You can help the marketing team by identifying customer advocates, connecting them directly with customers, passing on customer feedback, and generating content.
- You can help the support team by providing clear and accurate details on issues raised with you, treating them as equals, and streamlining communication between them and the customer during escalations.
- The strength of your relationships with your colleagues is just as important as the relationships with your customers.

CHAPTER 12

How Improved Productivity Leads to Customer and Career Success

I used to dread Mondays. My alarm would go off, and I would constantly hit snooze, knowing I had a full inbox and a calendar jammed with meetings. My Slack was already buzzing with escalations, and I hadn't had any coffee. I would start to panic: "How am I going to get through the morning, let alone the whole day?" This would lead to further procrastination and breaking out in hives.

My Monday anxiety was so bad that I was an irritable mess on Sundays. A change was necessary, as I was on a path that could have lasting consequences for both my personal relationships and my job. My path to becoming more effective in my role and pushing my career forward wasn't a new training course or a new diet. I decided to focus on how I could be more productive with my time.

Productivity is principally based on planning and preparation. Prioritizing your most important goals and structuring your schedule to focus on your top tasks will allow you to execute your overall plan and prevent you from being distracted and wasting time on items that have negligible impact.

You cannot become a strategic CSM without improving your productivity. This is increasingly relevant, as our work environments have evolved from mostly in-office to fully remote and hybrid models. It's more challenging than ever to keep yourself on track. To help with this, I highly recommend reading *The One Thing* by Gary Keller and Jay Papasan and *Atomic Habits* by James Clear. These books will help you with goal setting and creating the right habits.

The power of planning

What are the most important items you want to accomplish? The first step toward improved productivity is planning. This goes well beyond your clients and your company. You need to prioritize your personal goals before your professional ones. Once you do this, you can then focus on what you need to accomplish as a CSM. There are three parts to this: planning your goals, planning the associated activities to hit your goals, and then allocating the amount of time needed to perform those activities.

Plan out your goals

Before you get into your professional goals, start with your personal aspirations. Consider all the important aspects of your life. What improvements would you like to make in your career, your relationships, your finances, and your health? Lay these out and set out a plan to achieve them. While you can think five years ahead, start with what you want to accomplish over the next year.

Use the SMART goal framework as a way of flushing out the details. SMART goals are specific, measurable, achievable, realistic, and time-bound.[48] For example, if one of your goals is related to weight loss, it might look like this: "I want to lose five pounds by the end of the year." If you want to start saving for retirement, you may have something like: "I want to put $5,000 into my retirement savings next year." We'll also cover SMART goals as they relate to your customers' business outcomes in chapter 17.

---

48 Wikipedia, "SMART Criteria," last modified March 18, 2025, 16:19 (UTC), https://en.wikipedia.org/wiki/SMART_criteria.

Go through this exercise of writing out SMART goals for each of the major areas of your life. Concentrate first on your annual goals, then take those annual goals and craft quarterly goals. I did a similar exercise myself, which led to my writing this book. By breaking down my annual goals into a calendar quarter, I could then determine what I was going to focus on and what I wasn't. When you know what really matters to you, it gets easier to decide where to spend your precious time.

Once your personal goals are clear, focus on your professional goals. These are directly related to your role and should be jointly created with your manager. As an example, a CSM goal might be: "Annual retention rates need to improve by 10 percent in the fourth quarter" or "30 percent of your customers need to be referenceable by the end of the quarter." Having your goals written out and aligning them with your manager's guidance will put you on a clearer path to success in your current role and in your career.

Plan out your activities

Write out the activities you need to perform on a weekly basis to accomplish your goals. For instance, to hit your weight loss goal, you'll ensure that you walk at least ten thousand steps a day, five times per week. If you're taking a course to learn a new skill, write out what you will accomplish: "I will complete the first three sections of this data analytics course by the end of the month." In drafting this book, I set a goal of cranking out two thousand words per week and tracked that in a spreadsheet.

The activities required to achieve your professional goals should follow a similar format. These may include performing a certain number of QBRs each quarter or reaching out to a certain number of clients per month to ask them if they would be references. It may also include assisting with a customer webinar to achieve the goal of improving product adoption. Be sure to write down your goals and the supporting activities, as that's proven to dramatically increase the chances of achieving them.[49]

Plan out your time

Allocate the right amount of time to your goals so you can achieve them. The best way to do this is to leverage a technique called *time-blocking*, where you block out time in your calendar for the most important activities related to your goals. For example, if you have an exercise goal, block out specific times on your calendar for exercising. You need to do the same for your professional goals. Set aside dedicated time to get ready for that important client business review or to assess your client portfolio. In the next section, we'll discuss how to make this part of your weekly routine during your *Sunday night prep*.

Remember: If you don't control your calendar, others will. We often get sucked into the whirlwind of our day-to-day activities, then feel that we hardly accomplished anything. When your schedule is already mapped out, it's far easier to say no to distractions. And don't worry, if you push off that exercise class or don't go for that run, you can always adapt your plan to recover from minor setbacks. The key is to keep your plan in motion. Setting clear goals, organizing your tasks, and time-blocking can significantly boost the likelihood of achieving your objectives.

Expert tip: Plan your vacation first

Book your vacation time before you set any other type of annual or quarterly goals. We can forget to take time off, leading to last-minute vacation plans, or none at all, due to our hectic schedules. This isn't healthy. Get your vacation on your calendar months in advance—even if you need to change the dates later on. This gives you something to look forward to and will allow you to plan a real break

49 Mark Murphy, "Neuroscience Explains Why You Need to Write Down Your Goals if You Actually Want to Achieve Them," *Forbes*, April 15, 2018. https://www.forbes. com/sites/markmurphy/2018/04/15/neuroscience-explains-why-you-need-to-write-down-your-goals-if-you-actually-want-to-achieve-them/?sh=569367e79059.

and step away from the daily grind. You need to take care of yourself first so you can take care of your customers and your teammates.

Preparation

My productivity breakthrough came from Paul Teshima, who taught me how to defuse Monday morning stress. He carried out a ritual known as *Sunday night prep*, which consisted of reflecting on the past week and preparing for the week ahead. I've found that the thirty minutes I spend performing this activity on Sunday helps me sleep better, gets me fired up for Monday, and improves my overall productivity. A little prep goes a long way.

While it's called Sunday night prep, you don't need to do it on Sunday. You can do this exercise on Friday afternoon or even Monday morning. Whatever works best for you. What's important is that you take time to review what you've accomplished and prepare for your upcoming week so you can confidently execute your plan. To do this, reflect, focus, and schedule. I call this RFS for short. Let's go through each of these.

Reflect: Review your accomplishments and where you spent your time

Do you often feel like you are in a hamster wheel—working hard but barely making any progress? This is common, and something I've experienced as well. What works best for me is to take a moment to do a mini-retrospective of my past week. One of my own weaknesses is that I never feel I've accomplished enough. This has plagued me throughout my life and affected my relationships with friends, family, and colleagues. If you suffer from this too, the good news is that you can combat it.

Weekly journaling

After trying many techniques, I've found that regularly reflecting in a journal has helped me realize the gains I've made both personally and professionally, the obstacles in my path, and where I need to improve. I no longer compare myself against others but compare my current self to my past.

I start the first ten minutes of my Sunday night prep by answering a series of questions that help jog my memory and force me to reflect on the previous week. This requires me to be open and honest with myself. You get out of this exercise what you put into it.

Ask these questions every week:

- What am I most proud of this week? This question allows me to celebrate what I've accomplished. It's typically tied to my defined goals (career, finance, relationships, health, and skills) but can really be anything.

- Where did I not show up or perform my best? When I answer this, I consider the people I interact with (such as my family, friends, colleagues, manager, and customers), my work, my personal goals, my finances, and my health. I then follow this up and ask myself: Why is this happening? What is bothering me? Where am I stuck? What could I have done differently?

  These questions help me identify areas for course correction and adjustment. They also help me consider and address any underlying issues I may be facing. At this point, you might recognize that you need help managing a particularly difficult client or that it's time to consider changing your current role. I've found this question to hit the hardest.

- What is one thing I learned from the past week? How can I apply what I have learned? I take a moment to reflect on one lesson that I took away from the previous week. This helps me internalize what I've read, what I've learned from courses, and key takeaways from interactions with customers and teammates.

- (Optional) Where do I want to be in five years? Am I on the right path? What else do I need? This question allows you to think bigger but doesn't need to be asked every week.

If you're pressed for time, ask these questions instead:

- What went well? What were the wins? What goals did I accomplish or make progress on?
- What didn't go well? What didn't get done? What situation could I have handled differently?

You can use a pen and a notepad to do this or a journaling app. I use an app because that makes it easier to do annual reflections on my entries. That said, it's the act of consistently writing down your thoughts and feelings that will have the greatest impact. You'll have a greater appreciation of how much you've grown, which will help you realize how much you've accomplished and where you need to change or take action.

Review last week's tasks

After I've completed this exercise, I go back over the work tasks from the previous week and determine which ones I completed and which I didn't. If more than five items didn't get done or if I'm feeling overwhelmed, I'll try and determine the root cause by asking myself a series of questions:

- Am I taking on too much or have too much on my plate?
- Are there blockers that are preventing me from getting these tasks done?
- Do I need help accomplishing these tasks?
- What methods should I consider exploring to assist me in these tasks?

- Am I focused on the root issue, or am I putting a Band-Aid on the situation?
- Am I making progress on the core goals that I'm measured on?

This reflection helps determine if you're using your time effectively. If not, complete a time-tracking exercise or leverage the urgent-important matrix.

Time-tracking exercise: If you aren't sure how you're spending your time, you can do this simple time-tracking exercise. Start a new spreadsheet and add several categories that reflect your typical tasks. I've added some examples below, but these will depend on what your role entails:

- Customer meetings
- Meeting preparation and follow-up
- Internal meetings
- Customer correspondence
- Proactive customer communication (QBRs, etc.)
- Renewal or expansion tasks
- Internal enablement (product training)
- Customer support tasks
- Customer training
- Administration (account and contact updates)
- Other items that require consistent time, such as projects, data analysis, or manual tasks

Next, create three columns across the top: Last week, this week, and next week. Reference your calendar and any other data points you have to help you determine where you're spending your time. Fill in the estimated number of hours for each category in each column – it doesn't have to be perfect. Sum up the hours, and you should start to see some trends that indicate how you're spending your time. You can also use a time-tracking tool to track your activities over a two-to-three-week period, but for this exercise, you just need some estimates.

Next, start to assess how you can better use your time.

Ask yourself, what is taking up most of my time? Where am I not spending enough time? Are there internal meetings or projects where I'm not really needed or are no longer relevant, so I can shift that time to higher-priority items? This simple exercise should help you uncover some of your productivity challenges and open your eyes as to why you can't achieve your more important tasks and quarterly goals.

If you find you're spending most of your time assisting certain clients, question why. Do they need additional support? Do they warrant the time that you are spending? Should they purchase additional services? Should you offload some of your responsibilities to another member of your team? Are there product deficiencies that you're making up for?

Determine where you need help. Look for bottlenecks and broken processes. Identify routine and mundane tasks that can be automated. For example, if you are manually sending welcome messages to new clients, work with your manager or operations team to get those automated. If you routinely need to query certain data points for customers, work with your operations teams to create dashboards and reports for you. Better yet, create feature requests so this data can be sent to customers directly. Consider how you can leverage AI to speed up or eliminate these tasks.

If most of your time is being spent firefighting, sound the alarm to your boss. Call out problematic clients that are sucking the life out of you and others on your team. Break out of the mentality that you can't change your circumstances. While some things are out of your control, the investments you've made in developing internal relationships should help you figure out potential solutions to your problems.

The urgent-important matrix: The second approach to assess how best to use your time is the urgent-important matrix. A common issue for CSMs is that they tend to live out of their inbox and DMs rather than focusing on the critical tasks that directly impact customer retention and growth. This is an easy trap to fall into. You feel a sense of accomplishment when you're able to resolve client questions and issues. Your customers love your responsiveness as well. But are you ensuring that you will retain your customers in the long run? Are you focusing on the most important customers? Remember this: A happy customer doesn't mean they will renew. Don't convince yourself that being busy means you'll be successful. This is where the urgent-important matrix can help.

Stephen Covey popularized the urgent-important matrix in his book *The 7 Habits of Highly Effective People* (which I highly recommend). It's a simple grid that groups tasks according to their importance and urgency.[50]

Quadrant 1: Crises—*urgent* and *important*. These are important crises or time-sensitive tasks that need to be prioritized. For example, your manager asks for data for tomorrow's board meeting, or a client has escalated a bug due to their system being down.

Quadrant 2: Goals and planning—*non-urgent* and *important*. This is where you should be spending the majority of your time, but these tasks often fall to the bottom of the pile. Executing QBRs is an example of something non-urgent, yet important.

Quadrant 3: Interruptions—*urgent* and *not important*. These items should be delegated or tackled after more important items. This covers client escalations and urgent requests that may seem pressing but can either be routed to support or addressed later.

Quadrant 4: Distractions—*non-urgent* and *not important*. These are the activities you should stop doing as they have limited impact on your goals.

---

50 Emma-Louise Elsey, "The Urgent Important Matrix: What It Is & How to Use It!" The Coaching Tools Company, September 19, 2023, https://www.thecoachingtoolscompany. com/coaching-tools-101-what-is-the-urgent-important-matrix/.

They include spending too much time on social media or non-important Slack channels. This also involves eliminating tasks that you're required to perform because of product limitations.

	Urgent	Non-Urgent
Important	**Quadrant 1: Crises** Client escalations, time-sensitive requests from your manager	**Quadrant 2: Goals & Planning** QBRs, reviewing the health of clients, uncovering growth opportunities
Non-Important	**Quadrant 3: Interruptions** Client requests that can be delegated or addressed later	**Quadrant 4: Distractions** Busy work such as pulling data from multiple systems, social media, Slack

Figure 8. The urgent-important matrix

When a client raises an issue, it may seem urgent, causing you to drop everything else. Constantly clearing your schedule for these prevents you from achieving the more important tasks, such as setting up strategic conversations and performing at the SCSM level.

You need to determine whether the client escalation is genuinely an urgent issue or just something your client perceives as a crisis. For instance, they might be frustrated that a product feature isn't available yet. While you're empathetic to their concerns, there is a limit. Your hands may be tied and they can work around the issue for now.

Balancing responsiveness with productivity is key. This is where managing your time wisely comes in. Not every issue requires immediate action. Unless it's a true emergency, one request shouldn't derail your entire day.

Let the client know that you understand their concerns and that you will get back to them in the next forty-eight hours with an update. You can then get back to your more important tasks at hand.

"You have to stay in control of your own time, at all costs," says Nils Vinje, CEO of LeadershipMBA and CS thought leader. "You're the maestro here—don't cede control to your inbox or to one particular crisis just because it's getting the most immediate attention or heat from customers."[51] This may be difficult, but it's important to consider your overall duties and the consequences of prioritizing every issue that arises. In these situations, ask yourself: When you say yes to one thing, what are you now saying no to? When you take the time to dig into an urgent but unimportant item, either something else will get pushed off your to-do list or you will be forced to work late and burn yourself out.

To become a strategic CSM, you must focus on the most important items. Review unfinished tasks from last week and current ones, then sort them using the urgent-important matrix. For any project or initiative, assess: Is it still relevant? Should I stay involved? You should come away with a list of important items that require your attention. In the next sections, you'll pare these down and then schedule them into your calendar.

Expert tip: It may be time to call it quits

The reflection exercises outlined in this chapter are meant to help you gain perspective on where you're spending time, but can also cut deeper. You may start questioning if your current position or organization is the best fit for you at this stage in your career. As an example, if your CSM role is a facade for primarily handling support issues, no amount of productivity optimization is going to help you be a strategic CSM.

---

51 Nils Vinje, "Customer Success Time Management: How to Stop Firefighting and Start Managing Your Time as a CSM," Glide Consulting, February 19, 2016, https://glideconsultingllc.com/customer-success-time-management/.

If you find yourself spending most of your time on unproductive activities or tasks that aren't helping you toward your career goals, you need to let your manager know so they can attempt to help. If your feedback is ignored or if there are no plans to change your role or responsibilities in the near future, you may decide it's time to look for another position.

You should expect that there will be certain points where you'll need to carry more of the load on your team—that's part of the role. This usually happens if a teammate suddenly leaves, there's a temporary pause in hiring due to an economic downturn, or you have a chance to take on more responsibilities. Recognize the difference between a lack of growth opportunities and being overburdened. Everyone needs to assess their own situation and the surrounding circumstances. Just know that you have options, so seek out mentors who can provide you with objective advice.

Focus: Narrow down what you plan on accomplishing

After your weekly reflection, identify the key clients to prioritize and build a targeted action plan. Use these questions to guide your client review:

- **Planning for renewals:** Which of your customers are coming up for renewal in the next six months? What needs to happen to secure the renewal?

- **Transitioning from onboarding:** Which of your customers will soon complete their onboarding? How much time will be required from you once they are transitioned? Which clients are stuck in the onboarding phase and why? What needs to be done to get them unstuck?

- **Assessing customer health:** Which of your customers are in poor health? Who hasn't achieved their business outcomes? Whose value realization is still in question? What is needed to get them back on track? What help do you need?

- **Improving customer engagement:** Which customer has gone dormant recently? Where do you see opportunities to strengthen or establish ties with key decision-makers in your patch? Which of your customers do you need to schedule a business review or executive sponsor meeting with?

- **Encouraging customer advocacy:** Who among your successful customers might be willing to share their story via a G2 review or case study?

- **Uncovering expansion opportunities:** Which of your clients are ready to upgrade their current offerings or expand their usage? How can you help move this forward?

After wrapping up your client review, you'll be ready to compile a set of action items. This may include preparing for upcoming renewals, targeting clients with poor health, scheduling a few QBRs, reconnecting with certain decision-makers that you've neglected, or targeting a few clients to demonstrate your new product upgrades. With limited time, focus on the most critical tasks.

The ten to fifteen minutes spent in this focus phase helps secure renewals, drive growth, and avoid *oh-crap* moments—surprise customer churn notices that come out of nowhere. While you can't prevent some unexpected contract cancellations, proactive strategies such as these can minimize unanticipated losses. That's why preparation is key.

You need to see yourself as the CEO of your book of business and practice extreme ownership (see chapter 9). It's your responsibility to keep on top of your clients in the same way that a CEO needs to own the success of their business. Weekly monitoring through Sunday night prep needs to be part of your regular routine. Your manager will likely want to review the health of your clients, and this exercise will give you a valuable head start.

With your client priorities set, turn your attention to internal projects that also require focus. Just as you track client needs, staying on top of your internal initiatives ensures steady progress and clear communication with stakeholders. Determine which projects and initiatives have upcoming deadlines and which you should focus on for the upcoming week. Having these in a spreadsheet or project management tool can make it easier to track and review. Be prepared to provide updates on these projects to your manager or other project stakeholders. If you feel your time can be better used elsewhere, discuss this with the key project stakeholders or your manager.

This exercise gives you a clear set of action items. Leverage a task management tool to organize and prioritize your weekly tasks while tracking your progress. This allows you to review your accomplishments over time and is helpful for the reflection phase. You may want to leverage the urgent-important matrix to assist in the prioritization process.

Schedule: Review your calendar and map out your week

It's time to tidy up your calendar to maximize your time and ability to achieve your high-priority tasks. Start by checking what's already on your agenda for the week ahead.

Many people start the week without a plan, reacting to each day as it comes. This approach only gets you so far. By taking a moment to evaluate what's ahead, you can approach your time more strategically and anticipate upcoming tasks and challenges. But reviewing your calendar is just the start. You need to scrutinize the items on your calendar to maximize your precious time.

To assist you in your calendar review, ask yourself:

- What are the most important meetings for the week? Identify the currently scheduled meetings that will have the greatest impact on your long-term objectives. These may include QBRs, customer escalation calls, or 1:1s with your manager. If you aren't sure if a meeting falls into the *important* bucket, use the urgent-important matrix and determine how the meeting will impact your overall goals. Flag the meetings that need an extra level of preparation, then block out dedicated time to get it right.

- Are all the blocked times on your calendar necessary? Are there some meetings that you can skip or cancel? If your schedule still shows recurring meetings with customers you've already transferred or for projects that have already concluded, get rid of those so you can free up your time.

- Did any critical attendees decline? If a key participant declines an upcoming meeting, either delete it or reschedule it. Keep your calendar clean.

- Is the meeting cadence correct? If you have weekly or biweekly customer meetings, determine if these should be moved to monthly or quarterly to make better use of everyone's time. Several months after onboarding, the weekly meeting schedule that was once essential should probably be scaled back. Put any internal meetings under the same level of scrutiny. Never be happy with the status quo of your calendar—always look to cut down on meetings.

- Are there agendas for every meeting? Take a moment to review each scheduled meeting and ask yourself what the purpose is, why you're required to attend, and what will be covered. Reach out to the organizer for clarification if you're uncertain about your role. If you're leading the meeting, confirm that you have an agenda and have scheduled dedicated prep time during your week. For more on meeting preparation, see chapter 13.

- Which meetings are missing from your calendar? Based on your customer review, which customers should you be meeting with? Which of your colleagues do you need to engage with to complete goals? Schedule these in.

AI tools that sync directly with your calendar can help streamline this process. Once you've completed your calendar review, removed any unnecessary meetings, and scheduled necessary meetings, block off time in your calendar for meeting preparation, such as time required for QBRs. Next, review the tasks you identified from the focus phase and time block sections in your calendar based on their priority.

Time-blocking involves creating specific calendar items that are dedicated to specific tasks. You might reserve calendar slots titled "Renewal Planning" to tackle upcoming contract work or "Client Outreach Strategy" to develop plans for business reviews and vulnerable accounts. Be as specific as possible and indicate the account you're reaching out to, as well as the specific project tasks you are working on. This provides you with more clarity about what you should expect to accomplish in that designated time block. Don't rely on recurring time blocks, as those will mostly be ignored over time. Set specific time blocks each week.

You'll need to keep adjusting your schedule as the week progresses. At the end of each day, review your upcoming meetings and assess your task list to ensure those meetings are necessary and that you have set aside enough time to accomplish the highest priority tasks. You may need to switch gears and either decline, cancel, or reschedule meetings based on your most pressing needs. Because you've already planned out what the most important goals are, deciding what you need to push off shouldn't be difficult. If you're overwhelmed by what's on your plate, use your manager as a sounding board.

One of the biggest challenges for CSMs is trying to get too much done and then feeling like a failure when they don't achieve everything. To avoid that, be very deliberate about what you plan to accomplish. This section should take roughly ten minutes, making the entire Sunday night prep exercise around thirty minutes. Some weeks will take longer than others, depending on how many items are on your plate.

While this exercise may seem a bit awkward at first, you'll notice increased productivity and a stronger sense of achievement as you wrap up each week. It won't eliminate all the surprises that come at you, nor will it prevent you from hitting that snooze button on Monday, but it should put you in a better position to get ahead of issues and take control of them rather than the issues controlling you. There is no better time to start your Sunday night prep than now.

Expert tip: Sunday night prep can also include personal goals
You can also mix your personal goals into your Sunday night prep ritual. As an example, I list high-level goals such as how often I will exercise, the money I will put away for retirement, how much I will read, and other goals, such as a writing goal. These are part of my broader annual goals that I've broken down into monthly, and then weekly goals. I time-block my personal goals by creating specific tasks just as diligently as I do for work objectives. For example, I time-blocked the specific chapters of this book I was going to write on specific days.

At the end of each week, I review my performance on my personal goals as part of the review phase of Sunday night prep. Each month, I evaluate my performance and reassess my quarterly and annual objectives to confirm that they align with my intended direction.

Additional productivity tips

Try these additional productivity tips I've learned over the years:

- **Take advantage of AI tools.** Leverage AI tools for sending meeting notes to customers, doing customer research, sending replies to customers, analyzing data, creating project plans, and other time-saving activities. See strategicustomersuccess.com for the latest on this topic.

- **Automate or simplify customer communications.** If you're spending too much time creating QBR materials or renewal presentations, explore tools that could streamline the process—and consider recommending them to your manager.

- **Do the hardest tasks first.** Tackle your largest and most difficult tasks first thing in the morning. Getting them out of the way early will guarantee a sense of accomplishment for the day and put you in a better mood.

- **Do small things right away.** While you may have items that are not urgent or important, it's best to do them right away if they take less than two minutes. For example, when I review my email and Slack, I will answer right away if it takes me less than a minute.

- **Break down large projects into manageable tasks.** Taking on a larger project can seem overwhelming. Write out all the possible tasks required to complete the project and then set timelines for each task. This will help you determine which tasks you need to focus on each week and prevent feelings of paralysis when starting a project. Use AI tools to help you with this.

- **If you're stressed about something, write it out.** There can be times when you are so stressed that you lose sleep, and ruminating over the issues can compound the problem. Drafting out what the problem is and writing down possible solutions should help you feel more in control.

- **If you aren't feeling well, take the day off.** It's best that you rest up rather than trying to slog through client meetings and other work. This role is too stressful to handle when you aren't at your best. Take the day off and focus on you.

- **Review your calendar.** If your time is limited, prioritize reviewing your calendar over the reflection exercises. Don't skip the scheduling section. It's imperative that you plan out your calendar.

Putting this into practice

Go to strategiccustomersuccess.com and complete the "Preparing for Your Week Exercise."

Summary and key takeaways

Planning out your goals and completing the necessary weekly preparation will improve your productivity and overall well-being.

- Productivity encompasses two principal areas: planning and preparation.
- There are three components to planning: planning your goals, planning the associated activities to hit your goals, and then allocating the time needed to perform those activities.
- To properly prepare for the upcoming week, leverage the *Sunday night prep* routine, which involves three components: reflect, focus, and schedule.
- Reflect on what went well, what didn't go well, and where you need further assistance. Use techniques such as the time-tracking exercise and urgent-important matrix to assess whether you're spending your time on the items with the highest impact.
- Narrow your focus for the week by considering which clients and tasks need to be prioritized.

- Review your schedule. Remove any unnecessary meetings and add meetings and time blocks to ensure that you accomplish your prioritized items.

CHAPTER 13

How to ACE Client Meeting Preparation

We all have our meeting horror stories, and I've already shared a few. Here's another doozy. A CSM on my team had scheduled a client call to discuss a few items, one of which was a product issue that the client was very upset about. I attended the meeting to lend my CSM a hand, knowing it might be a challenging discussion. But I didn't realize how badly this was going to go.

I jumped on the Zoom, and I could tell straight off that something wasn't right. Our client attendees had switched off their cams and were dead silent. Our plan was to have our PM speak to them about a bug they were frustrated about, but unfortunately, he couldn't join right away. In an ill-fated move, we decided to cover some other agenda topics while we waited for the PM. That was a big mistake. We were getting one-word answers from our client, and it went downhill from there.

When the PM finally joined, the client tore into us, asking, "Why is it taking so long to resolve this issue?" They were also offended that we were wasting their time, as all they wanted to discuss were the product issues that were impeding their efforts. They were 100 percent right, and I was embarrassed about not being fully in tune with their needs.

What should we have done differently? For starters, we needed to improve our meeting preparation so we covered the right items in the right order. In addition, we should have focused on creating an atmosphere of trust and appreciation. We were too focused on our needs and not theirs. Fortunately, we were able to recover from this car crash, and I walked away with a valuable lesson.

You can't wing your way through crucial client conversations. Client meetings should be managed with the same degree of intensity and urgency that professional athletes exhibit for their key games and matches. Athletes see these moments as their time to shine, and you should see client meetings in the same light.

The time you have with your clients is rare and precious. Despite their hectic schedules, they've prioritized spending these moments with you. Okta recently reported that the average company uses ninety-three applications, while larger organizations use an average of 231 apps, and these numbers keep rising every year.[52] That means that it's even harder for you to get the time of day from your clients. Don't waste their time, and don't squander this golden opportunity. Ignore the following steps at your own peril.

What to consider when scheduling a client meeting

When planning your client meeting, ask yourself:

- What do I want to achieve?
- Who should attend?
- What materials are needed for the meeting to be productive?

Let's dive into each of these.

---

52 "Businesses at Work 2024," Okta, March 12, 2024, https://www.okta.com/sites/default/files/2024-04/Okta-2024_Businesses_at_Work.pdf.

What do I want to achieve?

You may want to finalize renewal terms or better understand an issue your client is facing. Even if you have a standing meeting with your client, you should always go into each one with a specific objective. This one step can drastically improve your meeting performance.

To facilitate this process, I leverage a special technique by sales guru and Chief Sales Scientist of Cerebral Selling, David Priemer. He suggests determining the *critical insights* that you want to gain from your customer before going into the meeting.[53] Priemer recommends completing the following sentence as part of your preparation: "If we don't leave the call with details about _____, then the meeting was a failure." For example, "If we don't leave the meeting with an understanding about the client's intent to renew, this meeting will be a failure." This is a simple tactic that you can leverage for your next meeting.

Who should attend?

The right mix of meeting attendees is important. While you don't want to waste people's time, you need to ensure you have the right people present, depending on the goals of the meeting. For example, if you're trying to confirm your customer's business outcomes, it's best to have your client's senior stakeholders present, as they are aware of their overall objectives and the metrics that will determine success.

The same holds true for attendees from your company. You may want your own executives there to leverage their expertise and influence. You may need a product manager to join to discuss the requirements of a new feature being planned. If the meeting is highly technical in nature, include colleagues with this skill set. Think carefully about who should attend to ensure

---

53 David Priemer, "Missing Key Details in Your Discovery Calls? Try this simple exercise," Cerebral Selling, September 2, 2018, https://cerebralselling. com/discovery-call-exercise/.

a fruitful discussion, and figure this out well in advance to avoid last-minute scrambles.

The client may dictate who they want at the meeting by informing you that a senior executive from their side will be present and even asking that you match the seniority level on your side. Make sure you take these requests seriously and try to "title match"—even if they haven't explicitly asked for it.

What materials are needed?

Ever heard the expression "Don't bring a knife to a gunfight"? Think of meetings in the same way. Consider what information you'll need to increase the chances of a productive meeting. For instance, if your customer wants to improve a certain metric, you'll need to gather some concrete suggestions and customer examples. If the purpose of the meeting is to resolve a specific issue, source examples and research from your engineering team. If it makes sense to have a few slides ready, build time into your schedule to craft these. Make sure you'll be equipped with the right weapons for battle. If you're not sure what to bring, ask the client or your colleagues for input. We'll tackle the preparation needed for specific meetings, including onboarding kickoffs, QBRs, and renewals in future chapters.

How to prepare for your client meeting

"There is one skill that rises to the top in this ambitious profession: preparation,"[54] Ashvin Vaidyanathan and Ruben Rabago emphasized in their book, *The Customer Success Professional's Handbook*. Preparation is critical for client meetings. To ensure your meetings hit the mark, follow the recommendations below.

---

54 Vaidyanathan and Rabago, Customer Success Professional's Handbook, 83.

Draft an agenda

I always create a meeting agenda—even if it's informal and there is only one item to cover. This ensures that we're aligned about the meeting's purpose, that we keep each other on track, and that we don't forget any significant topics. The purpose you previously defined should drive your agenda.

When you have high-stakes meetings with senior client stakeholders, it may make sense to set up a premeeting with your customer champion to confirm the agenda and get your ducks in a row. These pre-meetings can help you nail down the meeting priorities and focus, and determine which topics to avoid. For example, one of my client champions wanted me to help convince their boss to purchase one of our add-on products, so we concentrated the discussion on the current inefficiencies that could be overcome if they made this investment.

Confirm the meeting

Ever had a client no-show for your meeting or cancel at the last minute? This happens to everyone and seems to be increasing in frequency. There usually isn't any malicious intent by the customer, but for one reason or another, they missed your meeting. Sending a message the day before the meeting to confirm their attendance reduces the chances of them backing out or using the excuse that they forgot. I especially recommend this when you're meeting with executives. Technology can help automate this process.

If you want to take it up one more level, you can try *no-oriented questions*. Experience has taught me that meeting reminders by themselves doesn't guarantee that clients will show up. To increase meeting attendance, I use a technique called a no-oriented question—a term coined by Chris Voss, former FBI hostage negotiator and author of *Never Split the Difference*—to provoke a response. I list the agenda items and then ask, "Are there any agenda items you want to change?" No-oriented questions usually elicit responses, since they break the pattern of standard messages.[55]

Sharing the agenda in advance also allows clients to customize it to their specific needs. Your reminder could prompt them to share something they forgot about. You can even add a teaser such as "I can't wait to show you this new feature we launched as it will help you towards the goals we've discussed!" Their plate is already full—make sure this meeting stands out as time well spent. Don't assume your client will be there just because they accepted the meeting invite. You have to earn every minute.

Prepare meeting materials

Few things are more frustrating than securing a meeting with key stakeholders—only to realize you're missing the critical data needed to make it productive. For instance, if you're having a renewal conversation, you should have the customer's current contract terms and an outline of the proposed renewal pricing. If you don't, the meeting becomes a waste of everyone's time.

Meetings don't require presentations, but the act of preparing a presentation can help you think through your meeting objectives and ensure that you're not forgetting any critical points. Just don't use your slides as a crutch. They should be treated as aids to facilitate a conversation—not as the focal point. Writing out the points you want to convey, such as why you are justifying a price increase or the benefits of the client taking action now versus in three months, will assist you in organizing your thoughts and the flow of the meeting. Keep the text on the slides to a minimum so you don't overwhelm your attendees.

---

55 Nick Peluso, "Why You Need to Use No-Oriented Questions in a Negotiation," The Black Swan Group, April 10, 2023, https://www.blackswanltd.com/newsletter/why-you-need-to-use-no-oriented-questions-in-a-negotiation.

Show, don't tell

I like to think of meetings like a Broadway show. While you aren't there to entertain your clients, you do need to keep them engaged. Drive client participation by showing rather than telling—walk clients through new product features in the actual live or test environment, and present onboarding status updates using your project tracker. When training your clients or working through a product challenge, have your clients share their screens. Typical CSMs just talk at their customers and hope their clients aren't tuning out. Strategic CSMs engage their customers and seek out their participation.

Do your research on your meeting attendees

As part of your meeting preparation, scan the list of meeting attendees. This allows you to quickly learn more about who you'll be meeting. The more you know about the attendees beforehand, the easier it is to build trust and influence.

The most important advice I can give you is to review the LinkedIn profiles of any unfamiliar client attendees. LinkedIn tells you their job title, where they live, who in your network knows them, how long they have been in their role, how long they have been at their company, and the content they've shared or engaged with. This information provides you with the context you need about who this person is, what their perspective is, and what is important to them. You can leverage these details, as well as any recent company updates from Google News (or other sources), during your meeting to build a stronger connection and speed up the trust-building process. Newer AI tools should make this process even easier.

I remember a meeting with a client that could have easily gone sideways as it was a very tense negotiation. After reviewing their LinkedIn profiles, I saw that they lived in Brazil. During our meeting, I shared that I had traveled to Brazil a few years ago and mentioned some of the sites I had visited. That immediately put them at ease, as I had connected with them on a personal level. This set us up for a more constructive conversation.

If it's a more formal meeting, such as a QBR or on-site engagement that includes several people you've never met with, draft the following:

- List out all the attendees.
- Add titles for each person.
- Write out what you know about their roles in relation to your product. Are they the administrator? Are they technical contacts?
- Indicate which attendees are decision-makers. For example, are there senior leaders attending the meeting?
- Indicate their level of familiarity with your product. Simply mark down if it's low, medium, high, or not sure.
- Indicate whether they understand the value your product has delivered. You can use yes, no, or not sure.
- Indicate the attendees' current sentiment toward your company. You can use positive, negative, or neutral.

It's OK if you can't gather all these details. The act of preparing most of these details will better mentally prepare you and your colleagues and help avoid miscommunication while fostering broader participation. You'll avoid saying things like, "I thought you already knew about that feature," or the client saying, "I thought you knew about that already." Time in these meetings is limited, so make the most of it by gathering all the background information you can.

Do your research on your client's company

To prepare for your meeting, follow the 3C method outlined in chapter 2—learn about your client's company, who their customers are, and the challenges their business is experiencing.

Review past correspondence, support tickets, and product usage

One main advantage of a CSP is that it makes your critical client data more easily accessible. These tools allow you to scan your client's product usage, recent support tickets, and the latest correspondence in a matter of seconds. This provides additional context on issues the client may be experiencing, changes in their circumstances, and other relevant information. Certain AI tools can provide you with account summaries as well. Take a few minutes to prepare for your meeting by reviewing this data.

Don't forget to connect with teammates who have recently interacted with the client so you have additional context that may not be in the documented notes. This is especially important if you have various people interacting with the customer, such as sales, support, onboarding, or others.

Write out a list of questions you want to ask

The second most important step for increasing the chances of meeting success, beyond defining the meeting purpose, is writing out a list of questions. Preparing questions ahead of time forces you to consider what you already know about your client and what details you still require. These could be high-level questions about their business or very technical questions regarding a project you are working on. Once you've written them out, place the most important questions at the top of your list so they aren't missed. See chapter 17 for guidance on crafting effective discovery questions.

Expert tip: Prepare for their questions and objections
Preparing questions to ask your customers is a critical step for any customer meeting, but what about questions they may ask you? Take the time to prepare for their questions and objections when you're in a renewal or expansion conversation, or if you're proposing a challenging solution. An objection is simply a reason that your client may be hesitant to move forward with a renewal or upsell,

but the term could also apply to questions about a solution you've proposed.

You can find many great resources on objection handling, but for our purposes, it's important to anticipate your client's questions and concerns and to be ready for them. You may have a bank of common objections, such as questions they'll have about price and functionality. Think through the questions and objections they may ask you and come prepared with ways to alleviate any concerns they have and clear a path to move forward. You may even want to role-play scenarios ahead of time so you can practice your responses. You can leverage the motivational interviewing and discovery techniques in part IV to uncover your client's underlying needs and concerns.

Assign roles

If your meeting includes multiple people from your company, assign meeting roles before the meeting. For instance, you can assign one person to handle the introductions while another person takes the lead on the other agenda items. It can get very awkward and unprofessional when it's not clear who from your side is doing what. This is especially important when it's a high-stakes meeting, such as handling an upset client or meeting with a new client executive. Every teammate should know their role. For example, who is going to act as the meeting host who does the introductions and introduces the agenda? Who will run the main part of the conversation? If you have an executive from your company joining, what role do you want them to play? The better you plan this out ahead of time, the more productive the meeting will be.

ACE-ing the start of your meeting

To begin any meeting and build an atmosphere of trust, use the ACE framework. This three-step approach will bridge the gap between you and your customer and lay the foundation for a productive meeting.

The ACE framework consists of three parts:

- *Appreciate* your clients by thanking them for their time and personalize your introduction.
- *Confirm* meeting goals and review the agenda.
- *Engage* your clients. Ask your clients what else they would like to cover and where they would like to begin.

A: Appreciate your clients and personalize your introduction

This may not seem necessary, but thanking your clients for taking the time to meet with you is important in starting your meeting on the right foot. Kick off the meeting by saying, "Thank you for meeting today." When spoken from the heart, this acknowledgment shows you appreciate and value their time.

If there are only a few attendees, add a personal touch as you kick things off. Show genuine interest by asking about their family or picking up on something they've shared before, such as their hobbies, pets, travels, or a big milestone in their life.

Leverage the company research you compiled as part of the preparation phase and sprinkle it in when it makes sense. If they've just rolled out a new product, closed a funding round, or dealt with recent layoffs, that's probably top of mind for them, and you should bring it up because it could impact the outcome of your meeting. Referencing your research shows that you did your homework and came ready to play.

C: Confirm meeting goals and agenda

A frequent oversight for CSMs is skipping the agenda review and plunging directly into discussion topics. I made this mistake on the Zoom call I described at the beginning of the chapter. We started with the items we wanted to cover, and by the time we got to the issues they cared about, their anger had boiled over like an exploding volcano. This could've easily been avoided.

Beginning with the agenda and a brief outline of meeting goals helps synchronize everyone's expectations and focus. I usually start with the following statement: "The goal of our meeting today is to . . ." and list one or two overall meeting objectives. I then say, "I'm hoping that we can cover the following . . ." and then go through the agenda.

E: Engage your clients

At this crucial point in the meeting, give the clients the wheel and turn the conversation over to them. Open the floor by asking them, "What else would you like to cover?" and pause for at least five seconds. This question gives your clients the freedom to express whatever's on their mind. Their responses might surface unexpected topics, creating space for a deeper, more meaningful exchange.

If you see puzzled looks on their faces after you've gone over the agenda, you can ask, "Would you like me to give you more context on any of these items?" or "Is there anything in the agenda that I should define more clearly?" This ensures that everyone is on the same page and prepared for the discussion, which is especially necessary when you've just started working with new customer stakeholders.[56] Never assume that your clients understand the terminology you're using or that their heads are in the right place. They're probably moving from meeting to meeting, so read the room before you jump in.

---

56 Bob London, "How to Have More Strategic Customer Conversations," recorded webinar, posted September 16, 2020, by ChurnZero, https://www.youtube.com/watch?-v=xCTNfVGeMC0.

When the agenda is set, you can ask, "Where should we start?" This is a significant moment in the meeting, as you're ceding control of the conversation to your clients. You are putting their needs before yours, which lays the foundation for a more productive discussion.

Practice using the ACE framework until it feels natural. This approach strengthens client connections and builds trust, which are essential foundations for the strategic conversations explored later in parts IV and V, where the specifics of running the core components of meetings are also discussed. At this point, we'll skip ahead to how to successfully end your meeting and ensure that the proper steps are taken to keep everyone accountable.

Expert tip: Use icebreakers

Using icebreakers as part of your meetings can help build greater intimacy between you and your clients. When meeting a customer for the first time, ask a question such as "Where would you travel if you could?" or "What is something you enjoy doing outside of work?" The goal is to learn more about them as humans. I typically answer first to set the example and to give them time to think about what they want to share. If the call is with senior stakeholders, skip this step to maximize the use of their time. However, it's a perfect exercise when meeting with your day-to-day customer contacts or meeting in person.

Concluding the meeting and the follow-up

Assign action items

Ever been at a meeting where everyone agrees on the next steps, and then nothing happens? It usually comes down to a lack of accountability. My rule of thumb is that each action item always needs to have a single, clear owner and a defined due date. Never assign multiple people to be a task owner, as this can lead to confusion and inaction. Other people can assist the task owner, but as the famous line from the movie *The Highlander* goes, "There can only be one."

This rule also applies to tasks that your company is responsible for. Don't assign your company name as the task owner. Assign it to someone on your team or pencil in your own name until you determine the appropriate person. Never have any squishy action items that prevent you from holding your company and your client accountable. The other main reason for a lack of progress following a meeting is not properly assessing the client's motivation (see chapter 16).

When the client's responsibilities are unclear, ask the following questions:

- **Who on your team will own this task?** If you don't get a response, call out the customer by name: "[CUSTOMER FIRST NAME], can I put you down as the owner of this task?" This makes things very real and forces them to either accept responsibility or assign the task to someone else.
- **When can we expect this to be completed?** If the client can't commit to a due date, suggest a date and say, "Does this date sound reasonable?" You should also ask if any other priorities or holidays/vacations may prevent them from hitting the agreed-upon dates. Always get a specific date and not a general timeline like "later in the month."

At the end of the meeting, summarize any decisions made and the action items, including the owners and due dates. To gauge their commitment, ask, "Does this sound good to you?" If you get an enthusiastic "Yes!" or "This was great," you know you're headed in the right direction. As the meeting concludes, be sure to thank the client for their time.

Send a prompt follow-up

Ever get a rush of adrenaline after a successful client meeting? It's one of the positive aspects of being a CSM. You start humming along to Sia's "Unstoppable," feeling that your client is going to take the necessary steps to get on the right path. Maybe your client gave you verbal confirmation for their renewal, or they were in agreement with a solution you proposed. You're pumped! But as you're probably aware, you haven't really accomplished anything until the customer follows through on what was agreed upon. Now is when the rubber hits the road.

To continue the positive momentum from your meeting, send a follow-up to your clients within twenty-four hours that outlines what was discussed, the decisions that were made, if any, and the agreed-upon action items. Leverage a subject line or headline that not only summarizes the meeting but seizes your audience's attention. For example: "Phenomenal improvements in conversion rates over Q2 with room to improve" or "Efficiency is down, but we've outlined three ways we'll improve this in Q3."

Next, use bullet points with subheadings to summarize what was covered, so it's clean and easy to read. In addition, add the action items to a larger project plan or success plan so you can ensure that they are carried out and not buried in emails. Even just a shared spreadsheet that your clients have access to can keep these items at the top of their minds. If your action items are only in email, they can be lost, misinterpreted, and forgotten. With the numerous AI-powered note-takers out there that can draft follow-up emails for you, there is no excuse for not completing this step.

Always keep in mind that your client meetings are your World Cup final. They are your Stanley Cup playoffs. Your Super Bowl. Your NBA championships. Your Olympic gold medal event. Don't view those client meetings in your calendar with fear or dread. It's your time to shine. Spend the proper time to prep, go into it with a plan, and come out of it with specific actions, and you'll nail it.

Reflect on the meeting

One of my first bosses and mentors, Jeff Chapleau, used to ask me after client meetings, "How do you think it went?" This powerful question forces you to analyze what went well during the meeting and what could've gone better. Take a moment to reflect on the meeting and be honest with yourself. Did you achieve what you set out to do? Why or why not? Jeff knew my self-critique would always be harsher than his, and it was an effective coaching technique that helped me improve my client management skills.

You can also ask yourself, did I talk too much? Too little? Did I fail to jump in at a critical point? Did you probe more when you got an evasive answer, or did you stay at the surface level when you could have dug deeper? What could've made the meeting more successful? These are just a few of the questions you can use as part of your self-reflection. Don't hesitate to ask your colleagues for feedback—they may offer valuable insights.

I also recommend reviewing your meeting performance just like athletes review game tape. Go back through the meeting recording and critique your performance. Observe how the customer responded to your questions or didn't. Look at their facial expressions. Were they positive or withdrawn, or did you sense hostility? Try to determine the causes behind this. Some tools may allow you to ask for critiques but you could also download the transcript and use an AI tool to provide you with feedback on your performance.

For more significant client meetings such as QBRs or on-sites, send your clients a quick survey or just ask them for feedback. Use your meeting experiences to level up your skills so you can keep growing as a strategic CSM. Taking thirty minutes per week to review your meeting performance can immensely speed up your development. As an aside, there was plenty that went wrong in my early consulting days with Jeff. Reflecting helped accelerate my career, as I would use the lessons I learned to improve my overall performance.

Expert tip: Add key client contacts to your follow-up emails to keep them informed

Even if certain client stakeholders, such as decision-makers, didn't attend your meeting, it's still your responsibility to keep them in the loop on significant items. To accomplish this, cc these customer stakeholders on the meeting follow-up emails. You may even want to send a pared-down version of your follow-up that is tailored to specific senior client stakeholders to drive home certain points.

Don't assume that your client champion or point of contact is keeping their managers and other critical stakeholders updated. By proactively sending your own updates, you control the narrative and ensure everyone is in the loop. Remember, it's your role as a strategic CSM to sell the value of your products to your customers (see chapter 9).

Additional meeting tips

Follow these additional meeting tips:

- **Do morning meeting prep.** Even when I've fully prepared for a meeting, I still set aside time every morning to do a quick walk through of the meetings I have for the day. I like to review the agenda and visualize how the meeting will go. This gets me primed and ready to rock.
- **Brief your execs ahead of time.** If you've invited any executives, senior leaders, or your manager, provide them with a brief overview that gives them context on who is attending, some background on the client, the meeting's purpose, and what you expect from them. This ensures they're prepared and can actively participate in the meeting.
- **Fast-track intros.** For meetings with more than five attendees, ask the client to have one person run through intros of their attendees

and do the same on your side. That way, you don't spend half the meeting on introductions, and you can get to the meat of the meeting.

- **Use the meeting chat feature to ask questions.** When you have meetings with more than three stakeholders, set some meeting ground rules, such as posting questions to the conference chat or using the *raised hand* feature to ask questions. This approach promotes fluid dialogue while preventing overlapping voices and unnecessary interruptions. You can also skip the broad "Any questions?" approach, which usually results in a deafening silence.[57]

- **It's OK if you can't do every prep step.** We're all busy, so if you can't follow every step mentioned, don't stress. At the very least, focus on what you want to accomplish in the meeting and have faith in your abilities. Even taking a deep breath before you jump on your call or step into the room can calm your nerves and get you mentally prepared for what lies ahead.

- **Arrange the next meeting while you're on the call.** Setting up the next meeting or series of meetings live with the customer avoids the typical back-and-forth messages needed for this task and greatly increases your chances of maintaining the momentum you've gained. Just reassure the client as you're scheduling the next meeting that they can always reschedule—you just want to have it on everyone's calendar to keep everyone accountable.

- **End early.** Don't feel obligated to use the full time of the meeting. If you've planned out what you want to achieve from the meeting and you accomplish that, end the meeting. Give the client the best gift of all—time.

---

57 Devin Reed and Sheena Badani, hosts, "How to Deliver QBRs that Execs Love with Nick Mehta," Reveal: The Revenue Intelligence Podcast, episode 136, posted on April 25, 2022, by Gong.io, https://www.youtube.com/watch?v=V848zrTEG40.

Putting this into practice

Go to strategiccustomersuccess.com and complete the "The ACE Framework Exercise".

Summary and key takeaways

Customer meetings require proper preparation, opening remarks, and follow-up.

- Your client's time is precious. Prepare for your client meetings like a pro athlete prepares for their biggest games. This is your time to shine.
- Always ask yourself prior to a meeting, "What do I want to achieve?" This will keep you focused as you plan for your meeting.
- Be thoughtful about who you invite to maximize meeting effectiveness.
- To adequately prepare for your meetings, draft an agenda, confirm the meeting, prepare necessary materials, conduct research on the client attendees and company, review past correspondence, support tickets, and product usage, prepare questions ahead of time, and assign meeting roles.
- Use the ACE framework to kick off your meetings. Thank your clients for attending and personalize your introductions. After confirming the agenda and meeting goals, ask your clients what else they would like to cover and where they would like to begin.
- Always assign action items to a single owner and specify due dates.
- After the meeting, take a moment to reflect on how it went.
- Quickly follow up the meeting with a summary of action items.

PART IV

How to Conduct Strategic
Conversations with Your Customers

CHAPTER 14

What Does It Mean to Have a Strategic Conversation?

"Meeting with customers is like Christmas," Alex Shootman loved to say when meeting clients during his tenure as Eloqua's chief revenue officer. Initially, I dismissed this as Alex being out of touch—just another executive who didn't grasp customer success. The reality on the ground was far different: My customer meetings were often chaotic and required careful navigation. They were never like Christmas! But Alex's customer meetings always seemed to proceed smoothly. Was it just that customers saw his title and treated him differently? What was his secret?

Years later, I realized what Alex did differently. While Alex's title helped him get an audience with client decision-makers, that didn't guarantee a productive meeting. What did was his outlook. He saw these meetings as opportunities to gain real insights from our customers. His days were mostly occupied with internal company matters, so for him, being on the front lines and speaking to the people who paid our bills was like a holiday. Moreover, Alex didn't hesitate to ask our clients hard questions to get to the root issues, yet he did this in a nonintrusive way that made people feel heard and valued.

Alex used many of the techniques discussed in this chapter and the next few in part IV. These aren't superpowers reserved for people with senior titles. The barrier to transformative customer conversations isn't your job title—it's understanding how to navigate these high-stakes discussions effectively.

Many of us hesitate to broach sensitive subjects, like renewal intentions with customers, fearing we might not like what we hear. For example, you might choose not to challenge clients on feature requests, deferring the issue to your product team for resolution, as you would rather have someone else let the client down by telling them no.

In an effort to avoid difficult conversations, you may engage in shallow client discussions—ones that focus more on the features and functionality of your products. Solving customer challenges and being a product expert will make you a solid CSM, but it won't prevent you from receiving a surprise churn notice when you don't uncover that a new stakeholder is looking at one of your competitors. Fixating on your product will limit your ability to be successful in your role. You need to broaden your perspective and sharpen your CSM skills.

The key to preventing churn and driving expansion lies in your ability to foster more meaningful client discussions. It's time to evolve beyond being just a customer success helper—your role demands becoming a strategic advisor who drives positive customer outcomes. This is what being an SCSM is all about, and it starts with facilitating strategic customer conversations. This chapter provides the foundations for having these types of conversations.

What is a strategic conversation?

I define a strategic conversation as a candid and genuine dialogue with your customer which is primarily focused on uncovering essential details that are required to achieve a specific objective. Since a strategic conversation aims to help you understand your clients better and influence them in a certain direction, your goal is to get a better sense of their working environment, what is impacting or could impact them, what their root issues are, and how you could partner together. To do this, you need more than just empathy—you need to expose what's in your customers' heads and win over their hearts.

The focus of these discussions should go well beyond your product. In fact, they may not involve your product at all. Instead, you should see yourself as a truth seeker or someone performing an intervention.

These discussions often reveal hidden challenges. Through them, you might help clients break from ineffective patterns, talk them off the ledge, steer them in a new direction, or maintain momentum on existing commitments. These strategic discussions can help clients realize more value from your solution while staying on track with important goals like completing a training certification. By having strategic conversations, you take a step back from your normal routines and *get real* with your customers.

You may be asking, "But do these discussions truly make a difference?" The answer is a resounding yes! CS thought leader Nils Vinje reported, "In a study on customer loyalty in hospitality, researchers found that having high-quality conversations—that is, ones that went beyond the superficial level—significantly increased customers' relationship with and loyalty to the brand."[58] Strategic conversations can dramatically transform the CSM–customer relationship.

Every client meeting holds strategic potential, extending far beyond QBRs and executive discussions. Strategic conversations can happen at any time, with stakeholders at any level—so you must be ready to shift gears and uplevel the discussion when needed.

Strategic conversations often focus on uncovering business outcomes, easing tensions, managing renewals, spotting expansion opportunities, and guiding stakeholders toward action. On paper, this sounds simple, but in reality, it's probably the most challenging aspect of being a top-performing

---

58 Abby Hammer, "The art of strategic conversations in CS, learning opportunities from churn, ways to make CS a key business metric," *ChurnZero*, October 20, 2016, https://churnzero.com/blog/the-art-of-strategic-conversations-in-cs-learning-opportunities-from-churn-ways-to-make-cs-a-key-business-metric.

CSM. The good news is that we can borrow some proven methods from the field of psychotherapy and apply them to customer success. Let's explore the concept of motivational interviewing.

Leveraging the power of motivational interviewing

In the early 1980s, a clinical psychologist named Bill Miller discovered that many therapists were failing to curb their patients' drug and alcohol addictions. A common approach used at the time was to scold patients for their addictive behaviors and demand that they change their ways. That approach, as you can imagine, wasn't very effective.[59]

Scientific research has demonstrated that most people become defensive when they're told what to do because they're trying to protect their right to make their own decisions.[60] Any parent can relate to this—especially if you try to order your kids to go to bed. As a parent of three kids, I can tell you that this technique doesn't work. It just makes the situation worse!

Miller understood this problem. Command-and-control tactics weren't working, so instead of ordering his patients to follow his instructions, he started asking them questions and deeply listening to what they had to say and what the barriers were to helping them improve their lives.

Together with Stephen Rollnick, he developed a new clinical approach to treatment called motivational interviewing (MI). In clinical terms, MI assists patients in finding their own motivation to pursue a necessary change. You can leverage the power of MI to get inside your clients' heads and see the situation from their perspective.

MI is about putting your clients' needs before your own. It's about refraining from immediately offering a solution or advice or telling your clients what to do so they feel heard. It's about giving them the freedom to make

---

59 Adam Grant, Think Again: The Power of Knowing What You Don't Know (Viking, 2021), 151.
60 Thomas G. Plante, "Giving People Advice Rarely Works, This Does," Psychology Today, July 15, 2014, https://www.psychologytoday.com/us/blog/do-the-right-thing/201407/giving-people-advice-rarely-works-does.

their own decisions. As it pertains to customer success, the essence of MI lies in active listening, authentic curiosity, and guiding customers to discover their own drive for action.

As strategic CSMs, we need to help our customers break out of their bubbles so they can see new possibilities. But you can't just force your clients down a certain path or demand that they follow your directions. Before you can offer advice and expect your clients to change their ways, you need to truly listen to them, understand their underlying challenges, and determine how motivated they are to take action. Missing the mark here can result in your clients tuning you out or passively agreeing with you without genuine follow-through. There needs to be trust.

Your customer as a hero

My favorite film hero as a child was probably Luke Skywalker in Star Wars. Poor Luke didn't have it easy: His real mother died during childbirth; his adoptive parents were burned to a crisp; he discovered his real father was Darth Vader; and his love interest was his sister. Yet Luke, who came from a humble upbringing, learned the ways of the Force and became a Jedi knight who saved the galaxy more than a few times. I loved all of that as a kid.

The point here is that we all love heroes because they overcome adversity and accomplish some amazing feats. We can leverage these concepts in our strategic customer conversations by picturing our customers as heroes on their own journeys.

When you envision your customer as a hero, they don't just have a job—they are on a quest. Their world becomes more than just using your product. Your customers are on a mission to revolutionize their company. Getting into this mindset allows you to more easily climb inside your customer's head and pull you out of the weeds of your day-to-day.

To reveal your customer's journey as the hero of their narrative, ask yourself these key questions:

- **Who are they, and what do they do?** By understanding your customers more deeply, you can better visualize their transformative mission. If it's your first time meeting, you can say, "I'd love to hear a little bit about you. Can you tell me more about your role, your core responsibilities, and how this may have changed over time?" Even if you have scanned their LinkedIn details, having your clients tell you about themselves will tell you what is important to them and what makes them tick.

  Even if you've known your customer for some time, you can ask them if their role has changed at all since you last met, or if they anticipate any changes in their responsibilities in the near future. Showing a genuine interest in your customers will increase their trust and nudge them to open up.

- **What is their quest?** What are they trying to achieve, and why is it important to them? What is their desired future state? What constitutes a win for them? What is at stake if they don't complete this quest successfully? You are trying to unearth the business outcomes they need to accomplish, and the role that your products play in this.

  Customers tend to churn when they cannot complete their quest or can complete it in another way that doesn't involve your product. Find out what their quest is, what winning means to them, and if they are on the right path.

- **Who are the other characters in their story?** The characters that play alongside your primary customer contacts include both allies and foes. Allies could be their coworkers who help them achieve their quest, such as the IT or operations team. Foes could include their finance department, which doesn't want to give them the budget they need, or even their boss. Uncover the characters and how they relate to your primary contacts.

- **What obstacles are keeping them from completing their quest?** Challenges arise on every journey. Your customer might be managing multiple roles after workforce reductions or struggling with the complexity and performance issues of your products. It could be that one of their colleagues wants to switch to a competitor. You need to uncover those obstacles and clear the path so your customer can complete their quest successfully. In addition, you need to be empathetic to your customer's plight, as they may be facing substantial obstacles.

The next time you're jumping into a meeting, think of your customer as a hero in their own story and ask, "Who are they? What quest are they on? Who else is alongside them in their journey, and What is blocking them from achieving their quest?" While you may not think of your customer meetings as Christmas, like Alex did, having this customer-as-hero mindset will put you in the right frame of mind when commencing a strategic customer conversation. Imagining your customers as heroes in their own stories will force you to concentrate on learning more about their quests before you jump into solving their problems.

Putting this into practice

Go to strategiccustomersuccess.com and complete the "Picturing Your Customer as a Hero Exercise."

Summary and key takeaways

Leverage the power of motivational interviewing to guide strategic conversations, and adopt a customer-as-hero mindset to start on the right foot.

- Many CSMs like to play it safe. They avoid asking their customers tough questions and focus their meetings on what they are comfortable with—their products.

- A strategic conversation is a candid and genuine dialogue with customers that is primarily focused on uncovering essential details required to achieve a specific objective. It can also entail defusing tense situations and influencing others to take specific actions.

- Most people become defensive when they're told what to do because they're trying to protect their right to make their own decisions.

- Motivational interviewing (MI) involves truly listening to your customers and helping them find motivation to take certain actions.

- MI is a key component of strategic conversations, as it can help you uncover your client's desires to take action.

- Perceiving your customers as a hero on their own journey puts you in the right mindset to better visualize their world and allows you to put their needs before your own.

CHAPTER 15

How to Build Trust and Guide Conversations with OARS

I remember the dreaded day when I opened a client email that began like this: "Chad—I'm sorry, but we decided we're not going to renew our contract with you." I couldn't believe it. Despite all the effort I put in, they were still planning to churn.

I felt pangs of guilt as I absorbed this news. This client was a perfect fit for our product and our company. They had all the right ingredients to be one of our most successful clients, yet they had given up on us.

After some deep breaths, I contacted our head of marketing, who had a strong connection with the decision-maker. He set up a meeting with her so we could review their decision and somehow salvage the relationship. I was convinced that this was a waste of time and the client was a lost cause, but I went along for the ride.

When the dreaded day of the meeting arrived, I hopped on the call and thought, *Might as well get this over with and learn what we can so we can prevent this from happening in the future.* Once we completed the meeting pleasantries, I did my best to keep my composure and politely asked, "Can you provide more details about what led to your decision not to renew with us?" The client responded, "We really loved the idea of how your product would help grow our business, but we're finding that it doesn't have the impact we expected."

I then experienced one of the most embarrassing moments of my career—I completely froze and didn't know what to say next. Our head of marketing sprang into action and took over the conversation. "Thank you so much for taking the time to meet with us. You mentioned that you loved our product, but it seems like it's not providing value. Did I get that right?"

"Yes!" she exclaimed. "I don't think our new chief marketing officer will really understand its purpose compared to the costs involved. It's very expensive to operate."

"Oh, that makes sense in terms of the cost," he responded. "Regarding that, I know you are working with an agency. How does that factor into the equation?"

"It's a big part of it. It eats up a fair amount of our budget," she said. "We just don't have the resources for this."

"I understand. Resources are needed to make this a success. Out of curiosity, how many hours per week did your direct team dedicate to our product?"

She considered his question and responded, "I didn't really permit my team much time to use it. I had them focused on other tasks, so they probably didn't know what to do with it."

"If I had a magic wand and could somehow remove your agency from the equation, how much money would you save?" She admitted that they could save a lot of money if they didn't have to rely on their agency.

"OK," he said. "This is what I think I heard. You believed in what our product could deliver, and you mostly leveraged agency resources to run it up to this point. Due to the costs involved, you're not seeing the return on your investment, and you're concerned about how your new CMO will react."

"That is an accurate summary," she stated. I could feel the relief in her voice. She felt that she was finally being heard.

To my complete amazement, we started to unpack the true reasons behind their decision to leave us: We hadn't effectively communicated our solution's benefits, understood the true costs involved, or fully grasped our client's constraints.

As the conversation continued and we uncovered the core issues, I started to see the possibility of saving the relationship. What led the client to open up more? How was my colleague able to extract critical information we hadn't uncovered before? By asking questions—and by playing back what the client said. Was that really all it took?

At the time, I didn't realize that my colleague was using elements of the OARS framework, one of the core components of motivational interviewing.

That moment was a turning point for me. I realized that I needed to uplevel my own skills so I could have more productive client conversations. I committed to learning more about his approach and seeking advice from others.

Ever have that feeling of wishing the other person would stop talking so you can interject? You're blocking out whatever the other person is saying so you don't forget what you want to say. Many CSMs fall into this trap. Instead of being curious and listening to understand, they are just waiting for their customer to finish their sentence so they can provide the solution they think the customer requires. It's a real problem: It sends a message that you don't care what the other person is saying, even though you didn't have any malintent.[61] We're usually triggered by something our customers have said, and our natural inclination is to jump directly into solution mode. This is a mistake.

---

61   Dana Brownlee, "Are You Really Listening or Just Waiting to Talk? There's a Difference," Forbes, August 6, 2020, https://www.forbes.com/sites/danabrownlee/2020/08/06/are-you-really-listening-or-just-waiting-to-talk-theres-a-difference/.

Author Adam Grant agrees. In his book *Think Again*, he states, "Our first instinct is usually to start talking. Yet the most effective way to help others open their minds is often to listen."[62] Your desire to be helpful and address your customer's issue can backfire when you assume you understand what the client actually wants. My late dad loved to give me this advice: "Never assume, because when you do, you make an ass of yourself." He was spot on.

Rowing in the right direction: The OARS framework

To avoid making assumptions and practice active listening, use the OARS framework. It equips you to understand your customer's quest, who's on the journey with them, and the obstacles they face. It cultivates deep listening skills, helping you stay inquisitive and guide discussions organically rather than jumping to assumed solutions. Rather than merely executing requests, you'll learn to uncover and tackle strategic priorities.

It can be intimidating to have strategic conversations, which can be uncomfortable and unpredictable. You can discover skeletons in your customers' closets that you didn't want to know about, such as how they really feel about your company. But you have to put those fears aside. By engaging in genuine discussions beyond feature updates and issues, you forge stronger and trusted client partnerships. But how do you make this happen?

As mentioned, start by picturing your customer as a hero in their own narrative. Then use the four-part OARS framework:

- ***Open questions*** demonstrate your curiosity and desire to learn, as opposed to closed questions, which lead the other person down a certain path.
- ***Affirmations*** provide encouragement and acknowledge the positive behaviors that your clients may be exhibiting.

---

62 Grant, *Think Again*, 156.

- **Reflections** are an active listening technique and a central component of OARS. In them, you paraphrase or repeat what the other person said to you.
- **Summaries** tie multiple reflections together and may also include your own advice. They can be used to wrap up a discussion topic or meeting.

Open questions: Start the conversation with open versus closed questions

Open questions help uncover your client's underlying issues and business outcomes. But it's not just what you ask—it's how you frame a sequence of questions and follow up each question.

Think of open questions as a can opener for your customers' minds. Used properly, open questions have hypnotic powers that surface information that you may never have known existed. They're powerful because they let your customers talk about what they care about most: themselves.

Open questions typically begin with *what* or *how* rather than *why*, which can sound accusatory. Ask questions like:

- What does success look like to you?
- Tell me about what you're trying to achieve.
- What is one improvement you would like to see?
- What are the metrics that demonstrate you've made progress?

These types of questions sharply contrast with closed questions, which only require one-word answers—typically yes or no. Closed questions take away your customers' power as you control the conversation. This can be frustrating for them, as you're focusing on what you want rather than taking the time to listen to them. Closed questions can also give the impression that you're leading your customer into a trap, such as asking "Wouldn't you want to learn how to save money?" This can reduce trust and drive your customers away. Think about how you respond to retail store associates who ask you if you need help.[63]

Not all closed questions are bad. They can be useful for clarifying a remark or to obtain specific pieces of information. For example, when a client says they don't understand an area of your product, you may ask, "Did you take the training course on this feature?" This will give you the precise data point you need. Aim for seven open-ended questions per closed question once you've honed your strategic conversation skills.[64]

When using an open question, always consider the outcome you're trying to achieve. Are you trying to resolve a long-standing issue, determine what your client should focus on next, or extract details needed for an upcoming renewal? Ensure every question you ask has a purpose, avoiding a barrage of unnecessary inquiries. For this reason, you should prepare your questions ahead of time (see chapter 13).

Expert tip: Ask one question at a time and then shut up

A common mistake is asking multiple questions at once. For example, you may say to your client: "What is your number one priority in the next thirty days? Why is it the most important priority, and how will you know if you are successful?" This can overwhelm and confuse your clients. This is called the question-answer trap because it feels more like an interrogation than a two-way conversation. Instead, ask them a single question, then shut up. Stay silent and give your customers time to respond. They may be mulling over your question, so don't feel you need to fill the void. Mix reflections into your conversations to create natural breaks.

---

63 David Priemer, "The Hidden Force Accidentally Driving Your Prospects Away," Cerebral Selling, August 19, 2024, https://cerebralselling.com/driving-prospects-away/.
64 "Motivational Interviewing: Advancing Your Practice," Michigan Center for Clinical Systems Improvement, February 2016, https://www.miccsi.org/wp-content/uploads/2016/02/Day-3-Advancing-Your-Practice-in-MI-for-MiCCSI-2014.pdf.

As an added tip, don't appear to be reading off a script, or you'll seem cold and robotic. Have some prepared questions, but don't stick to them. The more curiosity you display and the more interested you are in your customers' businesses and needs, the more interesting and trustworthy you'll appear.

Once you've opened the door with broad, exploratory questions, you can guide the conversation deeper using targeted probing questions. By shedding light on their current reality, you help your clients become more open to exploring solutions.

Kristen Hayer, CEO of the Success League, recommends two types of probing questions: impact questions, which highlight the cost of inaction, and value questions, which illustrate the benefits of change. She adapted this from Neil Rackham's famous book *SPIN Selling* and applied it brilliantly to the world of customer success.

Impact questions

Impact questions "uncover the effects, consequences or implications of your customer's problem on their business."[65] This translates into something that is very tangible for your customer, such as wasted time, increased costs, or decreased revenue. These questions bridge the gap between customer goals and your product's value.

For instance, a client may have resisted upgrading to your premium analytics package due to the increased fees, without recognizing the hidden costs of their manual efforts. Questions like "What's your weekly time investment in report creation?" can help clients realize how an upgrade could free up

---

65 Kristen Hayer, "How to Engage Your Customer's Top Level Executives," SlideShare, March 29, 2018, https://www.slideshare.net/slideshow/how-to-engage-your-customers-top-level-executives-92318981/92318981.

countless hours. You have the power to illuminate your customers' inefficiencies with questions like these:

- What do you see as the cost to your business if these problems aren't addressed?
- How much time are you wasting due to those manual processes?
- Why is reducing time spent in this area important to you?
- What are the three best reasons to start using this feature we discussed?
- What happens if you don't achieve the goals you've mentioned?
- If we delayed this or did nothing, what would be the impact on you?
- Is this impacting anything else?

Value questions

Value questions help you clarify the tangible benefits your clients will receive if you help solve their problems. Rather than dictating solutions, ask thoughtful questions to help clients recognize opportunities for positive change.

For example, in the story at the start of this chapter, my colleague asked the value question "If I had a magic wand and could somehow remove your agency from the equation, how much money would you save?" The question was intended to help the client work through their challenges by generating ideas about how they could save costs.

Here are some sample value questions:

- If we helped you solve this problem, what else could you get done?
- By focusing on this area of your business, how much potential revenue could you generate next year?
- If we could reduce the manual tasks your team does on a weekly basis by 10 percent, how would that benefit your group?

- If we could consolidate your various systems, what would your potential cost savings be?

Impact and value questions can be very powerful weapons in your question arsenal. It's best to prepare these ahead of time so you can leverage them in your conversations as needed – especially when introducing new products. Consider the pains your customers may currently be experiencing, the possible drivers such as time, cost, and revenue that could influence them, and possible solutions that could address their pains. When it seems like your customers are struggling to recognize the impact of their problems or the value that could be achieved by solving them, use these aces up your sleeves to move the conversation forward.

Don't accept the client's first response: Use clarifying questions

Don't take the first response from your clients at face value. They may have misinterpreted the question, purposely withheld key details, or provided a high-level answer without much substance. Whatever the case, it's your job as a strategic CSM to dig deeper.

Take a moment to confirm your understanding of the customer's statement before moving on. Ask yourself if something wasn't clear or if there are details that may be missing from their story. This is a perfect opportunity to leverage a reflection, which gives you time to consider your next move. Then, ask a clarifying question to extract additional details or shed additional light on something they said. For example, if a client tells you that they want to achieve a higher return on their investment, you can leverage these clarifying questions:

- What led to that being such a high priority?
- Can you let me know what you meant by that?
- How do you feel we're performing today?

Always ask additional questions if you believe you require more detail or clarity.

Affirmations: Acknowledging the right behaviors with affirmations

Affirmations are forms of flattery and positive reinforcement that build rapport and encourage openness. You can leverage affirmations by acknowledging the progress your clients have made and the obstacles they've overcome. Just don't overdo it by laying it on too thick. Appearing disingenuous will have the opposite effect and erode trust.

Affirmations should be sprinkled into your client conversations at various times. Some well-placed compliments at the beginning of your meeting can start things off on the right foot. Doing this builds up your client's ego and puts them at ease. For example, you could mention the following to a customer as part of a regular meeting: "I've been so impressed with the recent changes you made to your processes. It wasn't a surprise to see that you received more responsibilities." or "I really admire how you set up our product so quickly. Do you ever sleep?" While sincere appreciation might feel awkward to deliver, research by influence expert Robert Cialdini shows that it builds the rapport essential for influencing others.[66]

Use affirmations at pivotal points in your conversation. If you hear your client commit to taking action or state their intention to change their behaviors, use affirmations to positively reinforce their statements. Your client may suggest that they realize they need to take a product training course, or that they recognize they aren't dedicating enough time to your product. You can respond with: "You are making a smart decision" or "I know you have so much going on, but I know you've got this." Make your clients feel that you're in their corner and that you have their backs.

---

66 Catherine Webb, "Influence, the Psychology of Persuasion — Key Insights," review of *Influence: The Psychology of Persuasion,* by Robert B. Cialdini, Medium, January 23, 2024, https://medium.com/@rvacatswebb/influence-the-psychology-of-persuasion-key-insights-2db3d7cf01f5.

Finally, affirmations can be used when your client doubts their abilities—especially when they relate to your product. For example, you could say, "I know it's been challenging to use our product, but look at how much progress you've made since we started working together. You are now a whiz!" You can also send messages to your client congratulating them when they achieve certain milestones toward their stated goals. Act as your client's cheerleader by recognizing their wins and how far they've come.

When concluding a conversation, you can use affirmations to applaud your client for their bravery for the positive steps forward they've taken. This provides the reassurance and confidence they need and improves the chances that they will follow through on what they have promised. Remember to leverage affirmations in your conversations, but don't overdo it.

Reflections: Your most powerful strategic weapon is reflections

While affirmations help encourage and reinforce your client's efforts, reflections show them that you're truly listening—and build deeper trust.

Think about it, how do you typically respond to your customers after they've answered one of your questions? You might say "That makes sense" or "I hear you," or offer a silent nod. That's a missed chance to create rapport—especially early in the relationship.

Meaningful listening requires more than basic acknowledgment to show you're fully present, and not multitasking. Reflections—repeating and rephrasing your client's words to clarify meaning and emotion—are a form of active listening.

According to Bill Matulich,

> Reflections are statements made to the client that mirror, give back, repeat, rephrase, paraphrase, or otherwise manifest what you hear the client saying or see the client doing, such as smiling or looking sad, for example. Reflections are really guesses or hypotheses about what is going on in the client's mind and heart, so you are reflecting on what you think the client means by what he or she says and what you think your client feels emotionally as well. Keys to good reflections are that they are delivered confidently as statements with your voice inflection going down rather than up at the end.[67]

You're not just saying that you understand—you're showing it by paraphrasing what they just told you. This is how you build rapport and trust with your clients.

Start off with these statements and then paraphrase what your client just said or state how you think the client is feeling:

- It seems like. . . *or* It sounds like . . .
- If I understand you correctly . . .
- What I am hearing you say is that . . .

To see this in action, let's return to the example at the beginning of this chapter. The client said, "We really loved the idea of how your product would help grow our business, but we're finding that it doesn't have the impact we expected." My colleague then reflected on what he heard: "You mentioned that you loved our product, but it seems like you don't feel it's providing value. Did I get that right?"

---

67 Bill Matulich, *How To Do Motivational Interviewing: A Guidebook* 2nd ed. (Bill Matulich, 2013), 17.

You know you are on the right track when your client agrees with your assessment, saying, "That's right," or nodding their head. Another positive sign is that the client keeps talking and divulging more information. You may even hear phrases such as "To be totally honest with you." This typically means you're breaking through their armor as they start to reveal their true feelings and concerns that they didn't previously divulge.[68]

You don't need to use a reflection every time your client answers a question, as this can take too much time and disrupt the flow of the conversation. You can also use reflections to defuse a tense situation, label a certain emotion you are sensing, or clarify important details.

What if your reflection isn't completely accurate? Won't you look foolish? Though this worry is understandable, imperfect interpretations often lead to valuable clarifying discussions. In these situations, your customer will typically correct you and may even divulge additional information. When you feel you may have missed a few points the client made, repeat what you heard and ask them if you missed anything. They will gladly point out what may have been overlooked, as they appreciate that you're trying to help address their concerns.

Expert tip: Mirroring

Another technique recommended by famed negotiation author Chris Voss is *mirroring*. In this case, mirroring doesn't mean mimicking how the other person is behaving. It's repeating the last word or the last few words the other person said as a question.

If the client says, "You know, we're really not happy with the support we're receiving," you would respond with, "The support you're receiving?" Repeating these last few words as a question invites the other person to divulge more details and "vomit information," as Voss calls it. It's as if you are imitating the other person, which creates an unconscious bond that acts like a Jedi mind trick.

---

68 Vaidyanathan and Rabago, *Customer Success Professional's Handbook*, 196.

> Mirroring requires practice, but it's extremely effective in uncovering additional information. It can be mixed in with reflections in your conversations as a powerful form of active listening.[69]

Summaries: Using summaries to build shared understanding

A summary is a key component of a strategic conversation. It allows you to summarize what's already been discussed and move toward action. It weaves together key insights and reflections from your ongoing dialogue, though it can also serve as an opening review of previous conversations. This gets everyone aligned around the topic at hand so you can either move on to another topic or take action on what's been discussed. It also gives everyone the chance to weigh in on your view of the situation.

For example, as part of a QBR, you may ask your client a series of questions to clarify their priorities. Then, you can use a summary to combine the various details you gathered and ensure they align with your customer's intentions. Summaries improve your customers' comfort level, as they know you're on the same wavelength as them, which builds trust, and allows you to reframe the conversation as you see it or to nudge the client in a certain direction.

Let's go back to the summary my colleague used: "This is what I think I heard. You believed in what our product could deliver, and you mostly leveraged agency resources up to this point. Due to the costs involved, you're not seeing the return on your investment, and you're concerned about how your new CMO will react."

My colleague reaffirmed why they bought our product and narrowed down their reason for churn to some root issues: Agency resources didn't make our product cost-effective, and she wasn't dedicating enough direct

---

69 Chris Voss and Tahl Raz, *Never Split the Difference: Negotiating as If Your Life Depended on It* (HarperBusiness, 2018), 34–36.

resources to give it a fair shake. She also acknowledged her fears of her new boss.

The goal of a summary statement is to have the client agree with your assessment. If you've accurately described your client's position, you should hear something similar to a reflection, such as "That's right," "Yes!" or "You nailed it." This indicates that you've established some influence over the other party that is based on trust. You have a solid foundation that you can build on.[70]

Row, row, row your boat

Even if you hate rowing or anything related to water sports, if you want to be a strategic CSM, the OARS framework is going to be your best friend. You should be consistently leveraging open questions, affirmations, reflections, and summaries as a critical part of your strategic CSM toolbox. It takes time to familiarize yourself with these concepts, so please follow the instructions in the *Putting this into practice* section below. Get out your OARS and start paddling!

Putting this into practice

Take the time to practice the various components of OARS. Go to strategiccustomersuccess.com and complete the "Practicing the OARS Framework Exercise."

Summary and key takeaways

The OARS framework is a key part of MI and something that is used continuously in strategic conversations. It consists of four elements: open questions, affirmations, reflections, and summaries.

---

70   Brandon Voss, "How to Build Rapport Quickly in Any Situation," The Black Swan Group, May 24, 2021, https://www.blackswanltd.com/the-edge/how-to-build-rapport-quickly-in-any-situation.

- Open questions, particularly those starting with *what* or *how*, are essential tools for understanding client needs and goals, but their effectiveness depends on proper framing, sequencing, and follow-up.

- Use impact questions to help customers understand the consequences of their problems (e.g., wasted time, increased costs).

- Employ value questions to help clients recognize potential benefits and opportunities for positive change.

- Follow up on initial client responses with clarifying questions to dig deeper and gain more clarity. Never accept the first answer at face value.

- Avoid the *question-answer trap* of rapid-fire questioning that turns dialogue into interrogation.

- Apply affirmations strategically to build rapport and reinforce positive behaviors.

- When your clients relay information, most CSMs respond with, "I get what you're saying," or "I understand," or simply nod their head. You can do better by using reflections: Paraphrase what the client just said or the emotion you feel they are exhibiting.

- Use summaries to weave together key insights and get everyone aligned.

CHAPTER 16

Nudging Customers to Take Action: The SOON Funnel and Assessing Motivation

Let's pick back up from where we left off in the last chapter, with the client who informed us they were churning. As you may recall, the client agreed with my colleague's summary of the situation. She then added, "We're open to figuring something out; I'm just not sure what that would look like at this point." My colleague asked, "Well, what would success look like for you?"

She paused for a minute and replied, "We want to further engage our customers to help us drive more revenue. It's a major company objective. We want them to refer us new business."

"It sounds like you want your customers to play a major role in your marketing efforts. How are you doing this today?"

"Well, we don't have a great way of doing this," she explained. "That's been our problem all along. That's why we wanted to use your product."

"That makes sense. We spoke about this briefly, but what are the real obstacles to engaging your customers?"

"Well, this goes beyond your company. I need to dedicate more resources to this. It's really important, and I know I can make an impact here. I guess I've been an obstacle, as I was focused on other initiatives."

My colleague responded, "I understand that you have a lot going on. I've been impressed by how you've been able to juggle everything. How much time would you say you have dedicated to a customer engagement strategy?"

"Maybe an hour a week at most. Not very much, to be honest."

He then summarized the situation: "So it seems that it's important to engage your best customers, as they can help with your company's broader goals. You have a good sense of the possibilities, but you just didn't dedicate adequate time to this."

"Yes, I think that is a good assessment of where we are."

"Thanks for confirming that. In your opinion, what are some options to get this project back on track?"

"Well, I just hired a new marketing manager who could really drive this. I had him working on a different project, but I think he could be really good at using your product. I could also use some of the data that your team was sending us to make a case to our CMO of the value of your product."

"Great, it sounds like we have a possible path forward. Chad and his team will train your marketing manager, and we'll come and present to your CMO. Let's build a schedule for this so we can keep on track. What are the next steps from your end?"

"I'm going to schedule a meeting with my marketing manager to review what we've discussed with them," she said, "and then look at the data that your team has sent us. Let's set a meeting for Friday to review where things stand."

"Great—will do!" he responded. "Thank you again for your time. We understand the pressure you are under, and we're committed to making you successful."

I couldn't believe how my colleague had turned the whole meeting around. What began as a churn postmortem call evolved into a masterclass on course correcting a client relationship. You may have noticed that various components from the OARS framework were used, including open questions, affirmations, reflections, and summaries. The client's openness to finding a solution, often referred to as *change talk*, was harnessed—a concept we'll delve into later in this chapter.

With the client willing to work together, my colleague asked the trigger question, "What would success look like for you?" Together with the client, he analyzed the challenges impeding their progress, considered available options, and planned actionable next steps to move forward. This solution-oriented framework mirrors something called the SOON funnel.

Transforming ideas into actions: Leveraging the SOON funnel

Up to this point, we've concentrated on the foundational elements of strategic conversations, which centered on the OARS framework. But what do you do when you want to spur your clients to take action? For example, how do you convince your clients to start adopting certain products or features? How can you persuade your customers to commit to a product upgrade? I always struggled in this area until I learned about the SOON funnel framework, which encourages your clients to self-discover possible solutions while nudging them toward action.

LifeLabs Learning designed the SOON funnel—success, obstacles, options, and next steps—to help leaders coach their employees through challenging situations. The company recognized that the types of questions leaders ask their employees lead to employees taking action, so it created a framework to simplify this process. A former colleague of mine, Brittany Barrett, brilliantly applied the SOON funnel to client conversations to achieve a similar purpose.

The SOON Funnel

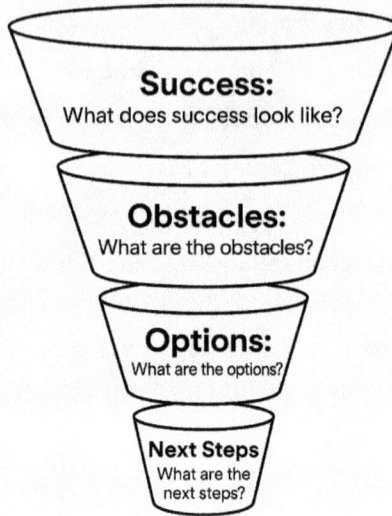

Success:
What does success look like?

Obstacles:
What are the obstacles?

Options:
What are the options?

Next Steps
What are the
next steps?

Figure 9. The SOON Funnel.

Success: What would success look like?

Success is what your clients aim to achieve. It's the gap between their current state and desired outcome. It's the goal of their journey. This could be simply onboarding your product successfully or achieving specific business outcomes. In the earlier example, the client defined success as increasing sales revenue.

Focusing the client on their definition of success can lift them out of the weeds and remind them of their ultimate objective. Success questions elevate the conversation and move the client to take action.

I refer to these types of questions as *trigger questions* as they have the power to redirect the conversation from issues to solutions:

- What would success look like for you (in this situation)?
- How would you define success?
- What metrics do you use to define success?
- How would you like things to be different from how they are today?
- What do you hope to achieve in the next ninety days (in this area)?

Once your client begins answering and painting a picture of success, it might be tempting to offer solutions right away. But you shouldn't jump right into solution mode. If you skip a few steps, it could derail the entire conversation. You first need to identify anything blocking your client's path. Before you can help clients move toward success, you must first understand what's getting in their way: obstacles.

Obstacles: What are the obstacles in the way?

Obstacles are the barriers keeping clients from achieving their defined success. This typically involves resource challenges, such as limited bandwidth or budget to fully leverage your products. Gaps in your product offering or key product bugs may also hinder their progress.

Additionally, clients may lack the necessary expertise to leverage your solutions or face internal blockers, like a resistant boss. Consider what or who may be impeding their ability to complete their quest.

To openly discuss their concerns, you can simply ask, "What obstacles stand in your way?" The scenario at the beginning of this chapter opened with this key question: "What are the real obstacles to engaging your customers?" You can also ask:

- What is stopping you from moving forward?
- What is holding you back?
- What might get in the way?
- What concerns you the most?

- What hesitations do you have?
- Whose buy-in do you need to get in your organization?

Your client may be stuck in their own bubble, unaware that they're the major obstacle. For example, they may claim your product is hard to use or not flexible enough. They may make assumptions or excuses to avoid the necessary changes for success. You need to be the bubble burster!

Dig into your customers' obstacles using the OARS framework. Share success stories or benchmark data showing they're below average and need to change. Ask them value questions such as "If we helped you solve this problem, what else could you get done?" This helps them be more open to moving past these obstacles, and it embodies the idea of radical customer candor (see chapter 9).

Your objective is to challenge your clients' assumptions and help them see things from a broader perspective. By documenting all their concerns and obstacles, you can identify paths to their desired outcomes.

Options: What are some possible options?

You've reached a pivotal moment in the conversation where you need to steer your client in a particular direction. While it's tempting to tell your client what to do, doing so could jeopardize the progress you've made. When tensions escalate or you're trying to change someone's behavior, they may be offended by being told how to act.[71] The better path is to work with your client on some possible approaches. Ideally, the conversation and insights will inspire them to come forward with their own ideas.

Clients need to own the solution, so ask what approaches they think might work—even if they aren't sure. In the example at the beginning of the chapter, the client determined on their own that they needed to dedicate

---

71 "You're Not the Boss of Me! Why We Don't Like Being Told What to Do," Cleveland Clinic, November 17, 2020, https://health.clevelandclinic.org/why-we-dont-like-being-told-what-to-do.

more resources. Don't underestimate your clients—involve them by simply asking.

Start with something like, "Let's work together on possible approaches to address the situation at hand." Asking for their help builds trust and makes them more willing to act.[72] Then, follow up this statement with one of these questions:

- What are some possible options you suggest?
- How can we help you achieve your objectives?
- What ideas do you have about how we can resolve this?
- How have you tackled this problem in the past?
- How else could this be handled? What other teams or people could be involved?

I often pair an affirmation with an open question. Picturing my client as the hero, I might say, "You've had to deal with so much since you joined your company. What you've been able to accomplish is really impressive. Based on your experience, what are some possible approaches you would suggest?" I use affirmations to boost their confidence and show them that their input is valued. Ideally, your clients will suggest solid ideas. If they're unsure or off track, offer your own recommendations.

How to present your recommendations and options to your clients in the right way

While it's better to have your client suggest a path forward, when they're indecisive, step in and take the reins. Research conducted by Matthew Dixon and Ted McKenna and described in their book *The Jolt Effect* found that win

---

72 Charles H. Green, "How Not to Create Corporate Trust," *Trust Matters Blog*, May 7, 2018, https://trustedadvisor.com/trustmatters/how-not-to-create-corporate-trust.

rates by sales reps increased when sales reps presented a personal recommendation when their prospects were stumped.[73] This applies to SCSMs as well.

When recommending solutions to your clients, you can take one of these three approaches or a combination of them: leveraging social proof, using storytelling, or suggesting two to three options.

Leveraging social proof: Social proof involves using relevant customer examples that support your suggestions. Start off by saying, "If it's OK with you, I would like to make a recommendation based on how customers who are similar to you have handled this situation. How does that sound?" If they agree, which they undoubtedly will, you can then proceed to relate relevant client examples: "A customer that is very similar to you did . . . which resulted in . . . Would you like to hear more?" This is much more powerful than just expressing your opinion with: "I recommend that you do . . ."

Social proof was popularized by psychologist Robert Cialdini in his book *Influence: The Psychology of Persuasion.* Cialdini maintains that if someone isn't sure how to behave in a certain situation, they will look to their peers for proper guidance.[74] You can leverage this psychological theory by imparting customer examples that your clients will latch onto.

Storytelling: Social proof and storytelling go hand in hand, and it's best to use storytelling when describing customer examples. Storytelling is a vital CSM skill to master. A simple storytelling technique is to outline the key details of the story, followed by a summary of the issue, and finally wrapping up with the happy-ever-after solution that led to a positive outcome.

When presenting your social proof customer story, give some context as to who the customer is and what they do. This can include the company size, the team that leverages your product, and the product features they leverage.

---

73 Matthew Dixon and Ted McKenna, "Stop Losing Sales to Customer Indecision," *Harvard Business Review,* June 24, 2022, https://hbr.org/2022/06/stop-losing-sales-to-customer-indecision.
74 "What Is the Social Proof Theory?," The Psychology Notes HQ, March 10, 2018, https://www.psychologynoteshq.com/social-proof/.

The more similar they are to your client, the better, and the more details you provide, the more real it will appear. In storytelling, always consider why the audience will care about what you're going to tell them.

Next, let them know the predicament the customer in your story found themselves in, which should be similar to your client's. Finally, explain what they did that solved the problem and the positive results they experienced. That's all you need to do in a nutshell. Prepare a few similar stories and practice them to ensure they feel authentic. Don't overcomplicate this.

Provide two to three options: Another proven tactic to get your clients to adopt your suggestions when there isn't a clear path is to provide them with a few options rather than just putting forward a single approach. By providing two to three choices, you're giving them a sense of control and autonomy. This works well in renewal negotiations. However, if you sense some strong hesitation from your clients during this process, it's best to skip the options and provide a personal recommendation, as suggested by Dixon and McKenna.[75] Just be sure you have established a trusted relationship first.

Expert tip: *What if* questions

A proven strategy to lift your clients out of the weeds and help them picture a future state is using *what if* questions as defined by Alan Armstrong. These questions are effective because they subtly guide clients in the right direction without directly telling them what to do.[76]

What if questions are designed to remove your client's self-imposed constraints. For instance, they may be overwhelmed by the complexities of your product and evaluating competitive solutions. After summarizing their challenges, you could use any one of the following questions:

---

75 Dixon and McKenna, "Stop Losing Sales."
76 "TPMS 0008 Nail It, Then Scale It ft Alan Armstrong," posted February 11, 2018, by Product Management Show, YouTube, https://www.youtube.com/watch?v=uCvR5Tb63Pg.

- What if we could provide you with additional resources at no cost?
- What if we started to meet weekly to work through these challenges?
- What if I connected you with another customer who had similar challenges?
- What if we offer you personalized training?
- What if we could improve your efficiency by helping you implement this new feature?

Getting your client to picture possible solutions and what the future may look like can move the conversation forward and break impasses. Have some *what if* questions prepared in advance.

Expert tip: Use double-sided reflections to drive the conversation forward

Clients often get caught up in tactics and lose sight of their bigger goals, leaving them stuck in quicksand and halting their progress. Double-sided reflections can be extremely helpful in getting you unstuck. They help you communicate to the client that they are struggling between two contradictory ideas: their desire to achieve their stated goals and the barriers that they are hung up on. As an example, when your client has told you that their goals are aligned with your product but they don't have the budget to move forward, you can say: "On the one hand, you have goals of improving efficiency, and on the other, you don't have the budget to achieve this goal."

Let's look at another example. If a client pushes back due to budget reasons, you can respond by saying, "It seems that you don't have the budget to leverage our product, but what about your goal to improve efficiency? How will you achieve that?" You can help your clients recognize how they are impeding their own progress and prompt them to find a resolution by playing back their conflicting statements.

Next steps: What are the next steps?

Having identified your client's objectives, the barriers they face, and the strategies to meet their needs, your focus should now be on driving them to take action. The best way to do this is to ask them, "What are the next steps?" Take a moment to ask this question rather than telling them. When the action items come from their own mouth, they'll be more likely to commit to them.

You can ask your client what the next steps are in other ways:

- What is the first step we need to take?
- Where should we go from here?
- What needs to be done to get this moving?
- What is the first task you are going to start on following this meeting?

Once the client outlines the next steps and you have a clear path forward, you can build out a success plan (see chapter 17 for how to create one). If you sense some reluctance or you don't feel they're fully onboard, it's best to assess their motivation.

Assessing your client's motivation

What if you detect some strong hesitancy to take action from your clients even after you've followed the steps of the SOON funnel? You may hear something like, "I want to start using these features we discussed, but I'm not convinced this will get us where we need to go." In MI, this is known as "Yes, but"—a clear sign your client isn't fully on board with the plan.[77]

When you hear a "Yes, but," or you can sense that your client is reluctant to move forward, you need to pause and further explore your client's concerns. Maybe you recommended a solution before the client fully understood the issue or opportunity. Or maybe they have yet to accept some

---

77 Matulich, Motivational Interviewing, 32–33.

responsibility for their predicament. You could have clients who are very set in their ways and are having a tough time accepting the changes they need to make. Perhaps your clients don't fully trust you yet. Whatever the case, you need to ease up on the gas and dig into what's holding them back.

When you find yourself in this type of predicament, explore your client's hesitation by using two key scaling questions:[78]

- On a scale of zero to ten, where *zero* is not important at all and *ten* is crucially important, how important is it for you to take action?
- On a scale of zero to ten, where *zero* is no confidence at all and *ten* is completely confident, how confident are you in taking action?

Note: You can substitute the specific task you want the customer to complete for *take action*.

Ideally, your client would be both highly motivated and highly confident in their ability to proceed, putting them at the top right of the motivation matrix (Figure 10). However, that rarely happens.

Some of your customers are highly motivated to get moving but have low confidence that they can perform what is required (top left in the motivation matrix). This may be due to a lack of skills, self-confidence, resources, time, budget, or faith in your product or your abilities.

Some of your clients are low on motivation but high on confidence (bottom right in the motivation matrix). In these cases, your client has the confidence needed to proceed, but they see this project as a low priority. They may also be overconfident in their abilities, so they don't believe they need to do anything or that your solution is worth the investment.

Ideally, your customers express what Bill Miller calls *change talk*—expressing a desire to improve their current situation. For example, if your customer chose *eight* for the first question, you know you're on the right track,

---

78 Matulich, Motivational Interviewing, 17.

as there is a willingness to act. If they selected a *three* for the second question, it's important to understand why they're hesitant to move forward.

You can dig further into their initial answers by using these two follow-up questions:

- For high numbers, you can ask, "Why did you pick the number __, and not a lower number?"
- For low numbers, you can ask, "What would it take to move it to a higher number?"

MOTIVATION MATRIX

Figure 10. The Motivation Matrix.

These follow-up questions test your clients' resolve and uncover hidden issues. For the client that answered an *eight* to the first scaling question, you want to hear something like, "I chose eight because this initiative is very important to my current priorities."

In a situation where you were pushing your client to use an additional product of yours as part of an upsell conversation, you may hear: "I really want to use your new product, but it's just too expensive." Your client's feedback gives you the necessary information you need to work through their uneasiness. You could offer a discount or some other incentive to move things forward. This is a perfect opportunity to use a *what if* question such as "What if I could lower the costs further?"

These questions can also unearth deep-rooted frustrations that have yet to surface. In the story about my Eloqua client from Texas who ended up churning from chapter 1, I should have assessed her motivation. These questions would have revealed that she had neither the motivation nor the confidence to renew with us. If I had followed up with a "What would it take to move it to a higher number?" question, I could have uncovered my client's trepidation about the complexity of our product. We could've then tried to build a success plan to address her needs. At the very least, I would have received frank product feedback that I could have passed on to our product team.

Assessing your client's motivation using these scaling questions can also break down the invisible wall your clients have erected. This shows how a little empathy and structure can turn hesitation into action. For instance, I've encountered a case where a client was enthusiastic about the plan we discussed but ultimately didn't follow through. We had come to an agreement that they would enroll in a workshop we offered, but they never attended one and continued to escalate issues to our support team instead of improving their product knowledge.

I decided to test my client's motivation by asking the two scaling questions. I uncovered that while she was motivated to act, her confidence score was low. She confided in me that she was overwhelmed by our product and wasn't convinced it would deliver value. I told her I would join her in the workshop to ensure that we took small steps and addressed any questions she had. This was enough for her to sign up and join the next workshop. Her support questions began to decrease as she began to gain more confidence in the potential of our product.

Don't expect an instant client turnaround. It may take several meetings and messages to convince your client to take action. Keep using these techniques and the other suggestions in this book to nudge your clients forward. Celebrate the small signs of progress and keep pushing for more when needed.

Mastering strategic conversations

You've now learned the basics of how to have more productive strategic conversations with your customers. It's now in your court to practice these concepts by doing the recommended exercises and trying them out with your clients. It's perfectly normal to feel uneasy the first few times you try these techniques, but practice is necessary to master them.

Putting this into practice

To become comfortable with the SOON funnel and assessing your customer's motivation, practice these techniques with a colleague. Go to strategic-customersuccess.com and access the "Practicing the SOON Funnel & Assessing Motivation Exercise."

Summary and key takeaways

Defusing a situation or capturing information alone usually isn't sufficient for a successful strategic conversation. The SOON funnel, a framework for strategic conversations that encourages clients to self-discover possible solutions while nudging them toward action, assists in driving your clients to action where they feel that they are the ones controlling the conversation. It has four components:

- Success
- Obstacles
- Options
- Next steps

To increase the chances that your clients will follow your recommendations, do the following:

- Leverage social proof.
- Use storytelling.
- Provide a few options.

If you detect any hesitancy from your clients or feel they are going through the motions as you work through the SOON funnel, use the two scaling questions to assess their motivation.

CHAPTER 17

Mastering Discovery and Defining Business Outcomes

A few years back, one of my clients whom I knew quite well was suddenly ghosting us. We were attempting to meet to discuss their renewal, but we just got crickets in return. As their contract was worth several hundred thousand dollars and the renewal date kept creeping closer, this was a massive concern. The CSM escalated the issue to me because of my relationship with the decision-maker, whom we'll call Brian. My CSM and I were both perplexed by Brian's silent treatment. Little did I know that there was trouble ahead.

After I sent Brian a few messages and didn't hear anything, I knew something was up. I sent him a short text: "I know a lot is going on. Can we chat for fifteen minutes?" I finally heard from him. He apologized for being MIA, and we set up a time to chat. The meeting was very awkward. Brian's discomfort showed, though he pretended the renewal was on track. I could tell that whatever was bothering him, he didn't want to talk about it right now.

I tried to get him to open up one last time using one of Bob London's discovery questions. Bob is the CEO of Chief Listening Officers and an expert in sales and CS discovery techniques. I asked, "Is there anything you hoped I would ask, but didn't? Or relieved that I didn't ask?" He said that there wasn't, and I decided to end the call, as we were just wasting each other's time at that point.

The next day, a new email from Brian appeared in my inbox. It was a long one. As I scanned it, my temperature jumped fifty degrees. He said, "Look, your last question was a good one. I'm hearing a lot of chatter about your company falling behind your competitors, and my executive team is questioning if we should still back you." I was floored and blindsided by his claims. I sent him a quick response challenging his points and asked him to meet again. I could see he felt relieved to get this out in the open, and he agreed to meet.

I went through each of his concerns when we caught up and then I arranged for our CEO to meet with his executive team so we could ensure both of our companies were aligned. I asked if there were any other obstacles I should be aware of as part of the renewal, and he assured me that this plan would put us on the right path. We eventually secured a multi-year renewal.

I realized that the "Is there anything you hoped . . ." question most likely prevented the customer from churning. Rather than just accepting the status quo and throwing in the towel, I confronted Brian and challenged him. That conversation reminded me how vital it is to ask the right questions at the right time—something Bob London's framework is built around.

Leading general customer discovery conversations

There is a misconception that only the sales team needs to conduct discovery conversations—that simply isn't true. Discovery isn't just for sales—it's a continuous process used throughout the customer lifecycle. It's about obtaining information from your customers so you can ultimately help them achieve their business outcomes. These strategic discussions reveal crucial insights about your customer's world, from their business objectives to their view of your partnership.

The problem is that many customers are tired of the usual discovery approach that they're subjected to. Run-of-the-mill questions like "What are your goals?" or "What keeps you up at night?" are well past their expiration date. They are boring and can cause your clients to tune out or provide surface-level answers that lack any substance. In many cases, your customers aren't being open and honest but rather humoring you with what you want to hear so they can get to their pressing tasks. You have to cut through this.

To elevate your discovery conversations and gain valuable customer insights, I recommend utilizing Bob London's discovery framework. London has created a series of discovery questions that he calls *disruptive questions*,[79] one of which I used at the beginning of this chapter. His questions are perfectly calibrated to get your client's mental wheels spinning. They are thought-provoking and guaranteed to get your client's attention. His techniques are based on thousands of customer conversations he's had over his career.

When conducting a discovery conversation, London recommends asking questions about the client's company before diving into questions about your product. After grasping their broader organizational priorities, he recommends drilling down into individual stakeholders' drivers and motivations. With these perspectives captured, the discussion can turn to exploring their experience with your offerings.

Focusing on their business first demonstrates you're interested in their success, not just your bottom line. This is how you win over their hearts and minds, build trust with them, and get to the real issues. It also helps you get a sense of their current situation and the quest they are on (see chapter 14 on visualizing your customer as a hero).

By zooming out to see the bigger picture, you can view your customer's challenges from a new vantage point. It's why the order in which you ask your questions and the substance of the questions themselves are so im-

---

79 London, "More Strategic Customer Conversations."

portant. As London says, when executed correctly, "The questions are the answer," as they have the power to reveal what's truly on your customer's mind.[80]

In addition, London's approach is especially appealing to senior customer stakeholders who would rather spend time on high-level discussions than waste it on product bugs or tactical issues. These questions can be very helpful at key points in the customer journey, such as the kickoff, the CSM handoff from onboarding, customer stakeholder changes, QBRs, or renewal meetings to ensure that your client's priorities are aligned with your product and your focus.

Let's look at how London's thought-provoking questions are structured to align with the customer's mindset and stage in their journey: exploring your client's organization, addressing client stakeholder priorities and challenges, and focusing on your company and products. As you read through these, consider which questions may be suitable for your upcoming client meetings.

Questions about your client's organization

These big-picture questions help you uncover what's most important to your customer's organization:

- "At the highest levels of your company, what is the top priority for the next six to twelve months?" London suggests following that question with: "What are the challenges and goals driving that priority?"
- "If I were a fly on the wall at your board meeting, what is the biggest challenge or priority I'd hear them discussing?" This is my favorite Bob London question because every executive can picture them-

---

80 Bob London, LinkedIn, (n/d), https://www.linkedin.com/posts/boblondon_the-questions-are-the-answer-in-customer-activity-7084881585803538432-6z2D/.

selves sitting with their board and weighing in on a heated debate. Even if you're not meeting with a senior leader, you can ask what they think would be discussed at the highest levels in their organization. You'll be surprised at what you learn.

- "What is the highest risk that might keep your company from succeeding?" This question can uncover expansion opportunities or provide advance warning that your renewal is at risk. For example, if your client is struggling to secure its next round of funding, that could affect their budget and how much they can spend on your product.

Questions about your client stakeholders

These questions are designed to give you insight into what matters most to your client stakeholders, the quest they are on, and how their role contributes to achieving their company's overarching goals. They should build on the questions from the previous section.

- "Out of your entire job description, what's the one thing your company is counting on you to accomplish in the first half of this year?" Even if they forget their job description, they'll know their primary focus.

- "What's on your whiteboard that absolutely needs to be off of it in the next thirty days?" This is my go-to question, as it effectively determines my client's number one priority. Their answer may surprise you, as their focus could be well outside your product. Look for ways your product can address their needs, which you can share later in the conversation.

- "What's the one thing that you and your team need to get better at this year?" This question can unearth additional challenges that you weren't even aware of. They may even mention how knowledgeable they need to be about your product, which is a perfect transition to the next category of questions.

Questions about your company and product

These questions will help you learn more about how your customer perceives your company and your products.

- "What's the biggest thing that has surprised you since you signed the contract with us?" This is what London refers to as a delta question. You are trying to determine how your customer's perception of you has changed over time. This question should only be used within the first twelve months of your customer relationship.

- "If I gave you a magic wand, what problem would you make disappear first?" This question is a favorite because it can open up the floodgates on all the problems your customers are experiencing. You can set boundaries for this question by qualifying where their wand can operate. For instance, if you just wanted to focus on their onboarding, phrase the question this way: "If I gave you a magic wand to improve your onboarding experience, what problem would you address first?"

- "Is there something we're great at? Better than anyone else?" This will help you understand how your clients compare you against your competitors. It's better than simply asking, "What do you love most about our product?" You'll usually receive a few positive stories about your product features that you never would have known about. I always share these with our product team. Be sure to ask follow-up questions when they mention your product's shortcomings.

- "If a competitor reached out to you today, would you ignore them or engage? On a scale of one to five, with one being you'd ignore them and five being you'd reply, how interested would you be in what they had to say?" I love this question as it can help gauge how your client perceives you. Observe your client's body language closely once you ask this question: Do they hesitate, look uncomfortable, and so on? I've found that I've had to ask this question in a few different ways to get my clients to open up. They may be sheepish or embarrassed, as they feel they are going behind your back. If they deny speaking to your competitors, say something like: "So you're saying your boss never asked you to check out our competitors?" When discussing competitors with your clients, dig a bit more than you normally would. You'll usually find some buried treasure.

- "What would make you a customer for life?" This is London's go-to question. It's usually asked toward the end of the conversation and can reveal some key details you weren't aware of.

- I have found this question from London remarkably effective to close a discovery conversation: "Is there anything you hoped I would ask, but didn't? Or relieved that I didn't ask?" This is the same question I used in the story at the beginning of this chapter. It's powerful because it allows your client to get something off their chest that they may not have been able to previously.

One note of caution: Don't keep asking the same questions, or you'll find that they lose their punch, resulting in generic and substandard responses. Just as knives need to be sharpened, your questions will lose their edge if you don't maintain them. Experiment by preparing variations of the disruptive questions geared to the specific meeting attendees. Spice things up! Picture yourself as a *question barista*, a term coined by author and sales expert

David Priemer.[81] Your handcrafted questions should pique your customer's interest because they are tailored to the purpose of the meeting and to the individual meeting attendees. When you hear your clients say, "That's an interesting question," you know you're on the right track.

Having trouble coming up with new questions? Leverage the various AI tools available to help generate questions for you and ignite your creativity. For example, feed in your client notes, previous call transcripts and some sample questions and ask your AI tool to do the work for you. You can then adjust them as you see fit. This simplifies the process and speeds up your meeting prep time. To create a question bank that everyone can leverage, share with your teammates the questions that have hit the hardest.

Leveraging discovery techniques in your client meetings

Engage in discovery throughout the customer journey to gain a deeper understanding of your customer's challenges and opportunities. Some of these conversations are planned agenda items that are part of formal QBRs and regular cadence meetings, but most are impromptu discussions that you can initiate. You need to be prepared for both scenarios, so let's take a closer look at them.

Proactively performing discovery during planned client meetings

Strategic meetings (kickoff calls, QBRs, and regular cadence calls) can feel mundane and boring, but with a bit of curiosity and some disruptive questions, you can punch things up. Furthermore, properly managed discovery sessions can deepen your customer relationships.

At Kustomer, CSMs were trained to ask one disruptive question per cadence call to uncover a new client insight each time. Asking these thought-provoking questions transformed the meeting from one that merely

---

81 "How to Do Better Discovery by Becoming a 'Question Barista'," posted May 5, 2022, by Cerebral Selling, YouTube https://www.youtube.com/watch?v=x-K7d-Avy-M.

focused on tactical issues, such as bug fixes and feature requests, to one that focused on items that truly impacted our client's business. This is how we changed our customers' perception of us so they saw us as strategic advisors.

To elevate your customer cadence meetings, let your clients know ahead of time that you'll be posing some open-ended questions. You should also add this to the agenda, so you reserve time for it. Next, prepare one or two disruptive questions to use. They can be from any of the three categories (exploring your client's organization, addressing client stakeholder priorities and challenges, and focusing on your company and products). Many of my CSMs gravitated toward the competitor scale question, the magic wand question, and the customer for life question. Try out different approaches to see what works for you, and as I mentioned, experiment by crafting your own questions to keep things interesting.

When asking a disruptive question:

- Let the client know you want to uplevel the conversation by saying something such as: "Now that we've covered the other items on our agenda, I would like to take a step back and ask an open-ended question. Is that OK?" or "I would like to shift gears and ask you some open-ended questions if that's OK." This gets them in the right frame of mind.

- Next, ask your discovery question.

- After the question is asked, stay silent and let the client respond. There may be an awkward silence, but that's OK. Resist the urge to say anything until they respond.

- Once your client responds, use reflections as needed and ask any necessary follow-up questions. Always focus the discussion on them and their needs.

- Based on what you've uncovered, you may need to work toward a solution and an action plan. You can leverage the SOON funnel (success, obstacles, options, next steps).

- Once the meeting is over, reflect on what you've learned about the client. If your calls are recorded, listen to them and assess your performance. For more guidance, review the exercise in the *Putting this into practice* section at the end of the chapter.

The art of agile discovery: Seizing any moment opportunities

While planned discovery is valuable, many of the richest insights emerge when you stay alert to real-time opportunities during client conversations. CS influencer and coach Carly Agar says that you need to be flexible as discovery can happen "at any moment." This is what I call *agile discovery*. Agar outlines certain phrases to listen for. Here are a few examples:

- "I'm trying to . . ."
- "It's important that we do . . . this year."
- "Can you help me with . . ."
- "I need your product to do . . ."
- "I'm not sure about . . ."
- "How are other clients . . ."[82]

If you hear your clients use these statements, your spidey sense should be tingling, telling you that you need to lean into what your clients are inquiring about. Avoid jumping straight into solution mode—unless the client is making a very straightforward request.

---

82 Carly Agar, "There's a huge problem with the way we teach CSMs to do discovery," LinkedIn, May 30, 2023, https://www.linkedin.com/posts/carly-agar_customersuccess-activity-7069281553566060544-9Uv8/.

Start by clarifying their statement or request so you understand the important details. You can use a reflection combined with an open question. As an example, you could say, "You mentioned that you need help with reporting. What are the specific areas of reporting you are struggling with?" After collecting more details on their specific request, it's important to step back and explore the underlying business issue or priority driving it. Seek to obtain the necessary context to deliver the best advice or guide them in the right direction.

Engage your clients by asking, "Would it be all right if we took a step back so I can gain a clearer understanding of your request?" Next, ask them questions about their company's focus and priorities, and relate them to their requests. This will allow you to assess the importance of the request, how it fits into their overall objectives, and how critical it is to achieve their business outcomes.

I've seen many CSMs fumble through these critical *moments of truth* because they don't dig deep enough to learn about their client's underlying needs. I define moments of truth as the critical moments between you and your customers when your next actions will either make or break their trust. To determine whether you may be in such a situation, ask yourself: "What is behind the question they just asked or the action they just performed?" If you're not sure, you can leverage a scaling question such as "From one to ten, how important is this issue to your decision to renew with us?" and then ask follow-up questions to understand the reason behind that score.

You now have all the tools you need to lead general discovery conversations. Let's focus on how to uncover your customer's business outcomes so you can take a more proactive approach to your client's success.

Expert tip: Include known details in your questions to build trust

When leveraging disruptive questions, you can improve their effectiveness by inserting known facts about your customers into them. Before customer meetings, I'll review any relevant information on my clients, such as their business outcomes or recent news stories (as covered in chapter 2). I'll then blend them into my prepared questions.

For instance, instead of saying, "What is the most important item you need to get off your whiteboard in the next ninety days?" I'd say, "The last time we met, you were focused on building more automations. What other pressing items do you need to get off your whiteboard in the next ninety days?"

Blending relevant information into your questions demonstrates to your clients that you came prepared, you're focused on their business, and that you don't want to waste time. This technique can be very effective when you're meeting your client for the first time, as it can quickly build trust. You're signaling to your clients that they don't need to repeat themselves because you've done your homework. This immediately elevates their confidence in your ability to assist them.

David Perell, founder and CEO of Write of Passage, suggests having several tailored questions ready to better understand specific aspects of your client's business. For example, if the client happened to run an excellent marketing campaign that had well above average results, ask them for additional details: "That was an amazing campaign. What did you do differently this time that led to such outstanding results?"[83]

These types of questions peel back the layers of your client's expertise, revealing nuanced perspectives that were previously invisible.

---

83 Ryan Hawk, host, *The Learning Leader Show with Ryan Hawk*, "Watch This to Level Up Your Communication Skills—David Perell," posted April 21, 2024, by Ryan Hawk, YouTube, https://www.youtube.com/watch?v=6qgd3pkIQuo.

It's more than just information gathering—it's about building trust, showing you genuinely care, and creating connections that resonate on a deeper level. As author Dale Carnegie wrote in *How to Win Friends and Influence People*, "To be interesting, be interested."[84]

Leading business outcome discovery conversations

Capturing your customer's business outcomes is a specific type of discovery conversation that you need to master, as it's a foundational component of your role. Your objective is to clearly define what your clients are trying to achieve with your product, so the renewal becomes a nonevent. Healthy product usage won't guarantee the renewal—only a clear understanding of business outcomes and progress does. It's also what being a strategic CSM is all about.

As a reminder, business outcomes are the high-level objectives that indicate whether your customers have achieved value from your product. Examples of business outcomes include improving efficiency, increasing revenue, and improving employee satisfaction. These are problems your clients are trying to solve, and often why they bought from you in the first place. To ensure success, you need to pair their business outcomes with measurable results and actionable goals that guide their efforts.

Keep these two critical factors in mind as you navigate business outcomes. First, if you work with multiple stakeholders for the same client, be sure to capture their individual business outcomes. Don't assume that everyone shares the same expectations for your product, especially if you're working with many stakeholders and teams. They each most likely have their own needs that you need to define and align with so you can ensure you are providing the right type of assistance.

---

84 Dale Carnegie, *How to Win Friends and Influence People,* (London: Vermilion, 2006), 89.

The second and more important point is to remember that your customers' business outcomes will shift over time. Factors such as organizational changes, business model adaptations, market dynamics, economic conditions, strategic directions, and stakeholder turnover can all contribute to this. For example, as your customers start deepening their understanding of your product, they uncover new possibilities they weren't aware of. You have to adjust accordingly to ensure that your product is configured to meet their current needs.

To get ahead of these changes, look for indicators that suggest a shift in their position. This could mean changes in their product usage patterns—leveraging new features, a decrease or increase in logins, or higher or lower consumption rates. Moreover, look for changes in their business, such as a new stakeholder, a change in their product offering, or a new company focus. Their current outcomes, success metrics, or underlying goals may need to be revised. Be vigilant and never assume that your customer's circumstances will stay the same. They never do.

The necessity of including senior decision-makers in business outcome conversations

Business outcome conversations usually take place during kickoff meetings, QBRs, renewal meetings, and ad hoc settings. When conducting these discussions, it's recommended that you inform your customers in advance about the topics you'll be covering. You should also provide a few questions for them ahead of time, so they're primed for the discussion. The more notice you give, the greater the likelihood of securing the attendance of senior customer stakeholders.

Are your day-to-day customer contacts helpful in these discussions? It can vary, but I've found that many of your primary contacts are only somewhat informed about their company's key business objectives. They are generally more concerned about how your product will make their lives easier than they are about their own company's high-level objectives.

You may also find that your primary contacts aren't fully aligned with what their senior leaders are trying to achieve. They are often thrown into onboarding meetings with little advance warning or saddled with owning your products on top of their existing responsibilities. Even though you'll improve their lives in the long term, they may resent having to work with you. This can even lead to some of your day-to-day contacts dragging their feet on critical onboarding tasks. For these reasons, it's best to involve your client's senior stakeholders in the business outcome conversations. This will ensure that you and your client are on the same page and that the meeting is productive.

Expert tip: Fostering a strong relationship with the decision-maker

Back in chapter 2, I stressed the need to identify the decision-makers within your customer portfolio because tracking your relationship and interactions with these key stakeholders is critical. But how should you engage with them?

You may be thinking, *I don't need to build a relationship with the decision-maker—that's what sales does*, or *that's what my boss will do*. Think you're in the clear? If the client suddenly churns, everyone will be looking at you and asking why no one saw it coming. It's your job to ensure that there is a strong connection with the decision-maker and that they recognize the value your product provides. You may work alongside other team members, such as your executive team, when engaging senior client stakeholders, but you own the responsibility of keeping these client contacts actively involved and seeing clear returns.

You need to get over any fears you may have when communicating with executives. Like you, they're simply humans doing their best to manage their responsibilities and achieve positive results. While it may be intimidating, you can foster closer relationships with them, which will elevate yourself in their eyes and increase your chances of being successful in your role. Here are my recommended tips to build a strong connection with decision-makers:

- **Keep it short:** Precision and clarity in communication are paramount when engaging with decision-makers and executive stakeholders. Keep your communications brief and to the point. Use bullet points and include relevant data and facts to support your statements. This makes it easy for them to decipher what you're asking of them or any information you are passing on. If you don't, they'll ignore it.

- **Begin your emails with a bolded summary of your request or the key point you want to express:** This clarity eliminates any guesswork on their part about your intentions or requests. Reread your emails and remove any fluff so the major points pop. You can also leverage AI tools to assist you. Take those few extra minutes to review your messages before sending them—it will make all the difference.

- **Send them bite-sized updates:** Regularly brief key client stakeholders on achieved milestones, meaningful progress toward business goals, and updates from past conversations. Since they're probably not closely monitoring your product's performance, providing your client decision-makers with concise, focused insights can help fill in the gaps in their knowledge. Moreover, don't just cc them when you send out your meeting recaps—tailor your summaries for the specific decision-maker.

- **Focus on what they value:** Executive stakeholders care most about their defined measures of success. When sharing progress, translate your insights into terms that reflect their KPIs. Focus your communication on their business results, since that's what truly matters to them. In addition, don't just present a metric in isolation—show how it's trending over time, so they have context about whether things are getting better or worse. Share critical updates and decisions that align with their priorities and interests.

- **If you don't know what they value, ask them or your primary contact:** Julie Persofsky, a go-to-market strategist and former colleague, advises you to include this simple question in your communication: "Is this in alignment with your goals?"[85]

- **Benchmarks can spark interest:** Your client executives like comparing themselves to their peers, so help them out! Offer them benchmark data showing where they stand relative to peers in your customer base. Grab their interest by highlighting a few quick wins that the data suggests they're perfectly positioned for. In addition, round out your benchmark data with data from trusted industry reports that add valuable context.

- **Don't expect a response:** You could send the most perfectly manicured executive update with the most insightful benchmark data or the most unbelievable value metric and still be ignored. Don't sweat it if you don't receive a response from your decision-makers. Always send a follow-up message. If you keep consistently sending items of value, they will start to listen, and may even engage with you.

- **Multithread:** Leverage your company executives to connect with your client's executives. This type of multithreaded relationship is something I mentioned in chapter 9 as a way to give your customers more access to people in your company.

- **Be a master connector:** Connect your client decision-makers with other client decision-makers. Look for opportunities to do this at industry events or when you know your decision-maker needs outside advice.

---

85 Julie Persofsky, "When your CSM team is getting stuck with the power user/champion and has lost access to the Decision Maker," LinkedIn, 2024, https://www.linkedin.com/feed/update/urn:li:activity:7069346142290907136/.

Leveraging these techniques is especially important when a new decision-maker is involved. Time is critical as they're likely reviewing all their vendors. You need to quickly prove your worth and earn their confidence. Share a highlight reel of their accomplishments and the value they've achieved and request a meeting.

There will be times when you find that none of these engagement techniques work. There could be many reasons for this. Most of the time, it's due to how your client perceives you. If you've been pigeonholed as the responsive helper, you'll need to intentionally shift their view to seeing you as a strategic consultant.

Tap into your leadership team's connections with key stakeholders to help reposition yourself. You need to do a hard reset to reframe expectations so you can step into a strategic CSM position. Draw from the methods discussed throughout this book, with special attention to the QBR framework detailed in chapter 19, as a way of starting this transformation.

What's important is to take a moment to consider the relationship you wish to build with your senior client stakeholders compared to the one you currently maintain. Ask yourself, what is holding me back from being a strategic CSM? It could be that you need more product training or that you need to refine the skills mentioned in this book. It's not your title—if you're providing value, senior stakeholders won't care about that. In certain cases, if the chemistry isn't right or you've damaged your reputation, transitioning off the account may be necessary. If you find yourself in this situation, seek out advice from your manager.

When initiating a business outcome discussion, restate the meeting purpose to ensure everyone is aligned. The objective is to understand their business outcomes, success criteria, and the steps needed to achieve this (the goals). Ensure the result is a joint success plan for tracking progress and mutual accountability.

Start at the highest level: Business outcomes

This is it. You've started one of the most important conversations with your client: defining their business outcomes. While it can feel intimidating, think of yourself as a private investigator, learning about their business to best help them achieve their goals.

Use these proven questions from Bob London to uncover your client's business outcomes:

- "At the highest levels of your company, what is the top priority for the next six to twelve months?"
- "If I were a fly on the wall at your board meeting, what is the biggest challenge or priority I'd hear them discussing?"
- "Out of your entire job description, what's the one thing your company is counting on you to accomplish in the next six months?"
- "What's on your whiteboard that absolutely needs to be off in the next ninety days?"
- "If I gave you a magic wand, what problem would you make disappear first?"
- "If you fast forward a year from now and tell me you're really happy working with us, how would things be different for you than they are now?"

After these high-level questions, ask clarifying questions to identify the most important outcomes, such as, "Why is this your top priority?" or "What makes this important for you now?" Make sure you have a full understanding of their outcomes so you can move on to the next stage, which is defining the metrics they'll use to ensure they achieve these outcomes.

Defining success criteria: The key to measuring business outcomes

With a clear understanding of your customer's business outcomes, the next step is to define success criteria. These are the specific metrics that will tell you—and your client—whether or not the desired outcomes have been achieved and are what decision-makers care about.

At Kustomer, we aimed to improve efficiency while maintaining high customer satisfaction. One success metric was reducing the average handle time by 10% for the quarter. In addition, another success criterion included tracking the client's onboarding of Kustomer, which was defined as turning Kustomer live for their team by an agreed-upon date.

Use these questions to uncover their success metrics:

- "What is the most important metric you are currently focused on?" This should be followed by: "How often do you measure this? Monthly? Quarterly?"
- You may need to reframe the question so it pertains directly to your product. For example, you could ask, "If it was a year from now, what metric would you use to determine your success with our product?" This closely aligns with the "S" in the SOON funnel described in chapter 16.
- "What's your actual [insert the metric here] today?" Follow up with: "Has this gone up or down in the past X weeks/months?" and "What is your target for this metric, and by what date do you need to hit that target?"
- "If you were to get promoted in twelve months, what would be the metric that drives that?"

It's fine to ask about business outcomes and success criteria simultaneously. What matters most is identifying a success metric that quantifies your product impact and is measurable within a specific timeframe.

Some customers may hesitate during this activity due to privacy concerns or lack of clarity on their metrics. This is your moment to nudge clients outside their comfort zone. One method is leveraging the social proof concept mentioned previously. For instance, you can say, "Our other similar customers have used [add in your success metric]. Does that resonate with you?" Even if your customer disagrees with that metric, that may be the trigger to move the discussion forward. Use the OARS framework to leverage active listening techniques and be empathetic while challenging your customer to achievable criteria.

Be mindful of clients suggesting unattainable outcomes. Address unrealistic expectations directly, saying, "Based on our experience with similar clients, your targets may be unrealistic. I recommend that you aim for X." Use the skills from chapter 9 to be direct while showing care. These can be uncomfortable conversations, but it's necessary to ensure that you are creating a foundation for success for your customers, your company, and yourself.

Specifying the goals needed to achieve the business outcomes

To complete the business outcome discussion, define the goals that will impact your customer's success metrics. A business outcome playbook (described later) will offer recommendations and real customer examples. But remember, before pitching your ideas, seek your customer's input using the SOON funnel to achieve the best results.

Begin by asking your customer for their input on potential approaches to achieve the agreed-upon success metrics. You can ask them questions such as:

- "What are some possible options to achieve this metric?" This closely aligns with the second O in the SOON funnel.
- "How can we help you achieve your objectives?"

After you've given your customer a chance to have their say, you can then chime in with your ideas. As mentioned previously, if you sense any hesitancy or that your client wants to pause, you need to switch from discovery mode to solution mode and suggest a path forward.

Convert your discussion points into concrete, measurable objectives using SMART criteria (outlined in chapter 13) to drive customer follow-through. Each goal should be specific, measurable, achievable, relevant to the business outcome, and time-bound so it's clear when it needs to be completed. "Implement automated routing by the end of Q1" is an example of a well-defined goal.

When framing the goals, ensure that the timeframe aligns with the success metrics timeline. For example, if the goal is to complete training to optimize product use, ensure the training is completed in time to achieve the expected business outcome.

When creating goals, start with the end date and work your way backward. Ask your client, "When do you need to achieve this?" Then, based on this completion date, you can put together a plan. Now that you have defined the success metrics and goals of your business outcomes, you need to document them.

From discussion to action: Building a joint customer success plan

Your customer's business outcomes need to be documented in a jointly created success plan to ensure they are acted on and to monitor the progress. Think of a success plan as your customer's roadmap that connects their business outcomes to your product's capabilities.

Your success plan should be simple. It should include the high-level business outcomes, the success criteria, and the associated goals. Success plans should also include tasks and milestones that indicate whether the goals have been accomplished. As mentioned in chapter 13 on running successful meetings, it's important to assign a single owner to each task and specify the due date. See Figure 11 for an example of a success plan.

Success Plan

Maple Leaf Software

Create Date	2/28/2026
Last Updated	3/1/2026

Business Outcome Summary

#	Outcomes	Success Criteria (Target)	Priority	Status	Notes on progress
1	Improve efficiency	10% of volume handled by AI agent by end of Q2	Medium	On Track	AI agent volume is at 7%
		Improve first response time by 10% by end of Q2	High	Derailed	First response time has only improved by 2%
2					

Success Plan

#	Goal	Success Criteria	Tasks	Task Owner	Due Date	Status
1	Launch two new agent automations	10% of volume handled by AI agents by end of Q2	Build automation #1	Suhaila Anneke	March 4, 2026	Completed
			Build automation #2	Suhaila Anneke	April 8, 2026	Completed
			Track results	Cory Veda	June 14, 2026	In Progress
2	Optimize automated routing to route by skill	Improve first response time by 10% by end of Q2	Document out the skills to be included	Julia Stáňa	January 16, 2026	Blocked
			Configure routing tool	Julia Stáňa	February 13, 2026	Not Started
			Track results	Cory Veda	February 27, 2026	Not Started

Additional Notes

Julia Stáňa has left the company so we need to wait until her replacement has been named

Figure 11. An example of a success plan.

Build your success plan in whatever tool works best, ensuring it's easily accessible for both you and your customer to review regularly. Remember, this joint plan should be owned by your customer because it's their success plan. As CS influencer and HubSpot CS leader Daphne Costa Lopes says, "You will not get any traction if you create the plan by yourself and try to push it into your customer."[86]

Additionally, a success plan is a living document that should be reviewed and updated regularly. When meeting with customers, ask, "What's changed since we last reviewed your success plan?" to monitor progress and ensure priorities are aligned. The success plan shouldn't be something you build that no one ever looks at again. If that's happening today, you need to reexamine how these plans are used and your overall success metrics. Something is broken.

The success plan doesn't replace an onboarding plan, which is a more comprehensive project plan (though the terms are used interchangeably).

86 Daphne Costa Lopes, "CSMs, here is how you set a Success Plan that works," LinkedIn, May 4, 2023, https://www.linkedin.com/posts/daphnecostalopes_customersuccessmanagement-csm-cs-activity-7059844113872900097-xuU9.

The success plan has a sole purpose: to ensure that your customer is on track to achieve value with your product. Keeping it on point will make this process easier and allow you to easily share it with the right client stakeholders to demonstrate progress.

Can you create and maintain success plans for all your clients? It will depend on the number of clients you manage. If you are managing fifty clients or less, aim to have business outcome discussions and a joint success plan for the majority of your clients. Prioritize clients based on their segment and upcoming renewals. In the future, AI-infused tools should make it easier for customers to create their own success plans or have them automatically generated. Look for ways to optimize this critical process to sell the value of your products.

Creating a business outcome playbook.

While success plans guide individual customer progress, a business outcome playbook serves as a tool to standardize your approach across multiple clients. So take the initiative to craft one with your team. Use this as your compass for directing meaningful business outcome dialogues with your clients. While you can build this on your own, it's more efficient and effective to involve your colleagues, as then it will contain more examples and you'll get it done faster. This should also be something that sales and CS collaborate on so there is a unified definition of your customers' business outcomes.

Here are the steps to build a business outcome playbook:

1. List out the business outcomes your products help your customers accomplish. Start by compiling a list of common business outcomes your products help achieve, based on customer conversations, and add them to your playbook. It's usually two to three business outcomes at most, such as saving time, driving revenue, or increasing employee retention. It should be obvious what these are, but if

you're struggling with this exercise, consult veterans from your sales and marketing teams.

If your product supports multiple industries and business functions, you should divide your playbook into categories and list the business outcomes that apply to each section.

2. Define common success criteria used to determine whether the business outcome has been achieved. As discussed, there can be several success criteria for each business outcome. It all depends on your clients' objectives. Create a list of possible success criteria for each business outcome and add this to your business outcome playbook.

3. Document the tactics or *plays* to help your clients achieve these business outcomes. Capture examples of the possible plays you can recommend to your clients to help them achieve their business outcomes. This will enable your client to accomplish the metrics you defined in the success criteria.

Listing out the plays in a playbook standardizes the recommendations and provides a more consistent customer experience. It also encourages a culture of sharing so you and your teammates can learn from each other. Each play should have different customer examples and results. You can leverage these customer stories as social proof when you're trying to influence your customers to take action.

So, what does this playbook look like? The following example shows how you might arrange the different elements of your playbook. Start with the high-level business outcome, add the supporting success criteria, and then add possible plays. This can be further broken down by customer segment, industry, and business process.

Examples of a business outcome playbook:

Business outcome #1: Increase revenue

Success criteria

- Increase revenue by 10 percent by the end of the second quarter.
- Improve conversion rates by 15 percent by the end of the second quarter.
- Fully onboarded in the Asia Pacific region by the end of the first quarter.

Plays

- Launch new checkout feature.
- Optimize current campaigns.
- Integrate data source A.
- Build custom reports A, B, and C.
- Take training courses X, Y, and Z.

Business outcome #2: Improve efficiency

Success criteria

- Decrease in average handle time by 10 percent in the second quarter.
- Launch pilot test of chatbot product in the first quarter.

Plays

- Implement automated routing.
- Optimize current automations.

- Build custom reports A, B, and C.
- Take training courses X, Y, and Z.

Putting this into practice

Practice the techniques covered in this chapter so you're more comfortable using them with clients by doing the following:

- Review the examples of discovery questions provided in this chapter. Choose just one question to ask at your next customer meeting.
- Go to strategiccustomersuccess.com and complete the "The Strategic CSM Discovery Exercise" to help you practice using various types of discovery questions.
- Optional: Download the "Success Plan" template from strategiccustomersuccess.com.
- Optional: Go to strategiccustomersuccess.com and download the "Business Outcome Playbook" template to create a simple first draft of your own playbook.

Summary and key takeaways

Leading customer discovery conversations and capturing business outcomes are two essential parts of becoming a strategic CSM.

- Customer discovery is an ongoing process beyond the presales stage. It's about understanding customer priorities, challenges, and perceptions to ultimately assist them in achieving their business outcomes.
- Disruptive questions, inspired by Bob London's framework, can transform discovery conversations. These thought-provoking

questions spark meaningful discussions, focusing on the client's business, priorities, and challenges rather than just your product.

- Agile discovery involves being flexible and attentive to clients' requests or statements such as "I'm trying to . . ." or "Can you help me with . . ." that hint at underlying challenges.

- Mastering the art of capturing your customer's business outcomes is crucial for driving value through your products.

- Define your client's business outcomes, set measurable success criteria, and specify goals using the SMART framework.

- Transform discussions into action by creating joint success plans that connect business outcomes with product capabilities. These plans serve as a roadmap for achieving customer objectives. Keep them simple, assign ownership, and use them as a living document to monitor progress and adapt to changes.

- Develop a business outcome playbook. List the business outcomes your product supports, define success criteria, and document tactics to achieve them.

CHAPTER 18

Handling Feature Requests and Rebuilding Trust with Upset Clients

"This leaves us vulnerable to litigation. Do you understand the position you've put us in?" My client's frustration radiated through my laptop speaker. Our company had messed up royally: emails sent via our platform lacked an unsubscribe link, violating anti-spam laws. My client was worried about a lawsuit. Even worse, the client reported the error to us rather than the other way around. They were understandably very upset. I felt like someone was banging on my head with a hammer while all my vital organs were shutting down.

After regaining my composure, I worked with my team to gather the details of what had happened. It turned out that we had inadvertently removed the unsubscribe links from their emails as part of a product upgrade. As this type of change was unusual, we skipped the routine checks we normally performed. The client was not going to be happy with this news.

Resisting the urge to take a vacation, I scheduled a call the next day with the client. I prepped as best as I could and braced myself to take some heat. I laid out the complete sequence of events, holding nothing back about where we had fallen short. I outlined our plan to prevent it from happening again and offered to meet in person. They agreed, and I flew to see them the following week.

As we rolled toward the gate, the weight of my solitude hit me—like a shipwreck survivor headed into shark-infested waters. I was told that the client's in-house counsel and a few of their executives would be attending our meeting. When I sat down and scanned the room, I could feel the death stares. This was going to be a spicy one.

Fortunately, I had a plan of attack. After we calmly completed the meeting intros, I jumped in, "It probably feels like we have no idea what we're doing and that we're complete amateurs. I can only imagine how frustrated you are that a few thousand emails went out without an unsubscribe link. I also know that you're worried that you're legally liable for this error that we made. You most likely want to kick us to the curb, as we know how important the trust you have with your customers is. We flew here today so we could go over with you what happened and how we handled this, and outline what we're doing to prevent this from ever happening again. We also want to discuss how we can make this up to you." And then I just shut up.

The atmosphere shifted—cold, stilted faces softened, and the silence lingered as our client stakeholders released their pent-up anger. At the beginning of the meeting, they were ready to pounce on us. But I didn't give them the chance because I expressed how they were feeling without them having to. They felt heard. They could see that we knew what was at stake for them, and we made it clear that we were all in on resolving these issues and repairing the damage.

I threw out the normal meeting game plan, including the ACE framework (mentioned in chapter 13), and used a technique called the *accusations audit*. Strategic conversations aren't just about discovery or uncovering your client's outcomes. You also need to know how to handle specific situations, such as handling customer feature requests and defusing tense situations like the one I just described.

Strategic conversations involving product feature requests

A core part of your role is capturing customer feedback and sharing it with your product team to help prioritize the most impactful features. Even if customers can submit and vote on features themselves, you should stay attuned to their needs and relay that information.

Your company has limited resources, so they can't build everything your customers desire. I know this is a hard pill to swallow, but it's the reality. We all want to do the best for our clients, but your company needs to stay focused on its overall objectives. They can't entertain every customer request—no matter how good they sound, and no matter how impactful you feel they'll be.

It's tempting to slip into the role of a waiter-style CSM, simply taking orders from your clients. This is particularly true when your clients request specific feature improvements. But you can't take these requests at face value. When customers propose new features, take time to explore the why behind enhancement requests. When you do this, you often uncover valuable context that leads to immediate solutions using existing functionality. More importantly, though, it builds stronger customer trust as you're demonstrating that you care about your customer's needs.

It's best to capture as much information from your clients as you can on your customer's product needs and include that in your submission to your product team. The more details you provide, the better, as it allows your product team to make more informed decisions. You should also let your client know that your job is to ensure that their product enhancements are reviewed, but you can't guarantee which items will be acted on or the timing. You'll do your best to convey their needs, which is why you want to have a strategic discussion with them. By explaining your process upfront, you can align customer expectations with realistic development timeframes.

Uncovering the true intent behind your client's feature requests

So, how do you do client discovery when it comes to feature requests? Here are the recommended questions to ask your clients when you find yourself in this situation:

- **What are you trying to achieve?** Occasionally, customers might suggest product improvements without fully considering their needs or what your product can presently accomplish. For this reason, you must dive deeper into your client's actual use cases. Use the OARS framework and simply start with a reflection such as "What I heard you say is . . ." or "It seems that you are trying to achieve . . . Did I get that right?" This approach validates your client's input while deepening your understanding of their needs. It may turn out that a solution already exists that they weren't aware of or that their need would be better handled by an additional product or app (that may not even be yours). Put the time in to understand what they actually want – not just what they say.

- **How important is this feature to you?** Use scaling questions to uncover how important a feature request is to your customer. You could say, "I'm trying to understand how critical this feature is to your needs. Can you assign a score between one and five, with one being the highest level of importance?" Then ask a follow-up question such as "Why did you rate this a one and not a two?" or "Between this feature and this other feature you requested, which do you feel is a higher priority?" This puts the onus on them to help set the priority. Add these to a spreadsheet so you can track your progress. This exercise will enable you to recognize the key features to advocate for when presenting to your product team or senior management.

- **How disappointed would you be if you didn't have this feature? Why is that the case?** This question can be used in conjunction with the previous question when the client is struggling to prioritize one feature over another. It will also tell you just how serious your client is about their enhancement request. If they state that their business cannot function without a certain feature, it will reveal its importance in their eyes. You can then work with your product team to prioritize it.

As you balance customer requests with your strategic product direction, you'll inevitably be forced to decline some features. Let's explore how to handle these conversations with care.

How to deliver difficult news to customers

We all hate delivering unpleasant news to our customers, but that's part of the job. When your customer deems their requested feature to be crucial to their business, always deliver the news directly rather than sending a message—unless there is no other way possible.

Delivering this over email or other channels lacks authenticity—it's like breaking up with your partner over a text message. Your message could fall flat or be misunderstood.

Avoid delivering bad news alone: Difficult messages can be more effectively conveyed when delivered alongside a product manager or leadership team members. That way, your customers know that this was a company decision, not just one you made. It may even lead to alternative solutions, as your product team may have some additional ideas to assist your client through their predicament.

Show appreciation first: Open the conversation with sincere appreciation for their feedback. Let them know their input is valued even when you can't accommodate their request.

Explain your decision clearly: Once you've set a positive tone, explain your decision to deny or postpone their request and the reasoning behind it. Be direct but compassionate. If an alternative solution exists, respond with, "While we won't be focusing on your request for the short-term, we've found that other clients have successfully addressed similar needs with this approach. [Explain the approach.]" Real-world examples from their peers can help clients embrace alternatives to their initial requests.

Highlight new features: If there is no immediate alternative, say, "We really appreciate your input, but due to other product priorities, we won't be focusing on your requests at this time." Next, emphasize your current product priorities, such as new features that are coming down the pipeline. You can even point out a few recently released features they've benefited from. Focus on what they stand to gain rather than what they feel they'll miss.

Offer future consideration: Finally, unless their requests are unreasonable, let them know that you may still consider this for the future, even if it's not on the immediate roadmap. Hopefully, your customer will become more reasonable at this point. You are pushing back on their demands, but doing so respectfully.

Consider some outside-the-box ideas to soften the blow: Sometimes, offering a client something extra can help smooth over a denied request. Consider offering additional services, complimentary products, or a pass to industry events—anything to make them feel you care about them.

How to handle unrealistic feature request expectations

We all have those clients who expect you to build every feature they ask for. Some may even threaten to churn if you don't build exactly what they want, when they want it, and to their exact specifications. How do you handle these types of clients? It typically depends on how important they are to your business. How much they spend with you today, their potential worth down the road, and the strategic importance of their brand should factor into this equation.

When facing these situations, begin by assessing your client's product needs and prioritizing each requirement using the framework from the prior section. If they demand features you won't or can't build within their time-frame, look for ways to break the impasse. Request a meeting with the senior client stakeholders to assess the request's importance and whether it's a deal breaker. Someone less involved in the day-to-day operations may offer a more impartial view.

If the client keeps pushing back and makes it clear that they will churn if you don't address their needs, escalate this to your manager and the product team. When approaching the product team, lead with metrics that illustrate the potential business value this feature could deliver or the revenue your company could lose if it's not built. For more complex requests, consider having a PM interview the client to capture the requirements accurately.

If you can't get your client's feature request approved, let them know—don't beat around the bush. Avoiding the truth will make the fallout worse and cost you any remaining trust you still have. Face the music and live with the consequences. If your client has made it clear they will be looking at your competitors due to this, inform your leadership (either directly or through your manager), and flag the account as at-risk in your CRM/CSP. This en-sures everyone understands the consequences and accepts the potential fall-out. You will, of course, do everything in your power to work around this issue, but it may not be possible to save them. At this point, your trusted relationship may be what keeps them. Remember, you can't save every client so don't view this as a reflection of your personal performance.

You may find that the product team will commit to building a feature, but the customer's and product team's timelines don't align. For example, the client would like the feature built in two months to coincide with their renewal, but the product roadmap is set for the next three months. Share with your customer the projected timeframe and when the feature could feasibly be incorporated into the roadmap. A well-established partnership, combined with practical short-term alternatives, often helps retain business while pursuing long-term solutions.

No matter how good you are at your role, you will likely face a situation where you need to deal with product gaps and unrealistic clients. Do your best in these moments of truth—they can test your resilience. Sometimes it's best to cut them loose to prevent wasted cycles. Don't take these burdens on yourself—leverage your manager and others as needed.

Strategic conversations in times of crisis: Handling upset clients

Up to this point, we've mostly focused on building or maintaining trust with our clients. But what do you do when you've broken that trust? Your clients may be upset for various reasons, such as prolonged product downtime, a significant bug impacting their productivity, or an indefinite delay of a promised feature. We've all needed to calm down an irate customer and find constructive solutions. In this section, we'll cover how to navigate difficult conversations with upset clients.

You usually have just one shot to get things back on track when your customer's trust has been damaged. I find that many CS professionals become defensive in these situations and deflect blame or waste the customer's time on unimportant items that do not address the root issue. Rather than defending your actions, lead with empathy, even if it's not your fault or the customer has their facts wrong. Trying to deflect blame or minimize the impact will only make things more difficult. If your client's upset, simply let them vent—do not interrupt or try to explain what happened while they're very emotional. Just let them get whatever they want off their chests.

Once they've shared their burning concerns, respond with, "I can completely understand why you are frustrated" or "If I were in your shoes, I would be upset as well." Then proceed with a reflection such as "It seems that . . ." or "I want to make sure I have all the details. You said . . . Did I get that right?" This form of active listening validates their issues and demonstrates why they feel the way they do. Seek clarification on any points that remain unclear.

With the customer now likely to be more at ease, you can proceed to the next phase of the conversation. Explain what happened from your perspective and outline a plan to address their concerns. If you don't have clear answers for them, that's OK. Be upfront about it and let your client know the progress that's been made, what assistance you need from them (if any), and when they can expect to hear from you. They must see you taking action—even without a definitive plan. Never bury your head in the sand—always communicate even when you don't have a solid update.

In these pivotal moments, when your company's reputation is at stake (and yours as well), it's vital to follow through on your promises. If you say you will update them later in the day, send them an update. If you owe them additional details on the issue's impact, get them those details. Failing to live up to your promises after a crisis can cause irrevocable damage to your relationship. These are the *moments of truth* described in chapter 17. These are the moments that will define your customer relationship and the faith they have in you and your company.

When your organization's actions have caused significant disruption to your customer's business operations, explore meaningful ways to make it right. Saying "sorry" may be insufficient. Work with your manager on the proper way to respond. Offering a credit or a larger discount at renewal are options, but only as a last resort. In the example at the beginning of the chapter, I gave the client a 50 percent discount for the next six months to reestablish our partnership. That was extreme but it helped us regain their trust. It's sufficient in most situations to acknowledge what happened and communicate the preventive steps being taken to mitigate future occurrences.

There are times when your manager's judgment may be clouded. They may be stuck in rules and procedures and too focused on what's best for your company. It's your job to represent the voice of the customer and stick up for them if you feel they are being treated unfairly.

Use an accusations audit to start difficult client conversations

It can be very intimidating to go into a meeting knowing that your clients are upset with you, especially when your company is clearly at fault. As I mentioned at the beginning of this chapter, I was petrified as I sat across from my client. What saved me was my preparation. More specifically, the *accusations audit* method gave me the confidence to overcome my fears.

So, what is an accusations audit? Author Chris Voss, whom I've previously mentioned, defines it as follows: "An accusations audit is taking a step back, and taking an inventory, doing an audit of all the possible negatives, names, accusations, slanderous things that the other side might be thinking about me based on the circumstances, or the environment, or their own paranoia."[87] An accusations audit uses a combination of self-deprecation and proactive emotion labeling to calm people down and create an environment of trust. It can be an extremely effective tool in your strategic CSM toolbox.

When preparing for a challenging customer meeting, begin by listing all the issues that are frustrating your clients and any resentment they may feel toward you. In the scenario I described at the beginning of the chapter, I noted that my client was upset because of the legal liability we had caused them and the numerous issues they had experienced with our software.

Next, write out statements labeling your client's emotions and their grievances. If your company is explicitly at fault, call that out. This isn't the time to hold back—get all the cards on the table. Here are some examples of accusations audit statements:

---

87   Chris Voss, "The Accusations Audit," MasterClass, https://www.masterclass.com/classes/chris-voss-teaches-the-art-of-negotiation/chapters/the-accusations-audit.

- "It probably feels like we have no idea what we're doing and that we're complete amateurs." This is the example I provided at the beginning of the chapter.
- "It probably feels like we're not being completely honest with you."
- "I can only imagine how frustrated you must be with our lack of progress on this bug."

By presenting these statements at the outset of your meeting, you defuse the bomb your customers were preparing to drop on you. By removing the fuse, you tone down their intensity. It doesn't mean the fire's out, but it sets the stage for a constructive discussion. Your customer feels heard and understood, enabling you to move the conversation forward. You can move on to highlight the steps you've taken to resolve the matter and communicate your plan for what comes next. Resist the urge to fill the silence after you speak. Allow your customer to take it in, letting them make the next move so you can gauge their reaction.

Despite your best efforts to prevent these situations, you'll find yourself with upset clients. Unlike my previous advice, in which I recommend that you sit back and listen, this is where you need to be upfront. Admit where you made mistakes and demonstrate to your clients that you see their pain and you're doing everything you can to make things right.

Putting this into practice

Complete the "Handling Client Feature Requests & Accusations Audits Exercise" at strategiccustomersuccess.com

Summary and key takeaways

You need to effectively handle strategic conversations involving customer feature requests and address challenging situations with customers.

- Engage in strategic conversations with your clients to comprehend their requirements and prioritize feature requests accurately.

- Communicate customer feedback to the product team with comprehensive details to bridge understanding gaps.

- When communicating your company's decision to decline a feature request, be transparent and emphasize recent product enhancements that deliver value.

- Rebuild trust with upset clients through empathy, open communication, and taking ownership of resolutions.

- Use an accusations audit to address negative emotions, defuse conflicts, and facilitate constructive conversations.

PART V

Strategic Customer Engagements in the
Customer Journey

CHAPTER 19

Fixing the Two Most Broken Meetings: Kickoffs and QBRs

HubSpot, a billion-dollar public company with thousands of customers, faced the same issue in its customer success organization that many other CS departments face: Every CSM managed their customers differently. Despite HubSpot's impressive customer acquisition and growth metrics, its churn rate remained a persistent challenge. It was only when HubSpot fine-tuned its CSMs' daily workflows that it saw a marked uptick in customer retention. So how did they do this?

They ran an experiment. They created two cohorts: one group of customers receiving ad hoc assistance from their CSMs and one that had more regimented engagements. For the first cohort, there was no consistency in how CSMs interacted with customers—they would swoop in and out as needed. In the second cohort, HubSpot developed a standardized engagement framework, maintaining regular communication with their customers. You can guess which cohort's customers were more successful.

Customers who were regularly engaged showed a notable increase in both gross and net dollar retention rates. It wasn't even close. HubSpot discovered that CSMs had a measurable impact when they engaged with customers at key moments in the customer journey, such as the transition point from onboarding to post-onboarding. HubSpot called these activities *value-driven engagements.*

Jeetu Mahtani, the former EVP executive vice president of customer success at HubSpot, explained what was happening here: "In the new world, you as a CSM are the strategic advisor, the thought leader who can ultimately help your customers do what you describe, which generates results from their business by using the strategic advice."[88] By empowering their CSMs to specialize in specific parts of the customer journey, HubSpot elevated the customer experience and adopted a more strategic approach to customer success, concentrating on key interactions.

Up to this point, I've provided you with the foundation and tools you need to build trusted relationships with your clients and demonstrate value through strategic conversations. This includes the 3C framework, OARS, the SOON funnel, and assessing motivation. These concepts need to be embedded at pivotal points of the customer journey.

In the following chapters, we'll dive into critical points along the customer journey. Figure 12 illustrates the customer journey as an infinity loop, with four key areas: onboarding, optimization, renewal and expansion. This is a more realistic portrayal of the journey your customers embark on as compared to the traditional linear diagram. Your relationship with your customers is ongoing and cyclical, not one-and-done. In this chapter, we'll explore the kickoff call, a key part of onboarding, and the QBR, which falls under the optimization phase. In the next chapter, we'll cover the renewal and expansion components of the customer journey.

---

88 "How HubSpot Built and Implemented a Value-based Customer Engagement Model," YouTube, Uploaded by Valuize, July 24, 2023, https://www.youtube.com/watch?v=rEc-WkDRcH4.

Customer Journey

Onboarding Renewal

∞

Optimization Expansion

Figure 12. The customer journey as an infinity loop

Building trust from day one: The power of strategic kickoff meetings

"The beginning of your customer relationship is critical and will lay the foundation that can set you up for success or churn. This is an opportunity to build trust right away, and it's equally important to keep that trust going throughout the customer journey."[89] Sabina Pons, the CEO and CCO at Growth Molecules, eloquently summarized the mindset you need to have when your customers enter the onboarding phase of the customer journey. The initial purchase stage is a euphoric moment for your customers. They see your product as a savior in their current predicament. Now you have the difficult job of delivering on what they believe your product can accomplish. This kickoff call is a key moment and a chance to either make or break the client relationship.

I'll be honest. Most kickoff meetings I've experienced as a customer have sucked. They were boring and mundane, filled with endless slides, or were all over the place without enough substance. Instead of invigorating me, they've

---

89 Sabina Pons, "How to Keep the Customer Fire Going," *Newsweek*, November 8, 2022, https://www.newsweek.com/how-keep-customer-fire-going-1757577.

often drained my energy with mind-numbing details or an overly superficial approach that made it feel like a waste of time.

When prepping for a kickoff meeting, how many of you copy your existing onboarding slides, add the new customer's logo, change out a few items, and then jump into the meeting with the customer? Too often, the meeting becomes more about checking a box rather than uncovering the customer's priorities, establishing trust, and setting the customer up for success. To set the stage for a long-term and mutually beneficial partnership, it's essential to rethink your kickoff meeting strategy.

Kickoffs that set the stage for strategic success

The initial moments of a kickoff meeting are often filled with eager anticipation for a CSM—similar to the excitement of a first date. Butterflies are fluttering in your stomach as you await to see the type of client you'll get. Are they going to be friendly? Do they have any idea what your product actually does, or were they just thrown on this call by their boss? Will they be one of your star customers or a problem child?

Your clients may also be nervous, wondering if they made the right decision by choosing you over your competitors. While they may be excited to start, they may lack patience because they have a lot riding on the success of this implementation. They're counting on your solution to achieve a key goal and may have specific launch timelines they need to hit.

It's important to consider the level of commitment from the customer stakeholders responsible for implementing and managing your products, typically your main points of contact or administrators. The speed of onboarding often hinges on the availability of these individuals and how motivated they are. They may already have several items on their plate, and now they have one more thing to worry about. Their commitment largely depends on how they view the significance of your product to their role. Regardless of your emotional state, shifting your focus and putting yourself in your customer's shoes is vital. Think about what they need and how best to engage them.

Let's start our transformation of this meeting by changing its name. It's time to do away with the dull and generic *kickoff call* and call it something more enticing. For example, renowned CS thought leader and CCO at ClientSuccess, Kristi Faltorusso, calls her kickoff meetings *partnership kickoffs*.[90] I recommend calling it a *strategic planning kickoff*, as that sets the tone for you to uplevel the discussion. It signals to the decision-makers or executive sponsors that their presence is needed. I've witnessed numerous instances where decision-makers delegated the implementation to a subordinate without clearly setting expectations or fully explaining why they made the purchase in the first place. This led to unnecessary confusion and challenges that could have been avoided.

To eliminate confusion, the customer decision-maker must join the kickoff call and clearly explain their vision and decision to work with you. Train your sales team to inform customers that your kickoff meetings are different from other vendors they've worked with. It should be ingrained into their heads that decision-maker attendance is mandatory, as strategic planning kickoffs get everyone aligned around the right objectives and clarify the path moving forward. This speeds up the implementation and ensures that their vision of what your product will achieve becomes a reality.

It's important to value your client executives' time. Decision-makers should only be needed for the first twenty to thirty minutes, after which they can leave. Let's discuss how to run this meeting so you and your clients get the most out of it.

---

90 Kristi Faltorusso, "I improved retention and onboarding success by making a change to the first step in the onboarding process," LinkedIn, January 22, 2025, https://www.linkedin.com/posts/kristiserrano_i-improved-retention-and-onboarding-success-activity-7287859438860861442-mriD/.

Establishing the CSM as a strategic advisor

Skip the mind-numbing parts of a typical kickoff meeting, such as reviewing your onboarding process and the contract details—start with why they chose you and what they aim to achieve. As their strategic CSM, you should lead this part of the conversation to establish yourself as the client's strategic advisor. It shows your genuine desire to understand the client and their business.

After the introductions, map out their business landscape using the 3C framework. This includes their core offerings, customer base, and primary pain points (see chapter 2). Clarify critical timing constraints affecting their project priorities. Next, define their business outcomes, success criteria, and the specific goals they want to achieve (see chapter 17). By tackling this first, you'll engage the senior stakeholders and prioritize the right goals. Even if their business outcomes aren't well defined, it's a starting point that you can work from and rally around. You can always fine-tune this later. You'll know your conversation is on the right track if they start asking questions and have their cameras on.

This can also be done at scale for smaller clients. Either collect their business outcomes directly in your application or via a survey tool. Because you're dealing with higher customer volumes, get creative and experiment with different approaches.

Defining expectations and roles while preventing a breach of trust

After the first part of this meeting, your customer's engines should be revving and they should be eager for more. You've engaged them, taken the time to understand their business, and defined what is most important to them. Next, set clear expectations so everyone understands their roles and responsibilities. Specify your customer's high-level responsibilities, immediate next steps, and other critical project success factors. Senior client stakeholders should be present to prevent a game of "broken telephone." They can con-

firm their team's resource allocations for your product and eliminate potential accountability gaps.

In addition to defining what's expected from your clients, outline how
you'll support them during onboarding and beyond. Clarify how your various customer-facing teams, such as support, will engage with them on an
ongoing basis and the best way to access them. For instance, it's important to
clarify how a CSM will interact with senior stakeholders at various points in
the customer journey to secure their involvement at future meetings such as
QBRs. Ensure you are positioned correctly as your client's strategic advisor,
not their go-to person for all their technical questions.

At this stage, you can review the contract and statement of work (if
applicable) to ensure everyone is on the same page. As you've defined their
business outcomes, you can determine whether any necessary products or
services are missing from their agreement. Resolving any inconsistencies
right away is essential, as leaving them unchecked can damage your client's
confidence in you over time.

Lastly, while you have the decision-maker's attention, call out any thorny
issues that could derail the project. For example, sales may have promised a
tight deadline, or there may be a tricky technical requirement that wasn't fully scoped out. Like the contract review, it's best to immediately address any
key issues that could erode your customer's trust. Once you've completed
this portion of the meeting, you can give the decision-maker the option to
drop off the meeting or stay on.

Also, consider discussing while the decision-maker is present something
Kristi Faltorusso calls *the customer promise*.[91] The customer promise defines
what the customer can expect from your CS team. This includes how often you'll meet, the expected turnaround times when they reach out to your
team, and your commitment to listen to and act on their feedback. This

91 "Customer Success: Orchestrating the Customer Journey." Intellishift, 2020, https://
intellishift.com/resources/blog/customer-success-orchestrating-the-customer-journey/.

builds trust and allows the decision-maker to step back from this project, knowing they've left it in capable hands. Work this into your process regardless of whether the decision-maker is present or not.

With the critical alignment boxes checked, you can move on to important yet routine matters, such as reviewing the project plan, outlining the timeline for each phase, and identifying the specific actions your client needs to complete. Delving into these finer details gives the client a clearer picture of their accountability and the precise resource and effort requirements. Give the decision-maker the choice to stay or cut out early for this part. In addition, you should establish preferred communication channels, such as a project portal or Slack channel, and schedule upcoming meetings.

For larger, more complex implementations, scheduling a welcome call with senior client stakeholders before the strategic kickoff meeting can be beneficial to clarify roles and identify participants for the onboarding process. Keep these short and to the point.

Reinvigorating your kickoff meetings

Kickoffs need to be reimagined. Think of them as strategic launching pads—they can pull in key decision-makers, establish you as a catalyst for change, and create momentum for lasting impact. To achieve this, you must put their story front and center rather than focusing on your process. This will improve your understanding of their needs, elevate their perception of you, and set the relationship on the right path for a long-term partnership.

QBRs: It's time for a makeover

Remember those restaurant makeover shows? They showcased struggling restaurants being completely revamped to improve their chances of delighting guests and staying in business. The same type of change is needed for QBRs.

The former COO of customer success software Catalyst, Kevin Chiu, called QBRs a "Waste Your Time meeting."[92] He also said QBRs are often "just about vendor metrics" and that "the customer doesn't know where they came up with that data."[93] I agree with him. We've made QBRs serve our purpose and forgotten about the most important player—the customer. QBRs have been turned into a big production that focuses more on the aesthetics of our slides than the meeting outcomes.

Despite the current state of most QBRs, I still believe in them. They're essential touchpoints that reveal two crucial things: whether your clients feel they're getting real value and the honest health of your relationship. They pull you out of the day-to-day whirlwind of customer meetings and your inbox and allow you to focus on what's most important. They also typically involve a larger audience, including your customer decision-makers.

But that's not all! QBRs help you avoid potential issues and stay in tune with how your customer's needs may change. Are there new stakeholders that you should be aware of? Have their KPIs changed? Has the state of the economy impacted their business? QBRs help you handle these questions and more if they're done correctly. The problem is that QBRs have lost their effectiveness, so we need to mix things up. In this section, I'll examine the limitations of QBRs and discuss practical strategies for improving their impact and positioning you as a strategic CSM superstar.

QBRs are broken

The way QBRs are delivered today results in three main issues:

---

92 Kevin Chiu, "Catalyst put 100 CROs/CCOs/VP of Sales/CS in a room to debate," LinkedIn, November 10, 2023, https://www.linkedin.com/feed/update/urn:li:activity:7128785445978542080/.

93 Kevin Chiu, "The 7 Deadly Sins of Customer Success," posted January 24, 2024, by Catalyst Software, YouTube, https://www.youtube.com/watch?v=k1nATHk1wSA.

1. **Reviews are boring**. How can we make this meeting any less interesting than by calling it a *review*? Do you remember doing a book review in primary or middle school? Your peers were probably bored out of their minds. Many of your customers are having the same reaction to your QBRs.

   The problem with QBRs is that they often focus heavily on past events. In many cases, your clients may be overloaded with information that isn't relevant to their current situation. In addition, many of the slides presented in QBRs are full of vanilla crap that was designed to make the process easier for the CSM rather than drive business outcomes. This approach reduces the impact of the meeting and can turn your decision-makers off from attending any future QBRs.

2. ***Quarterly* doesn't make sense**. "Very few companies want a quarterly review from their vendor," says Gainsight CEO Nick Mehta.[94] And he's right. The truth is that your customers don't have the time—especially the senior customer stakeholders. QBRs should be conducted based on your client's needs and your team's capacity—not because *quarterly* is in the name of the meeting.

3. **Your company's needs come before customers' needs**. Too often, QBRs revolve around our internal objectives instead of addressing what our clients truly value. For example, QBRs may be used to sell more of our products, such as advanced reporting, instead of focusing on our customer's most pressing priorities. Your customers are more interested in solving their problems than learning about your new products and getting sold to.

---

94 Reed and Badani, "QBRs that Execs Love."

CS influencer and Head of Growth and Business Development of Sturdy, Aaron Thompson summed this up well: "QBRs are by definition SELFISH. They are about US and OUR Product/Service and how much it's made a positive impact on our customer's life. They are so often never about the customer's business strategy like they should be. Or what Business Outcomes we've helped them to achieve." [95] His point is that we tend to focus on our own products and short-term needs, whereas customers care primarily about how those products align with their objectives.

Bob London, whom I've mentioned in previous chapters, agrees and also calls for a QBR makeover. He says, "QBR fatigue is real,"[96] and, "Your customers aren't engaging. Because your customer success, account management or sales team spends too much time talking AT them. Presenting slide after slide about YOUR PRODUCT or solution."[97] The other issue is that the data presented often lacks context and isn't tied to your customer's goals.[98] Your customers feel disconnected from the meeting rather than being the story's main character.

A complete change to the traditional QBR is needed. The conversation itself should be the focal point of these sessions, so it's more about your customers and their needs than a desire to check off a box in your CS platform. Let's explore the steps needed to accomplish this.

95 Aaron Thompson, "QBRs Are Stupid," LinkedIn, January 31, 2022, https://www.linkedin.com/pulse/qbrs-stupid-aaron-thompson/.
96 Bob London, "QBR fatigue is real. For customers and vendors alike," July 29, 2023, LinkedIn, https://www.linkedin.com/posts/boblondon_qbr-fatigue-is-real-for-customers-and-vendors-activity-7091024581582303232--qs5/.
97 Bob London, "UBR Training," BobLondon.co, n.d., https://www.boblondon.co/ubr-training.
98 Daphne Costa Lopes, "Why Most EBRs Fail and How to Fix Them," Unconventional Growth, n.d., https://6458037.hs-sites.com/why-most-ebrs-fail-and-how-to-fix-them.

The death of the QBR and the rise of the strategic checkpoint

To fix this, we must first scrap the presentation-first mentality to transform QBRs from monologues to dialogues. We want customers to lean in and engage with us; presentations only create a wall between you and your audience. Visual aids such as slides or dynamic web pages are still needed as the foundation of the QBR, but they should be leveraged to spark a discussion, not dominate it.

QBRs should follow a board-meeting-style approach, with materials shared in advance so customers can review and prioritize key discussion points. Most of your analysis should be contained in an appendix or separate document, ensuring that only the critical insights tied to your customer's business outcomes are prominently displayed, while still making additional data available if needed.

The finishing touch? Take a page from the kickoff playbook to make it clear from the start that you're breaking away from the old business review routine. Banish the term QBR or EBR (executive business reviews) and leverage a more adept name, such as *strategic checkpoints*. James Alarcon, on my team at PathFactory, came up with this name as part of overhauling our QBR processes, and we saw a 40 percent increase in decision-maker participation.

The core elements that make up a strategic checkpoint include:

- A balanced conversation where you and your client participate equally, instead of a one-sided presentation
- A focus on your client's business outcomes along with a plan to achieve them (This contrasts with typical QBRs that focus mostly on your product, not on your client's business.)
- A condensed look-back section—it should only take up a small portion of the meeting (20–25 percent at most). The bulk of the discussion should focus on the present and chart

the path forward, instead of the traditional focus on reviewing the past.

Adjust the cadence depending on how you've crafted your customer journey and your segmentation strategy. Rather than quarterly, they should be conducted based on your clients' needs. High-value clients and those with strong growth potential may benefit from more frequent strategic checkpoint sessions, while a digital strategy should suffice for your lowest-tier clients.

Many of these decisions may be out of your hands, but it's something to consider and recommend to your manager to improve your productivity.

Regardless of the approach, the end goal is the same: providing personalized insights and recommendations. When done right, strategic checkpoints deliver real value and build the kind of trust that turns clients into long-term partners.

Conducting strategic checkpoints

Follow these nine steps to transform your QBRs into strategic checkpoints that your customers will look forward to (use technology to streamline as needed):

1. Introduce the concept: Strategic checkpoints (SCPs) can be introduced via email, but it's best to do this live. This allows you to sell the value of these engagements, differentiate them from past QBR attempts, and address any questions your customers may have. Ask your main contact to help secure the decision-maker's attendance and set expectations.

You can use this script in a live meeting or in an email message:

Tanya,

We're taking a new approach to our business reviews. Instead of a typical QBR, I'd like to schedule a strategic checkpoint.

Instead of focusing mostly on product usage, we'll address your business needs. This includes confirming your goals and priorities. We'll also briefly discuss your past results so we can map out a go-forward plan.

Can you provide some possible days and times for us to meet? We'll need sixty minutes. Thank you in advance.

Yours truly,

Your amazing CSM

You can also include one or two personalized data insights in your communication that can sweeten the pot and drive urgency, such as:

- "You are 10 percent below the benchmark for [metric X]. As part of the strategic checkpoint, let's discuss how this may be impacting your overall results and how we can improve it."
- "Congrats! [Metric X] has increased by 20 percent in the last three months. Let's discuss how we can capitalize on this and what we should focus on next."
- "I want to share some ideas on how other clients have tackled [outcome X]."[99]

---

99 Inspired by McCulloch, Seven Pillars of Customer Success.

Remember that your main goal at this stage is to schedule a meeting, so don't convey too many details. This is just a teaser for the main event.

2. Gather information before the meeting: Meeting with your client beforehand helps create a more meaningful SCP. During this premeeting, align on the agenda, including their priorities, challenges, progress on goals, and any positive results from using your product.

Let your day-to-day contact know that you want to partner together so that the decision-maker has the most accurate view of the current situation. Then, you can have a fruitful discussion when you meet. Additionally, ask what shouldn't be mentioned to prevent unnecessary tangents or embarrassment.

Ask your client these questions before the strategic checkpoint to help you determine the best discussion topics to focus on, who should be in attendance, and some possible meeting outcomes to plan for (many are repeats from chapter 17):

- What is the most important topic being discussed right now at your organization's highest level? Why is it the most important item?
- What is the biggest challenge or obstacle faced by your team today?
- What has to be off your whiteboard in the next thirty days?
- What progress have you made against your business outcomes since we last met?
- What's one success you've had by leveraging our product? Why do you consider it a success, and how did it impact your business? What's one area you would like to improve?
- What topics would you like to discuss when we meet? What should we prioritize? What areas should we avoid?

This should be considered the most essential preparation task, as it frequently reveals key information you weren't aware of. You could also streamline this process by sending your client a digital version of the questionnaire before the meeting.

3. Do your analysis, but put most of it in the appendix: It's common to see QBRs overloaded with too much information. The challenge is that the noise can easily overshadow your message, or the client may fixate on irrelevant details, steering the conversation away from the core issues. Focus your data and analysis on their business outcomes and the key points you want to emphasize—everything else can go in the appendix. This way, the extra data is available if needed, while you can stay focused on the most pressing items.

4. Start with an executive overview: The executive overview should be the first slide of your strategic checkpoint. The goal of the overview is to provide a one-slide summary to the decision-maker that explains the current situation and recommendations in less than five minutes. It should entice them to want to learn more and spark questions. In addition, you should assume that any customer stakeholder may read this slide, so make sure that anyone can understand it—even if they have little context on your company or products.

Include these items in your executive overview, keeping the story you want to tell in mind:

- Progress against outcomes: State the progress that has been made against your client's business outcomes. This should be a quantitative update that includes the previously defined success criteria from your joint success plan. These metrics should resonate with the decision-maker and highlight any relevant client successes.

- Challenges: List the major challenges or obstacles preventing your client from achieving their outcomes. Don't pull any punches. If your client is underperforming or if you don't feel they are dedicating enough resources, get this on the table. It's best to do it now and address it while you can.

- Recommendations: List a few recommendations that should be explored based on your analysis and preparation. Make it clear that these points are intended to inspire ideas for the upcoming discussion and are not set in stone.

Create the executive overview only after preparing all other slides and gathering client input.

5. Summarize the customer's achievements and your key data insights: Following the executive overview, the next two to three slides should focus on the progress toward the customer's business outcomes and emphasize their key metrics. Where did they surpass expectations and where did they come up short? Craft a narrative that depicts your customer as a hero in this journey so they can picture themselves in their own story. In addition, provide a few bullet points that offer context on the progress achieved or highlight factors that may have negatively impacted results.

Draw attention to the insights and trends on the key metrics slides, including data demonstrating the breadth and depth of product usage. Call out any areas of concern where the client may be struggling or where adoption is below the average for similar clients. Just be sure the data is relevant to their use cases. Don't waste their time with useless information on features they can't use.

When done correctly, your insights should highlight strategies they hadn't considered before or encourage them to double down on existing practices. Show your true value by bringing to the table fresh perspectives that might be off your client's radar. This is also an opportunity to highlight positive wins, showcasing your main point of contact.

Expert tip: Enhancing your data insights—provide context and take a customer-centric approach

As you delve into data analysis for your strategic checkpoints, consider:

- Providing an explanation with your metrics. Include some short bullet points alongside the metrics in your materials to help clients grasp the meaning behind the data. Is the data trending up or down over time? How does it measure up to other initiatives the client has executed? How does it relate to their business outcomes? How does it stack up against similar clients? Ask yourself, "What story am I trying to tell from this data, and how does it fit into the larger narrative I need to convey?" By providing this context, you can help direct the client to act appropriately.

- Including benchmark data, which can offer valuable context, highlighting where your client exceeded or fell short of expectations.

- Coming with a point of view. In my experience working with hundreds of customers, the most valued CSMs aren't those who answer product questions the fastest. It's those who dare to question assumptions and challenge their customers. When preparing for your client meeting, come with your own perspective—don't just regurgitate the data. This goes hand in hand with the idea of radical customer candor introduced in chapter 9. Be that mirror for your clients and point out their warts and blind spots, but do it respectfully.

6. Prepare two to three discussion topics: Drawing on your analysis and premeeting preparation, formulate two to three discussion topics to form the core foundation for the checkpoint meeting. The first discussion point should clarify your customer's business outcomes or explore how their strategy may change.

Additional points might include insights from your data analysis or concerns brought up by your client. Shift the focus of discussion topics away from day-to-day issues so you can focus on the items with the highest leverage. These topics should cut to the core of their challenges or possible opportunities, such as:

- You told us that increasing conversions was your top priority last year. Is this still your top priority? Has anything changed that has impacted this objective?
- We've noticed that the UK team has decreased its usage while new countries are starting to leverage the product. What has changed in the business that is causing this? How will this impact your needs going forward?
- You mentioned that cost savings are a top priority for you. Can you provide more context on what this means and how it may affect our collaboration?

A single well-crafted discussion slide can reshape your entire meeting. As a word of warning, don't allow these discussion topics to merely mask blatant upsell pitches. If you plan to introduce new products with additional fees, you should clarify those intentions beforehand.

7. Send discussion topics and presentations in advance: To ensure that the discussion topics will be effective and that the meeting focuses on looking ahead rather than behind, send your presentation to your client at least forty-eight hours in advance. Make it clear that they must review it beforehand, allowing the majority of the meeting to be dedicated to strategizing the key priorities for the next year or quarter.

You can use this script as part of this communication:

Hi Tanya,

I'm excited about our upcoming strategic checkpoint. I've attached the slides for our discussion next Tuesday. Please review them before our meeting.

Here are three discussion points I recommend we cover:
o   Topic #1
o   Topic #2
o   Topic #3

How do these sound to you? Do you have anything you would like to add?

Looking forward to meeting with you, and let me know if you have any questions!

Yours truly,

Your amazing CSM

8. Confirm the next steps at the end of the meeting: Let's assume you had a productive strategic checkpoint because you prepared and followed these strategies. Now you will have several action items and next steps. So end the meeting by summarizing any decisions made and confirm the next steps. The worst thing you can do is conduct a great discussion and then leave the meeting without defining concrete actions.

9. Send a follow-up and craft a success plan: As part of your follow-up, send a detailed summary of what was covered and the action items. Celebrate the wins and highlight any challenges and how you'll work together to overcome them. Create or update the joint success plan so you can track progress over time. Make sure you follow through on any commitments you've made.

Don't squander the positive sentiment and energy that emanated from the SCP. You had a great meeting—now make it count.

Putting this into practice

To strategically engage your clients and uplevel your CSM–client relationship:

- Review your current customer kickoff meeting and kickoff processes. Compare your current approach to the "Strategic Planning (Onboarding) Kickoff Meeting Checklist" on strategiccustomersuccess. com and determine where you can improve.
- For your next QBR, ask your client questions before you start your preparation, send your slides well in advance, and focus on a few discussion points rather than going through each slide. Consider working with your CS leader to rebrand your QBRs as strategic checkpoints. You can download the "Strategic Checkpoint (QBR) Checklist" on strategiccustomersuccess.com.
- Optional: Download the strategic checkpoint (QBR) template at strategiccustomersuccess.com.

Summary and key takeaways

You need to transform kickoff meetings and QBRs:

- Traditional CSM practices need to evolve into strategic engagements that focus on the customer's business outcomes.
- Kickoff meetings should be transformed from slide-driven presentations into strategic discussions, building rapport and trust from the beginning. This will also increase decision-makers' engagement.

- QBRs have become mundane and unproductive, resembling more of a vendor-driven data dump than a meaningful conversation. However, the concept of QBRs still has value if we shift the focus back to the customer and their needs. To accomplish this, they should also be rebranded into strategic checkpoints.

- The term *review* suggests a backward-looking perspective. Shifting the focus to strategic checkpoints, emphasizing active discussions and forward-thinking solutions, can rejuvenate these meetings—especially for decision-makers.

- Implementing strategic kickoffs and checkpoints requires careful planning and preparation. By gathering relevant information and crafting engaging discussion topics, organizations can ensure that their meetings are productive and impactful. Following up with clear action items and commitments further strengthens the client relationship and drives progress toward shared goals.

CHAPTER 20

Driving Revenue Through Renewals and Expansions

"The client just rejected our latest proposal. We're going to have to start the renewal process from scratch and since I'm not going to make any money on this, I can no longer take this on." We just had a multi-million-dollar renewal negotiation blow up in our face, and I was now handed this hot potato after our sales team bowed out. Since their commission was based solely on upsell revenue, the sales team had no incentive to engage, as this deal would be a downsell and ARR would decrease. This was one of our highest revenue clients but they were struggling due to the COVID-19 pandemic. At the eleventh hour, they brought in legal counsel to push down our prices which ultimately killed the deal on the table. I was now going to have to figure out how to clean up this mess. Upsell or not, we were still talking about millions of dollars at stake.

The problem was that the sales rep working the deal didn't identify all of the key client stakeholders. After several grueling rounds of negotiations, we managed to scrape together a two-year deal—though I definitely earned a few gray hairs along the way. I vowed never to let that happen again and developed strategies to bring consistency to the chaos of renewals.

Streamlining your renewal strategy for improved results

As mentioned at the beginning of this book, I'm not going to debate who should own renewals within your organization. This will depend on many circumstances that are outside the scope of this book. Furthermore, I'm not going to get into a discussion about which renewal methodology is best—whether it's MEDDIC, MEDDICC, or MEDDPICC. After all those acronyms, I need a medic. Plus, this is outside the scope of this book.

I intend to help you improve your approach to renewals by examining two key strategies: the joint renewal plan and the renewal presentation. Implementing these processes will enhance your renewal discussions, increase the likelihood of a successful renewal, and identify possible risks before it's too late. These will leverage many of the SCSM concepts already covered in this book and build upon them so you can put them into action.

Engage clients early with a joint renewal plan

Have you ever thought a renewal was a done deal, only to have the client bring in their procurement team at the last minute to push for better terms? Has your renewal been unexpectedly delayed due to confusion about the various steps to complete it? Has a client churned at the last moment, right before they were going to sign the renewal? These challenges can be mitigated by collaborating with your customer to create a joint renewal plan (JRP). Something I wish we would have used for the renewal negotiations I described at the top of this chapter.

A JRP is very similar to a joint success plan. Just like a success plan lays out the specific actions needed to achieve your customer's business outcomes, the JRP lays out the steps involved in processing a renewal successfully. Both plans actively engage the client and are openly shared with them. This isn't the time to discuss price or start the negotiations. You're just defining the process.

To start the renewal planning process, schedule a meeting with your client roughly 120 days before the renewal to introduce the JRP. Let your clients know you'll walk them through the JRP to make the renewal as painless as possible.

There are three components of a JRP overview meeting:

1. Confirm the various stakeholders involved on both sides.
2. Verify the client's business outcomes and review the progress achieved.
3. Define the steps needed to complete the renewal.

1. Confirm the renewal stakeholders. Identify all stakeholders early to avoid ambiguity about who is involved in the renewal process. Communicate to the client who will be overseeing these efforts on your end and outline any supporting roles, such as legal. Are you handling the renewal? Are you bringing in an account manager? Let your client know who they'll be speaking with.

Most importantly, take this opportunity to finalize who will be participating in the renewal conversations from their side. Don't assume your main point of contact is the only player. Identify the decision-maker, other influencers, and whether the client's legal or procurement teams will be involved.

Kyle Coleman, former CMO of Clari, offers an excellent tip for uncovering the decision-maker. Instead of asking directly who the decision-maker is, ask: "Who would feel left out if we moved forward and they weren't included in this decision?"[100] This gets you the answer you need without possibly insulting your customers by making them feel less important.

Another great question from Coleman is "Who has the ability to stop this renewal from happening?" These questions will help you figure out who

---

100 Kyle Coleman, "The wrong question to ask: 'Who's the decision-maker?',"
LinkedIn, December 1, 2022, https://www.linkedin.com/posts/kyletcoleman_
sdr-sales-revenue-activity-7008921964614438912-ItvI.

all the key players are. To explore any internal politics within your client's organization, you might ask, "What's something about this renewal process that I should ask you that I may not have?" Certain key details might arise that have the potential to derail the renewal.

After determining the relevant participants, outline the timing for their involvement. For example, do you need to schedule time with the decision-maker to review the past progress? Will procurement be brought in at a later stage to confirm the renewal terms? Factor in their turnaround time, as it sets the tempo for the renewal process. Larger organizations and deals tend to require more approvals.

2. Verify the client's progress toward their business outcomes. The JRP doesn't require a complete strategic checkpoint. As part of the JRP, your objective is to validate the client's business outcomes and the progress made toward them. This allows you to highlight successes or challenges that could help or hurt the renewal. For instance, the client may be blocked on their business outcome attainment due to a product gap or a lack of resources on their end. Make sure you've identified the impact that each stakeholder in the renewal process expects to see.

The positive effect of this step has been verified by Erik Peterson and Tim Riesterer, authors of the groundbreaking book, *The Expansion Sale*. In a study they did with over 700 B2B buyers across a wide variety of industries, they found that during the renewal discussions, "The participants in our study reported greater trust in the provider when the provider's message first documented results."[101] Even if the outcomes weren't fully achieved, the authors still found that just the act of communicating progress against the stated goals had the most positive outcome on renewal rates. This is all about establishing credibility so that your customers are reassured they should continue to invest with you.[102]

---

101   Erik Peterson and Tim Riesterer, *The Expansion Sale: Four Must-Win Conversations to Keep and Grow Your Customers*, (McGraw Hill, 2020), 42.
102   Peterson and Riesterer, *The Expansion Sale, 42.*

To verify business outcome attainment, use statements combined with open-ended questions. You can lead with, "From our last checkpoint, we had discussed the need to increase revenue by 20% by the end of the year. It seems we are well on our way to attaining that. What is your perception of our progress against your goals?" Document any concerns from this conversation and adjust your renewal strategy to address them. If new stakeholders or business challenges arise, ensure they're reflected in your renewal plan.

3. Define the steps needed to complete the renewal. During your joint renewal planning session, walk through the standard renewal milestones and proposed schedule. Identify any special requirements your customer needs as part of their procurement process. For example, if your client wants you to demo your product to a new senior stakeholder, bake that into your overall renewal plan. Aim to have the agreement signed a week before the renewal to allow room for addressing any unforeseen complications.

Outline all steps involved and work backward from the renewal close date to account for legal reviews, client vacations, and other possible obstacles. This avoids any surprises on both sides and ensures a higher success rate of on-time renewals.

Treat the JRP overview conversation as a chance to learn more about your client's needs and uncover relevant information. Think of yourself as a pilot carefully aligning your plane with the runway for a safe landing. Follow the runway lights and the control tower instructions to land the plane successfully and prepare for the next flight.

Once the JRP is in place, ensure it's kept current and regularly communicate updates to the client.

Hammer it home with your renewal presentation

No matter the size of the contract, you can't take any renewal for granted. You must consistently demonstrate delivered impact and future possibilities to increase your clients' chances of staying with you in the long run. This is the essence of the renewal presentation, a tool you can use for clients of all sizes. The renewal presentation should address pricing and other renewal questions, making the decision to stay with you as easy as possible for your clients.

This is also an opportunity to discuss expansion and upsell opportunities (which we'll cover later in this chapter). These may include upgrading (or downgrading) product tiers or adding new product offerings.

When preparing the presentation, focus on the story you want to communicate. Ensure that every data point and argument in your presentation serves the narrative you are creating. For example, although they've achieved their key objectives, there may be potential for even more impressive results.

The renewal presentation can be delivered in a meeting or asynchronously, although it's recommended that you present it live so you can address any questions—especially if there is a significant renewal increase. It should be crafted to be easily understood and capable of standing alone, as it may be distributed throughout your client's organization. At a minimum, it should consist of these sections: the executive summary, supporting value points, new features and services, future outlook, pricing options, and next steps. Let's dive deeper into each of these.

- **Executive summary:** Create an executive summary outlining your clients' progress and major accomplishments. Leverage the results as defined by their success criteria. If your client's business outcomes have been identified and they've achieved their desired results, this part should be straightforward. Similarly to the strategic checkpoint, complete this slide last, as it summarizes the results from the other data you've gathered.

  In your summary, highlight any unmet goals. Though it may feel counterintuitive, being transparent about both successes and areas for growth is key. Greg Daines found from his research that "Customers with measured results stay 6 TIMES LONGER on average than those that don't measure."[103] Daines' research backs up what was also reported in *The Expansion Sale* regarding the positive benefits of communicating progress. Even when the numbers aren't stellar, acknowledge them briefly before focusing on the future.

- **Supporting value points:** The next slide of your presentation should spotlight additional key achievements and value milestones from your partnership. For example, show the percentage of licenses used or other consumption metrics such as messages sent. Incorporate supporting data highlighting how deeply they engage with your product, provided it presents you positively. Like the executive summary slide, you can include a few key areas where your client can improve. Being transparent about these areas helps build trust.

- **Features and services delivered:** Price increases at renewal times are common. It's important to present how you've improved your products and other offerings since the last contract negotiation. Create a slide that outlines new product features they've benefited from in the past year that are included in their existing contract. Highlighting additional offerings, such as a newly launched user community or educational programs, can help demonstrate the added value you've introduced.

- **Highlight what they should look forward to:** Add a slide or two that showcases what the future looks like. Your client wants to be assured that they've hooked their horse to the right wagon, so shine a light on the trails you'll be blazing. Share the headlines of your product roadmap, process updates, and whatever else may be relevant. Explain how these updates and changes align with your client's needs. When appropriate, share insights about additional funding

---

103 Greg Daines, "Hold Customers Accountable," gregdaines.com, November 17, 2023, https://www.gregdaines.com/post/hold-customers-accountable?postId=d8aad279-5917-4c4f-b204-42854722d8cc.

your company has received to highlight its financial strength and growth.

In addition, this is an opportunity to leverage an ROI calculator or other tools that highlight how future investment on their end will pay off in the long run. This strategy closely mirrors the concept of *painting the future* when working with an at-risk client (described in chapter 8). You're instilling confidence in your clients that you're the right partner in the months and possibly years ahead and that you're the one that they can trust.

CS leader and author Wayne McCulloch sums this up in his book *The Seven Pillars of Customer Success*: "The customer doesn't choose to stay with you because of the historical value you've driven for them—they stay because of the vision and promise of the future you have painted with them. They trust you because you have driven value in the past, but they will continue to work with you because of the future value you promise to provide."[104]

- **Position possible expansion or upsell opportunities:** Highlight any expansions previously discussed, as well as recommended add-ons based on their needs. See the next section for more on this topic.

- **Outline pricing options:** With their value story established and future product opportunities outlined, it's time to transition to the pricing discussion. Expect that whatever you present will be passed around, so it's essential to clearly explain the reason behind your pricing—especially if there is an increase. If everything goes according to plan, the first part of the presentation should make the value they are receiving and will continue to receive abundantly clear. This should temper any concerns over a modest increase.

When your client pushes you on price, it's best to give them options so they can choose what best suits them. For example, you can

---

104   McCulloch, Seven Pillars of Customer Success, 192.

offer different price points based on the agreement's longevity. A one-year agreement will incur a 5 percent increase, but a two-year agreement may only incur a 3 percent increase. This pricing section should be customized based on previous discussions and align with the client's future business outcome aspirations.

- **Outline the next steps:** Wrap up the presentation by outlining the next steps from the JRP. If you're meeting live, you should seek a commitment from your clients by asking them if they foresee any barriers in the process. Confirm with them what action needs to be taken next to ensure that the renewal is processed before the renewal date. Get a definitive answer on the approval processes and confirm that this aligns with what is laid out in the JRP.

Implementing a JRP and a solid renewal presentation can bring more rigor to your renewal process. No matter how well you execute these strategies, you'll still face customers churning. This is the sad reality of the life we've chosen. But when you have consistency in your approach, you can better evaluate what's working well and what isn't. Let this serve as a guiding principle as you level up your renewal process: If they're renewing, you're growing, and when they churn, you learn. Embody the growth mindset and always look for ways to improve—no matter how successful your renewal rate is.

Driving revenue growth: The strategic CSM's guide to expansion

Regardless of what falls under your responsibilities, you should be actively pursuing revenue expansion opportunities. Shake off any shyness or concerns that asking your clients for more money may compromise your trusted advisor role. Accept that commercial responsibilities fall on everyone's shoulders—whether it's in your job description or not. Evolving into a revenue-focused role is critical for the long-term survival of the CS function and is a core component of being a strategic CSM. While some old-guard customer success thought leaders fought to keep this separate from the CSM role, it's been to the detriment of the CS industry.

More forward-thinking CS gurus have shifted their approach. Customer success expert Lincoln Murphy explains that "Expansion is the start of success," which makes it a critical sign of customer health. When your clients aren't growing, take it as a warning sign that there could be underlying issues that require more investigation. Murphy adds that expansion shouldn't be portrayed as a sales motion but rather as a natural development in achieving your client's business outcomes.[105] Helping your customers to adopt and consume more of your products is part of your job, enabling them to be the heroes in their own stories. This perspective alleviates the uneasiness, as expansion becomes just another part of the overall customer journey.

Mastering the art of growing your client's wallet share can also accelerate your career growth. Any direct impact you have on your company's topline will get you noticed and potentially open up new opportunities for you. You need to accept that generating revenue is now intrinsic to customer success, a necessary shift that elevates the strategic impact of CSMs. It comes down to execution: The right approach enables you to maintain strong client partnerships while achieving exceptional results.

Before discussing how to do this, let's define the terms upsell, cross-sell, and expansion.

Upsell: Upsells involve upgrading customers to a more advanced tier or expanding their existing product capabilities with a related add-on feature or product. For example, your customer may have started with your basic prod-

---

105   Johan Nilsson and Lincoln Murphy, "Upselling for Success: Why Simple Retention is a Red Flag," Impact Weekly podcast, May 22, 2024, https://podcasts. apple.com/cd/podcast/upselling-for-success-why-simple-retention-is-a-red-flag/ id1656206843?i=1000656413088.

uct offering and then upgraded to the enterprise product to take advantage of your advanced integrations.

Cross-sell: Cross-selling involves introducing complementary but distinct products to current customers, often selling into new departments. For example, your sales team may have purchased Salesforce's sales solution while your support team later purchased the support solution.

Expansion: Expansion involves offering your clients more of what they currently have. This can include additional licenses, data, or other consumption components such as messages. For instance, if you host your product on Amazon Web Services (AWS), you will pay more when you require additional storage.

To keep things simple for the scope of this book, I'm consolidating these various revenue-generating methods under the term expansion. Ultimately, clients are expanding their usage—whether by increasing the number of users, consuming more data, or adopting more features or products.

The need for an expansion playbook

As I mentioned, expansion should be a natural evolution for your customers. In many cases, it is. For example, customers using Amazon's AWS will naturally expand their storage as they reach their limits. Problems often arise when client-facing teams—such as sales and customer success—have competing objectives or lack clear processes.

I recall a nightmarish meeting with a retail client facing numerous product issues. My sales counterpart asked me to tag along, and I agreed, hoping to learn more about the client's pain points. But mid-conversation, he rushed to pitch a high-priced solution that completely ignored their actual needs. The customer's face turned an even deeper shade of anger. "How can you expect us to invest more when your current solutions aren't delivering?" they asked. I tried to shift the focus back to solving their immediate problems, but it was too late. That meeting broke the relationship beyond repair, and they churned soon after.

That experience taught me a valuable lesson: Pressuring clients to expand before they're ready can irreparably harm client relationships. Part of your role as a strategic CSM is acting as the customer's voice of reason. You must balance the pursuit of hitting short-term quarterly revenue targets with the customer's long-term best interests. To guide this process, you need a comprehensive playbook that outlines growth stages, clarifies team roles between CS and sales, anticipates objections, and details operational steps. This also solidifies the strategic CSM as a contributor to revenue.

Typically, expansion playbooks define rules of engagement for each role. For instance, they might outline how CSMs are credited for identifying opportunities before transitioning them to sales (sometimes called a CS-qualified lead, or CSQL for short). Although the complete playbook isn't covered here, we'll explore two critical expansion strategies: uncovering expansion opportunities and tracking expansion potential.

Uncovering expansion opportunities with the SPOON funnel

Let me stress this point again: Let go of any hesitation you have about asking your clients for more money when the product or feature you're selling aligns with their business outcomes. If your offering matches their requirements, the challenge becomes less about the solution and more about timing and articulating the value proposition.

I once had a customer who wanted to consolidate all their data from various tools, including ours, into one accessible location. We offered an add-on that perfectly matched their need—we could pass our data into their data warehouse so they could access it easily in one spot. However, they weren't convinced it was worth the additional fees. The turning point came when I zeroed in on their key frustration: the time sink of manual data uploads. This breakthrough moment made me realize I needed to adapt the SOON funnel for expansion discussions.

I introduced the concept of the SOON funnel in chapter 16 as a critical component of strategic conversations. As you may recall, it includes four key elements: success, obstacles, options, and next steps. Expansion conversations demand a more nuanced approach because you're asking your clients to open their wallets wider. This requires an additional step, which involves uncovering your client's pain points, as I did in the story I shared earlier. I call this the SPOON funnel, with *P* representing your customer's *pain*. Therefore the SPOON funnel has five components: success, pain, obstacles, options, and next steps.

Like the standard SOON approach, you must first understand what success means to your clients. This could entail their business outcomes or a short-term goal that they've been tasked with. Defining what success means to the client can ground everyone on what's most important so you don't become too fixated on the solution. In the example above, success for the customer meant housing all their data in one data warehouse. To uncover possible opportunities, consider these questions:

- What's on your whiteboard that absolutely needs to be off in the next ninety days?
- If we were in your team meeting, what's the most important topic being discussed right now?
- What is a new initiative your team plans to work on this year?
- If I gave you a magic wand, what problem would you make disappear first?

By asking about their priorities, you may start to uncover their pain points. This is the moment to surface the real business problems behind their frustration. Carefully structured open-ended questions will help surface their pain points. For instance, to gauge how important it was for my client to consolidate their data, I asked them, "As it relates to reporting, what are you finding the most challenging?" Surfacing these issues gives your client tangible evidence to support their funding request to senior leadership.

Once your client reveals their pain, you can leverage impact and value questions (as mentioned in chapter 15). For example, I used the following: "How much time do you currently waste on manual processes?" and "What impact would it have if we could streamline these processes for you?" These open-ended questions help your clients picture how much time and money they are currently wasting and how your product add-ons could benefit them. I've found these discussions cathartic for my clients, as they've probably been dealing with these issues for some time, and I'm giving them a breath of fresh air.

Once you expose their pains, mine for potential obstacles that could derail the deal, just like in the normal SOON funnel. For instance, if the client has other competing priorities and doesn't feel they have the time to work on this project, or a technical gap may disqualify them from your offering, you must expose that at this stage. Your expansion playbook should cover handling common objections.

If you can move past this phase, lay out the options available as part of this upgrade which includes costs and different packages if your products have some variability. If there is agreement on a path forward or at least a consensus to keep the conversation going, finalize the next steps so you can move toward securing the expansion. Leveraging the SPOON funnel simplifies the steps in the expansion process. Leverage all the techniques covered in part IV of this book, including the OARS framework and assessing your client's motivation.

Another technique I like to use is offering a *no-cost* option. I present it when I take clients through their possible choices to address their pain points. Examples of no-cost solutions include uploading data manually instead of via a paid solution or self-onboarding a product instead of purchasing additional services. This positions you as a trusted advisor, as you've given your customers various approaches to solve their problems. Through the discovery process, it should become obvious that the paid solution becomes the logical choice, but providing options makes people more confident in their selections. This is part of motivational interviewing: You're helping your client find their motivation to take action by laying out all of the relevant information so it makes it easy for them to decide for themselves how to proceed.

Tracking expansion potential

Many CSMs fall into the trap of taking a one-size-fits-all approach, treating all customers the same. This strategy can leave valuable clients underserved, leading to surprise churn and missed expansion opportunities. It's essential to thoroughly understand your book of business, including those clients coming up for renewal, those ripe for expansion, and those at risk. CSMs often prioritize the clients who scream the loudest, but with this strategy, you are operating as a firefighter or waiter—not as an SCSM. Real strategic prowess lies in creating significant value, not in the number of hours you clock. To level up requires additional planning and preparation using a tool we introduced earlier: the client tracker.

Return to the account tracker you created (see chapter 7), and fill in the *growth potential* fields to indicate whether your clients have a low, medium, or high chance of revenue growth within the next twelve months. Including a field to indicate estimated future ARR will provide an even clearer view of which of your clients are the most valuable. This estimate should be based on real data and not be solely based on your gut feel. It could include expansion opportunities already identified in your CRM or based on additional information captured from sales and the client itself. It can also be based on adoption metrics which are known to lead to potential expansion or third-party data such as LinkedIn that indicate employee growth numbers.

Include specifics of both the actual and projected data that clearly show the clients with the highest growth potential. Let's have a look at an example (Figure 13). In situations where adding users directly impacts your expansion potential, consider tracking these specific indicators:

- Current seat utilization percentage: This tracks the seats used compared to the seats purchased.
- Seat growth percentage (past thirty days): This indicates the growth in the number of seats used in the last month.
- Projected seat growth—six months: This is your estimated seat growth percentage in six months.
- Projected seat growth—twelve months: This is your estimated seat growth percentage in twelve months.
- Current ARR: The current annual recurring revenue the client is paying.
- Projected ARR—twelve months: This is the estimated amount of ARR in twelve months.

Company Name	ARR	Seats Purchased	Seats Used	Seat Utilization	Seat Growth % (30 Days)	6 Month Growth	12 Month Growth	12 Month Projected ARR
Company A	$100,000	100	100	100%	10%	50%	85%	$185,000
Company B	$40,000	40	40	100%	5%	15%	30%	$52,000

Figure 13. The growth potential section of your client tracker

You could also list the revenue projection for each additional add-on or upgrade if you sell additional products. Last, you could track the current business units or teams that you work with and the potential business units within your customer's organization that you could sell into. The ultimate goal is to have a revenue projection for each customer and for your overall portfolio.

Make it a regular practice to refresh each account's growth potential. This assists you in your weekly Sunday night prep sessions (as covered in chapter 12) as you determine where to focus your time. Not sure what your client's revenue potential is? Set up a meeting with the right client stakeholders and have a strategic conversation. AI tools can also be leveraged to identify new opportunities by analyzing customer behavior and trends.

Don't wait for your manager to do this. To rise to the level of a strategic CSM, practice extreme ownership by owning the process of identifying customer growth opportunities—regardless of your current metrics.

Some final words of advice on expansions

Expansion selling can be tricky. New products might not be fully ready, and pricing strategies can still have kinks. Plus, it's hard to gauge the right timing to sell when client priorities shift. With this in mind, here's my final advice:

- Read the room: The most important guideline, which bears repeating, is to read the room. Don't be that cringy person who keeps pushing a sale after the customer has made it clear they aren't interested. This just makes you appear tone-deaf and unprofessional. You'll also lose any credibility you have. In addition, stop your colleagues from proceeding down this path if you see a car crash in the making. Learn from the experience I shared earlier in this chapter. Focus on your customer's priorities and break out of selling mode when it's clear the customer doesn't want to move forward.

- Revenue is there for the taking: Expansion opportunities often emerge when you least expect them, so be ready to shift gears quickly. Dan Ennis, who leads Scale Customer Success at Workato, shared a counterintuitive insight that makes this very clear: Some of their best expansion opportunities came from engaging with customers who provided negative feedback in their NPS surveys. Dan and his team recognized this and were prepared to introduce additional product offerings if it made sense.[106] While these customers may appear unhappy, they are looking for a solution to their problems. Just make sure that it aligns with their needs.

If you don't believe that CSMs should be tied to revenue growth, consider another profession. This is now an essential component as the role moves away from the helper and waiter mindsets. You must prepare questions before your meeting to maximize your effectiveness and flush out your client's business requirements. In addition, you should leverage an expansion playbook so you and your team can consistently mine for opportunities.

This doesn't mean you should ignore creating long-term value for your customers and establishing trust. As I've argued throughout this book, these are the foundational elements of customer success. Yet surfacing expansion opportunities should become a natural habit, not something to be feared. As you uncover your customers' business outcomes and build out their respective success plans, product add-ons should be a central component of these plans.

Failing to identify potential expansion opportunities is a disservice to your customers, who could benefit from these add-ons, and to your company. I've seen too many situations where my clients purchased a feature we offered from a competitor because we failed to educate the customer. You need to see expansions as a positive sign that your customers believe in you, and you should always look for ways to grow revenue.

---

106 Andrew Marks, host, "Enabling Customer Success Managers as Revenue Growers," CSM Mastermind podcast, episode 60, April 23, 2024, https://successcoaching. co/blog/enabling-customer-success-managers-as-revenue-growers.

Putting this into practice

To help you master the concepts in this chapter, you should:

- Access the "Renewal & Expansion Checklist" at strategiccustomer-success.com. Leverage this for an upcoming renewal or expansion and write out what worked well and what could have gone better.
- Optional: Download the "Joint Renewal Plan" and "Renewal Presentation" templates from strategiccustomersuccess.com.
- Optional: Download the "The Client Tracker" at strategiccustomersuccess.com to track potential expansion opportunities and customize it based on your organization's unique expansion options.

Summary and key takeaways

To master the transformation into a strategic CSM, you need to improve your commercial responsibilities for key moments in the customer journey. This includes enhancing your renewal processes and identifying, monitoring and possibly closing expansion opportunities.

- Strategic CSMs have a clear view of their renewal forecast and client expansion potential.
- Uplevel your renewal processes by implementing JRPs and renewal presentations.
- Use the SPOON funnel to uncover expansion opportunities by focusing on your clients' pain points.
- Segment your clients based on future growth potential, not just their current revenue.
- Create an expansion tracker to ensure you are prioritizing the opportunities with the highest potential.

CONCLUSION

"The relationship therapist of the sales team."

"The fire extinguisher of churn."

"The 'I hear what you're saying' nodding specialists."

"The king/queen of the 'happy customer' castle."

"The 'just checking in' ninja."

"The shoulder to cry on."

"Digital babysitters."

"Professional excuse translators."

"The 'I know it's frustrating, but let me show you a workaround' experts."

These are just a few of the hilarious responses I received when I used the AI prompt: "Funny ways that people describe customer success managers."[107] Though amusing and relatable, these conventional definitions of a CSM need to change.

Strategic customer success management represents a fundamental evolution in how organizations approach customer relationships and value creation. The transformation from traditional CSM to strategic CSM isn't just a title change—it's a complete reimagining of the role's scope, impact, and importance. This change coincides with customer success's greater focus on revenue generation, whether some people like it or not.

---

107   Claude 3.7 Sonnet, AI-generated conversation, February 9, 2025.

As you learned, a key aspect of this shift to being an SCSM is transitioning from solely emphasizing product knowledge and adoption to prioritizing the customer's business and their desired outcomes, including:

- The ability to align product capabilities with customer objectives and drive measurable business impact.
- The skills to navigate complex discovery conversations and senior stakeholder relationships to drive action.
- The wisdom to recognize that revenue expansion is the natural result of consistently delivering meaningful customer value and not something to be fearful of.

The main lever that differentiates an SCSM from a CSM is the ability to master strategic conversations. This book has extensively covered several practical frameworks and techniques, such as the 3Cs, OARS, SOON and SPOON, storytelling, asking difficult questions, and assessing motivation. These techniques deliver value when woven into every pivotal moment in the customer journey, from kickoff meetings to renewal discussions.

In addition, these same approaches can be used in every customer meeting. Whether you are welcoming new decision-makers, uncovering core challenges, navigating customer concerns, or managing feature request expectations, these skills are essential for elevating the CSM role.

This isn't an easy transformation, and this book won't solve all your problems. You're probably navigating through multiple constraints and challenges that create obstacles to becoming a strategic CSM. You may have an incompetent boss, a poorly defined role, messy data, insufficient tools, too many tools, problematic clients, and buggy and incomplete products to deal with.

You may be stuck with the name QBR, have to deal with churn that you had no way of preventing, or experience being ignored by your sales team.

These can suck the life out of you, but you must recognize that every company suffers from these problems. While most of these items are out of your control, you can take charge of your first ninety days in a new role rather than relying on the generic employee onboarding plan. You can better manage your time by planning out your week. You can prepare better for your meetings and at the very least focus on the meeting objective. You can experiment with some of the concepts in this book and make small changes to your habits and processes. You can change your mindset and set an example for others to follow.

Don't wait for your manager's guidance—it's not coming. Don't wait for someone to train you—create your own training opportunities. Focus on what you can control rather than what you can't. I believe everyone has the potential to be a strategic CSM. The only thing holding you back is you.

A few additional parting thoughts

This book isn't the definitive guide to being a CS professional—far from it. This industry is evolving too fast for that, and the CSM role can encompass many different responsibilities depending on the organization. In addition, technology—especially AI—is drastically changing how companies do business, which will result in changes to the CSM role in the near future.

It's important to keep ahead of these changes. I've been doing CS for over twenty years and sustained a high standard over this time by embodying the idea that "You're never done." That doesn't mean you don't celebrate victories such as a killer quarter or turning a large at-risk customer into a massive customer advocate. It means that you can't become complacent. You have to keep evolving in our ever-shifting reality. Adapt, adapt, adapt.

After all, these forces will continue to shift the CSM's responsibilities and the purview of the customer success department. But whatever happens, customer success will always rest on two foundational pillars: trust and value. The two terms are inseparable: Trust enables value delivery, while demonstrated value builds deeper trust. This virtuous cycle creates sustainable, long-term customer relationships that benefit you and your customers. You can accomplish this by leveraging both technology and the power of human connection, especially in the enterprise segment.

Moreover, the value and trust equation isn't just with customers—it also applies within your organization. SCSMs must continue to provide value to the other functions in their organization, whether that's sales, marketing, or product, and establish trusted relationships with them.

In essence, becoming a strategic CSM is all about resilience and grittiness—core parts of a growth mindset. Surviving a near-death experience in Scotland pushed me to seek out a new career path and taught me that life is too precious to accept the status quo. As I finish this book, I'm facing yet another health challenge, which I plan to battle with the same ferocity.

To be clear, you don't have to survive a near-death experience to be a strategic CSM, although there may be days when you feel you have. What is required is some edginess. That's why I stressed that you need to practice radical customer candor and be comfortable with saying no to people from time to time. You must have the courage to ask difficult questions and dig deeper into Pandora's box, which you pried open in your discovery conversations.

Mastering these skills took me several years, and I've shared several of my failures along the way in this book. The good news is that you can fast-track this process by completing the various exercises at strategiccustomersuccess.com. The most effective way to internalize the lessons in this book is through deliberate practice, which these exercises allow for. It's not easy, but tackling each exercise one at a time and slowly building up your competencies will put you on the right path to long-term success.

My hope is that as you apply these concepts, you'll grow not only as a CSM but as a strategic force in your business. You will not only succeed in your role but ascend in your career. You will be a giver not just within your company but also in the greater CS community and beyond. The transformation from traditional CSM to strategic CSM is more than a career progression—it's an opportunity to fundamentally impact how businesses create and deliver value in the modern economy. I'm excited to see how you leverage this knowledge and make it your own. Let's keep learning and growing together.

Chad Horenfeldt
May, 2025

NEXT STEPS

As I've mentioned throughout this book, your journey to becoming an SCSM is far from over. It's now up to you to build the right habits that will incorporate the ideas and processes covered in this book. Go to strategiccustomersuccess.com, where you can take the following next steps:

- Access the various free exercises mentioned throughout this book.
- Access my free recommendations, including books you should read, technologies you should leverage, and other CS thought leaders you should follow.
- Download professional CS templates from my store.
- Sign up for email updates to get regular content from me on practical applications of customer success.
- Have me train your team to transform them into strategic CSMs.
- Hire me as a personal coach.
- Have me speak at your next event.
- Access the bonus chapter "What May Be Holding You Back from Being a Strategic CSM."

I would also love to hear what you learned from this book and the successes you've accomplished. Please leave me a review on Amazon and reach out to me directly.

ACKNOWLEDGMENTS

My goal in writing this book was to share my knowledge, acquired both from my direct experience and from all the wonderful people in the customer success space and beyond. I want to thank you, the readers who took the time to read this book. At times when I was discouraged or overwhelmed with the task of writing it, it was you I thought of and that helped me push through. Feel free to message me directly on LinkedIn or email me at chad@strategiccustomersuccess.com.

Over the years, a few people have encouraged or inspired me to write this book, so I want to start by thanking them: Nils Vinje and Wayne Mc-Culloch. In his book *30 Day Leadership Playbook: Your Guide to Becoming the Leader You Have Always Wanted to Be* Nils explained the importance of creating frameworks and turned me on to self-publishing. This helped me organize my thoughts and gave me a clear path to publish my ideas. Wayne kept nudging me, "Where's the book?" which I appreciated as it gave me the courage to go for it.

I want to thank my editors from Beacon Point LLC — especially Robin Samuels—for their attentive and constructive feedback. They were true partners in this process, and I couldn't have asked for a better editing company. They pointed out several aspects of the publishing process I hadn't considered. I would also like to thank Alejandro Martin from Bloom Design Agency for the wonderful book cover designs and book formatting. This team made this process as easy as possible.

I want to thank my good friend, Dave Tepper, for reviewing my book and providing thoughtful advice. Thank you, Kristi Faltorusso, for writing the foreword to this book and helping me promote it. I met Kristi when I had just arrived in NYC, and I knew she would be someone to watch. Her steadfast commitment to the CS industry and to her friends and family inspires me. I also appreciate her encouragement throughout this process.

I've had the pleasure of working with some incredible people, and I wanted to thank two specific people who really inspired many aspects of this book and helped me get my start: Jeff Chapleau and Paul Teshima. Jeff gave me my first break in technology and the opportunity to discover my true passion for customer success. He also provided me with the guidance I needed to start my professional career in technology and leadership. Paul Teshima gave me my second break, which landed me at an early SaaS company. He demonstrated how culture can make or break teams and set a positive example to aspire to.

Several people mentioned in this book helped me shape my thoughts on strategic customer success. I want to first call out Adam Grant, whose book *Think Again* introduced me to the concept of motivational interviewing. I dug into this concept really deeply because it helped me put a framework around my daily practices. The second person who struck a deep chord was Bob London. His approach to customer discovery blew my mind as he helped me take the abstract concept of being a *challenger* and make it a reality. He's also one of the nicest and most generous people I know.

I want to call out several people that I mentioned in the book or who provided a spark in my creative process: Aaron Thompson, the late Alan Armstrong, Alex Shootman, Allison Pickens, Andrew Marks, Ashvin Vaidyanathan, Benjamin Hardy, Bo Bandy, Brad Birnbaum, Carly Agar, Chris Voss, Dan Ennis, Dan Steinman, Daphne Lopes, David Priemer, Donna

Weber, Drew Clarke, Emilia D'Ánzica, Erika Villarreal, Greg Daines, Jeff Pedowitz, Josh Schachter, Julie Persofsky, Kevin Chiu, Kia Puhm, Kristen Hayer, Lincoln Murphy, Linda David, Maranda Dziekonski, Mark Organ, Mary Poppen, Mikael Blaisdell, Nick Mehta, Paul Henderson, Peter "PJ" Johnson, Prashanth Jothi, Rod Cherkas, Ruben Rabago, Ryan Hawk, Sabina Pons, Todd Eby, Vikas Bhambri, Ziv Peled.

I would be remiss if I didn't take a moment to thank the many incredible people I've had the privilege of working with over the years, including former managers, colleagues, and, of course, the amazing individuals I was honored to lead. There are far too many people to mention here, but each of you has contributed in some way to this book, and you may even remember some of the stories mentioned.

I am deeply grateful to the many customers I've had the opportunity to collaborate with throughout my career. You've had a lasting impact on who I am today. I still hear from many of you on LinkedIn, and if you're reading this, I'd love to reconnect—send me a message! I mentioned a few customers in this book, including Drew Clarke, Heather Foeh, and Bo Bandy.

Growing up in Toronto, I was lucky to have two loving parents who did their best to put me on the right track. I didn't realize until many years later that my dad most likely inspired my path to customer success because he spent most of his career at DuPont selling X-ray film to hospitals. He taught me the importance of building strong customer relationships and working hard. My mother taught me to keep pushing and to raise my standards. There was a turning point in my primary school years when she ripped up my finished social studies project because she didn't think it was up to snuff. I redid it and got the A. I now forgive you, Mom.

My children, Matthew, Judah, and Amelia, are definitely my toughest customers, but they've taught me so much. In fact, they played a key role in helping me refine many of the techniques discussed in this book. Their support has made me more empathetic and better equipped to identify the underlying causes of complex issues. Most importantly, they've taught me the importance of connection. They know that I care deeply about them and want the best for them. I love each of you and thank you for giving me the space to write this book.

When I told my wife, Allie, I wanted to write a book, she wasn't surprised at all. She probably wondered why I had waited so long. She has been so incredibly supportive of me during this time. From the weekends when I was locked in my office to the days when I worked too late the night before and was a mess, she has always been there. While I know parenting is a partnership, I give her full credit for the wonderful people our children have turned into. She is a wonderful wife, mother, sister, and daughter—and best friend to me. I love you, Allie, with all of my heart.

ABOUT THE AUTHOR

Chad Horenfeldt is a seasoned customer success executive with over two decades of experience in SaaS. He is currently the VP of Customer Success at Siena AI, an autonomous AI customer service platform specifically designed for commerce teams. Prior to this role, Chad held key positions at companies such as Meta (Kustomer), Updater, Bluecore, Influitive, and Oracle (Eloqua), where he honed his expertise in customer success and customer experience strategies. Chad has been part of an IPO while at Eloqua and of two major acquisitions, one by Oracle and a second by Meta.

Beyond his professional endeavors, Chad is a recognized thought leader, frequently sharing insights on customer success through various industry publications and speaking engagements. Among his many contributions, Chad authored a section on customer advocacy in the book *The Customer Success Professional's Handbook: How to Thrive in One of the World's Fastest Growing Careers—While Driving Growth for Your Company*. Chad graduated from Western University with a Master of Arts in history and completed a postgraduate diploma in applied information technology. He is originally from Toronto, Ontario, but now lives in Northern New Jersey with his wife, three children, and dog, Timbit.

I NEED YOUR HELP!

Thank you for reading my book.
I would love to hear your honest feedback and your takeaways from this book. Can you leave me a review?

Please take two minutes now to leave a helpful review on Amazon, and let me know what you thought of this book:

strategiccustomersuccess.com/review

Thanks so much!

Chad Horenfeldt

www.ingramcontent.com/pod-product-compliance
Lightning Source LLC
Chambersburg PA
CBHW071538210326
41597CB00019B/3034